CHOOSING MERCY

Other Books by the Author

Shaken Faith: Hanging in There When God Seems Far Away

Coincidences: Touched by a Miracle

The Pummeled Heart: Finding Peace through Pain

A Parent Alone

What Do We Really Know about Aging?

Marriage Encounter: The Rediscovery of Love

Joseph the Huron

Charles John Seghers: Pioneer in Alaska

CHOOSING MERCY

A MOTHER OF MURDER VICTIMS PLEADS TO END THE DEATH PENALTY

Antoinette Bosco

ORBIS BOOKS

Maryknoll, New York 10545

The Catholic Foreign Mission Society of America (Maryknoll) recruits and trains people for overseas missionary service. Through Orbis Books, Maryknoll aims to foster the international dialogue that is essential to mission. The books published, however, reflect the opinions of their authors and are not meant to represent the official position of the Society.

To obtain more information about Maryknoll and Orbis Books, please visit our website at www.maryknoll.org.

Library of Congress Cataloging-in-Publication Data

Bosco, Antoinette, 1928-
    Choosing mercy : a mother of murder victims pleads to end the death penalty / Antoinette Bosco.
        p. cm.
    ISBN 1-57075-358-X (pbk.)
    1. Capital punishment. 2. Capital punishment – United States. I. Title.

HV8698 .B67 2001
364.66 – dc21

                                                            00-049173

I dedicate this book to
Charles Grosso, Robert J. Zani,
and to all my imprisoned friends,
to Msgr. Edward J. Donovan, Mercy Sister Eileen Hogan,
Father Vince Connor, and to all the chaplains
who work with the men and women confined behind bars—
who have so inspired me to see truth.

CONTENTS

✤✤✤✤✤✤✤✤✤✤✤✤✤

Acknowledgments   9

Introduction   13

One   The Murders   19

Two   Beginning the Healing Process   36

Three   Raising My Voice   57

Four   Plunging into the Debate   74

Five   A New Door Opens—and Prisoners Become Kin   93

Six   Calls Come In—and I Am the Learner   110

Seven   Behind the Bars, Seriously Flawed Prison System   130

Eight   The Other Victims   150

Nine   Leadership from the Pulpit   165

Ten   Concern about the Death Penalty Grows   181

Eleven   So Much Known—So Much to Be Done   200

Postscript   221

Sources and Notes   229

Recommended Books   237

Resource Groups against Capital Punishment   238

ACKNOWLEDGMENTS

I long ago learned that it takes more than one person to write a book. What is given to you by each person who somehow makes a connection with you is always the crucial piece you need to create your mosaic that is to be called a book. Truly I don't know where to begin when I try to gather the names of the people to whom I owe deep gratitude. Each one helped me assemble the information I needed to make the case for mercy, while yet acknowledging the incredible pain of grief caused by the evil deeds of some people who make us feel the world would be a better place without them.

I first want to note my friends from the two groups in which I proudly claim membership. My heartfelt thanks go to my friends from Survivors of Homicide for sharing their crushing stories with me—Dr. Samuel Rieger and his wife, Wanda, Shirley and Larry Bostrom, John Cluny, Rev. Stuart Brush and his wife, Laura, Helen Williams, and Mikki Brady; and to those I have talked to and come to know from Murder Victims Families for Reconciliation—Rennie Cushing, Rev. Walter Everett, Marietta Jaeger, Pat Bane, Anne Coleman, Barbara Lewis, Bill Pelke, Bud Welch, Shakeerah Hameen, and Sonia "Sunny" Jacobs.

Without help from people I met along the way, mainly from being on the same panel or program, or interviewing and working with them in some way, a decided richness of information would never have become available, and so I thank the late president of George Fox College, Dr. Edward Stevens; the sheriff of Bigfork, Montana, Joe Geldrich; the two homicide detectives who broke the murder case, Ward McKay and Arlyn Greydanus; Mimi and George Klocko and the other members of Delaware Citizens Opposed to the Death Penalty; Connecticut Representative Richard Tulisano and Bishop Thomas Gumbleton, outspoken opponents of executions; Richard Dieter of the Death Penalty Information Center; Sue Porter, Mary Boite, Clare Regan, and others of the Judicial Process Commission in New York State; Debbie Morris, a victim who wrote on forgiveness; anti–death penalty author Herbert

Haines; John and Maureen McNamara, Frank Fitzgerald, Sister Dorothy Briggs, and others I've met who work in prison ministry; the prisoners at Greenhaven in Stormville, New York, who have become my respected friends; Art Laffin of Pax Christi, brother of a murder victim who works for peace, justice, and nonviolence; John Armstrong, commissioner, and Eileen Higgens, warden, in the Connecticut Department of Corrections, who bring heart and concern for inmates to their very difficult positions; Sister Elaine Roulet, chaplain, and the women she works with in the Bedford Hills Correctional Facility; John MacKenzie, an inmate, for seeing the importance of bringing prisoners and victims together for understanding and healing; Lawrence Hayes, an innocent man who spent years on death row; priests who have shared their experiences with me, Msgr. John Gilmartin of Long Island, Father Vince Connor of California, Father John Fitzgerald of Long Island, and Father James Fanelli of Connecticut; Hernando Méndez, for putting a false conviction behind him and moving on to live a good, productive life; April Grosso, for showing me the power of a daughter's love for her father that prison bars could not destroy; Paul Grondahl, for being the best of what a reporter should be, when he courageously exposed the truth of what goes on in separate housing units (SHUs, or simply The Box).

So many people who have helped me come from the religious community and deserve more thanks than I could ever express: Pat Clark, coordinator of Religious Organizing Against the Death Penalty Project; Frank de Rosa of the Brooklyn, New York, diocese, who invited me to make an anti–death penalty video with Bishop Thomas Dailey, Bud Welch, and Camille Bodden, a father and mother respectively of a murder victim, and Kevin Doyle, a capital defense lawyer; the people of the Bruderhof community, active abolitionist workers; Bishop Thomas Costello and Bill Cuddy of Syracuse, New York, supporter and co-developer of a model anti–death penalty program for a parish; Bishop Charles Chaput of Denver, in gratitude for letting me reprint his anti–death penalty talk; Stephen Russo, for an innovative parish effort to bring attention to seeing the death penalty as a "pro-life" issue; Mercy Sister Camille D'Arienzo, for her years of inspiring work for life.

I learned a new level of respect for people who have the most difficult job of all in a pro–death penalty nation—the capital defense lawyers. For the time they spent with me and the expertise and concern they showed me, my humble gratitude goes to Gerald Smyth, the chief public defender for the state of Connecticut, and the very human, caring Capital Defense team he has assembled, lawyers Karen Goodrow, Ronald

Gold, and Barry Butler, assisted by social workers, investigators, and secretaries.

Very special thanks go to my cherished friends David and Linda Kaczynski, who have inspired me with their courage and their convictions about the importance and beauty of life, brotherhood, and forgiveness. I am proud to have David's wisdom in this book. Another friend who rates special gratitude is Scott Christianson, author of *Condemned,* an astounding book about the years of executions in the notorious New York prison Sing Sing. Because of his generous assistance, I was able, finally, after decades of wondering, to get information about my Aunt Margie's brother, executed in Sing Sing in 1928. Until Scott came along to help, the story had been family lore; now it is documented fact.

One man is very special to me and always will be, Bill Simonsen, the reporter at the *Bigfork Eagle,* who cared enough for truth—and I believe for John and Nancy, though he had never met them—to give his unrelenting attention to the murder case. While no other media reporters were interested enough in a small town double murder to do any investigating reporting, Bill kept faithfully pursuing the story, constantly in touch with me. He became my strongest, and sometimes my only, link with what was going on with the case and the court. To this day, Bill and I remain friends.

To write a book on a subject inherently controversial, such as this one, the greatest help one can have is the support of family, and how blessed I am with my family! They encouraged me from day one, sending me pertinent clips as they found them, assuring me always they were with me on this work. My very special, loving thanks go to my sisters Rosemary and Jeannette; my sons and their wives, Paul and Sue, Frank and Judi, Sterling and Bernadette; my daughter Mary vanValkenburg and her husband, Rick; and my daughter Margaret Minier. You are the ones who keep the light on in my life.

And then a book doesn't get published without a great editor calling to tell you, "Write it, we want it." It was a call from Michael Leach that gave me that invitation and convinced me he is really a mind reader. It had been more and more on my mind that I should write a book about how my personal experiences had led me to become ever more convinced that the death penalty is wrong, that mercy is the way of Christians. Now I had been given an invitation to do that, with a great bonus—I'd be working with one of the best editors in the business. For such a vote of confidence in me, a real honor, I shall be ever grateful to Michael Leach.

INTRODUCTION

The headlines in an editorial in the *Bigfork Eagle,* the weekly paper of a small town in northwest Montana, on August 25, 1993, literally screamed out the warning: "Era of Unlocked Doors Ending."

The editorial began, "Murder in Bigfork. A grim reminder that as remote and quiet as Bigfork seems, real world, big-time problems can—and have—reached into our backyards.

"Last week, the bodies of John and Nancy Bosco were found, shot to death in their Ferndale home. An intruder, apparently intent only on death, cut the phone lines and electricity, then crept into the Boscos' house through a basement window, climbed stairs to the master bedroom and shot John and Nancy to death. . . . "

All too often when we read a story that begins this way, the victims come across as statistics, two people murdered. John and Nancy were not statistics. They were my son and daughter-in-law.

I got the news of the brutal murders on August 19, and that day I learned a new definition of torment. I had had to accept much death in recent years—my father, my sister-in-law, my son Peter. Death from almost any cause, even from accident, can somehow be dealt with rationally. But if the death is caused by murder, there is a collapse in the heart and soul that cannot be described.

For murder is the entrance of the worst evil imaginable into your home, into all the safe places of your life, forever shattering any illusion you might have had that good can protect you from evil. Evil becomes all too real to you and never again can you even for an instant question its power. My beloved son and his beautiful wife were dead at the hand of someone I could only believe to be, at that moment, an agent of Satan.

I found myself screaming, sometimes aloud, sometimes with silent cries tearing at my insides. I tormented myself, wanting to know who was the faceless monster that had brought such permanent unrelenting pain into my family. I wanted to kill him with my own hands. I wanted him dead.

13

But that feeling also tormented me, for I had always been opposed to the death penalty. I felt now I was being tested on whether my values were permanent, or primarily based on human feelings and expediency. With God's help, I was able to grasp the truth again, that unnatural death at the hands of another is always wrong, except in a case of clear self-defense. The state is no more justified in taking a life than is an individual. And so armed, I found myself speaking out on a national platform, pleading against the death penalty for anyone.

In the year 2000, the death penalty debate in America began to surface with a new urgency as voices against official killings were raised in legislatures, on news broadcasts, in professional legal and medical associations, and in virtually every religious community in the country. With the truth about the inequities and mistakes on death row starting to emerge, Americans, in mid-2000, were beginning to feel some discomfort as they heard such facts as these: over 3,600 people are currently on death row; more than 675 persons have been killed in the past twenty-four years—some surely innocent—by legally sanctioned gassings, electrocutions, hangings, lethal injections, or firing squad bullets; 88 death row inmates have been freed in this time, some after new trials, some with convictions overturned on appeal, some having new DNA proof of innocence; more than 65 inmates whose crimes were committed when they were juveniles are on death row; Texas has executed 8 juvenile offenders since 1985; 26 states have allowed the execution of mentally retarded defendants; application of the death penalty is skewed racially and by income.

The new concerns about this deadly "solution" for ridding the country of murderers were well expressed by Professor Anthony G. Amsterdam at a conference discussing "Global Movements towards a Moratorium on the Death Penalty," held in October 1999 at Columbia University:

"Some of us are concerned with what the death penalty does to societies and systems of law that use it—with how it distorts and erodes the fabric of our moral and our legal norms as those must be twisted and emptied of meaning in an effort to justify taking human life on the basis of procedures that we know to be fallible, error-prone, and inescapably responsive to the urgings of vengeance, prejudice and primal rage.

"Some of us simply are sick of the insidious hypocrisy that is the necessary price of pretending that imperfect human institutions are good enough to make decisions about who should live and who should die and get them right."

The new millennium began with another strong voice when Pope John Paul II appealed to the entire world, urging all nations to abolish the death penalty. He cited the year 2000, which he proclaimed a Holy Year, to be a "privileged occasion" for promoting universal respect for life and the dignity of every person. Ninety countries still hold on to capital punishment, and, sadly, one of these is the United States, the only Western industrialized country to practice this barbaric punishment. The Holy Father was certainly directing his appeal for ending the death penalty to our nation, which in 1999, with ninety-eight killings, ranked third worldwide in the number of executions carried out.

Death penalty mania has been sweeping the country for over two decades, ever since the Supreme Court reinstated this ultimate punishment in July 1976, holding that "the punishment of death does not inevitably violate the Constitution."

Yet, in the first nine months of the new millennium, some major developments took place which indicate the climate may be beginning to change for the better when it comes to American attitudes toward the death penalty. What has come to light is the truth about the failures of this deadly system, particularly that innocent people have been put to death even when there is viable evidence that they may not have committed the crime. The American Bar Association, citing that the judicial process is seriously flawed, called for a moratorium on executions on February 3, 1997, until the process is overhauled. Then, in January 2000, Illinois governor George Ryan, a traditional supporter of the death penalty, put a halt to executions in his state. Appalled by the fact that thirteen death row inmates in Illinois had been found to be innocent since 1977, he declared a moratorium until there is reform legislation that can fix the volumes of errors that accompany convictions in capital cases. With this first sign of hope, people who have worked for years to abolish the death penalty have begun a "Moratorium Now!" coast-to-coast campaign to get all the thirty-eight states that allow the death penalty to follow the example of Illinois. While their true goal would be the end of executions, moratoriums would at least be an action now that could stop the killings, while, hopefully, more Americans would begin to see the wrongness of executions and this perhaps would lead to a strong national voice demanding these end, period.

The Massachusetts Council of Churches has put out a five-sentence statement which best sheds light on why people are beginning to be uncomfortable with our escalating murders in the death chambers of our prisons: "Capital punishment is subject to error by fallible judges and juries. It is not a demonstrated deterrent to violent crimes. In fact, the society that sanctions official vengeance may be setting an example of the brutal devaluation of life that it wants to deter. One of our most serious concerns about the death penalty is the well-documented fact that the color of one's skin, the size of one's bank account to purchase legal services, and the skills of legal counsel, often have much to do with who actually is executed. This discrimination against ethnic minorities and the poor is a chief reason for eliminating capital punishment."

While this statement addresses matters that seriously should be examined in the realm of conscience, it does not deal with a major argument for keeping the death penalty: that without this extreme punishment for brutal killers, families of murder victims will not receive justice. Nothing could be further from the truth. The pain of losing a loved one by the horrible act of murder is not lessened by the horrible murder of another, not even when it is cloaked as "justice" and state-sanctioned. It is only a delusion to believe that one's pain is ended by making someone else feel pain.

Some may quickly criticize me as being some kind of Pollyanna because I am opposed to the death penalty and also believe that murder victims' families should seek to be merciful, not vengeful. Not true. The murder of my son and daughter-in-law plunged me into a position where I have had to examine—really examine—the gains and ills of the death penalty. I had to confront my soul when I learned that they were murdered by an eighteen-year-old named Joseph Shadow Clark, who after confessing to this horrible crime faced the death penalty. I had always been opposed to the death penalty, as I stated before, but where did I stand now when cold-blooded murder had so permanently crashed my life? Let me tell you that when you are in that pit, alone with your searing pain, you can't play cat and mouse with honesty. With tears and prayer and begging the Lord to tell me where I should stand, I found my way and was given to know that to want more unnatural death by the hands of humans would be wrong. I could say that Shadow Clark, who ended the earthly lives of my son and daughter-in-law with a nine-millimeter semi-automatic gun, must be punished for life, but I could not say, Kill this killer.

I am in a minority position. The latest polls show that the majority of Americans still favor the death penalty. I know, especially from anti–death penalty talks I've given, that far too many people of many different faiths are in league with pro–death penalty advocates. Many may agree with the pope on abortion, but they're not with him when it comes to this issue of life and death for violent criminals. Not long ago I was asked by a Catholic pro-life group to give a talk, and when I said, yes, but I would also include the need to respect life when it comes to convicted criminals, they withdrew the invitation.

No one can deny that capital punishment is a question that causes confusion and pain. Even dedicated human rights advocates struggle with the arguments for and against—because brutal murder can challenge all of us in a way that puts our heads and our hearts at odds. I've had to look deep inside myself and ask, am I so noble, so altruistic as to still believe that Shadow Clark, this taker of innocent life, deserves to live?

That's why the death penalty puts us on the edge of a sword. The uncertainty, confusion, and anguish it generates offer strong testimony that the death penalty may be the most wrenching moral dilemma of our time. For the issue can't really be dealt with from our human perspective, but only through finding our higher selves.

Advocates of the death penalty say that a murderer forfeits his or her right to life. Maybe that's true, but I don't believe we can be the ones to make that judgment.

I know the claim that vengeance can make on your soul when you are devastated by the injustice of losing a love at the hand of a murderer. It fills every part of you, with rage tearing the very molecules of your existence. Yes, you feel like destroying the person who has so permanently clawed away a vital part of your life. This rage puts you on the point of a defining moment that will determine who you will become and what will happen to your relationship with God.

There are many victims of homicide who become self-righteous in their demand for the death penalty and say, as did Richard Thornton, the husband of the woman murdered by Daniel Ryan Garrett and Karla Faye Tucker, who was executed in Texas in February 1998: "I want to say to every victim in this world, demand this, this is your right." And he repeated, the night she was executed, in raging self-righteousness, that we victims have a right to hate, to demand death for the murderer and call it "closure" when the death house deed is done.

Advocates for death cannot assume that all victims will be ready and anxious to jump on their bandwagon. It is not surprising, however, that in this era of rah, rah death-penalty advocates, a victim who is opposed to this kind of terminal solution is sometimes seen as a traitor.

I know that criticism. It has often been poured on me. All I ask is that people listen to the powerful lesson some of us have learned when murder enters our door—that unnatural death is an evil, no matter whose hand stops the breath.

Thanks to the grace of God, there is where I stand. I have written this book as an invitation to others to co-experience my journey that has led me to this place. It is my prayerful hope that all will stand here with me.

ANTOINETTE BOSCO
Brookfield, Conn.
Summer 2000

Chapter One

THE MURDERS

August 19, 1993, was one of those nice summer days when you feel you should be outdoors reading a book or having a picnic. It was a Thursday, with only one day left of my two-week vacation from my position as executive editor of a Connecticut newspaper, and I should have been relaxing. But I was very restless. I called a cleaning company to come and shampoo my family room rug. Then I phoned the piano tuner to set up an appointment for the next day. I knew why I was feeling very uneasy that day. I was worried because I hadn't heard from John and Nancy, and that wasn't like them at all. They had been on a trip to Colorado, expecting to be back home in Montana by mid-week. But they hadn't called, and I couldn't get through on their phone.

"Toni Bosco, you're ridiculous," I kept telling myself. "John's forty years old and you're acting like he's supposed to check in with you so you won't worry about him." As it got to be late afternoon, I picked up a book I had purchased at a book sale just one week earlier. It had surprised me to see this book which took me back to when John was a baby. It was called *St. John Bosco and the Children's Saint, Dominic Savio,* written by Catherine Beebe in 1955. I had named my baby John Dominic, after those two saints, and I thought it was quite a coincidence that I now found a book about them. I couldn't wait to tell him.

I was flipping through the pages when the phone rang. I picked up the receiver and said, "John?"

It wasn't my son. It was Montana's Lake County Sheriff Joe Geldrich, who called me to tell me shattering news. "Are you Antoinette Bosco?" he asked. "Yes," I answered. "Do you have a son, John Bosco?" "What's wrong? What happened?" I literally shouted. "I'm sorry to have to tell you this, but we have a crime scene here. He and his wife are dead."

I couldn't talk. Somehow I was immediately calm. "Can you tell me what happened?" He said he had no information at that point, but would

19

let me know as soon as he had something to report. He gave me some phone numbers and expressed his sympathy.

I was alone in the house and my imagination took over. It's all a mistake, I kept saying to myself. The police have the wrong people. They must be in a different house. I had never seen John and Nancy's house because I hadn't yet made arrangements to visit them. They had bought the house and moved to Montana only a few months earlier. Yet I could visualize it because we were on the phone almost every other day, from Connecticut to Montana, and John and Nancy, excited about their new home in their new state, had described the house in detail to me. They had planned a trip to Colorado, and the last I spoke to them it was, "Have a good trip. I'll talk to you in a week." Only now I wasn't hearing their voices. It was a sheriff with a deadly message. I still had the book in my hands, and looking at *Saint John Bosco* in big letters, I fell into a chair and sobbed.

Sheriff Geldrich soon called back and gave me some details. He said a neighbor had gone to check out John and Nancy's house, saw their van in the driveway, still packed, tried the door, still locked, and noticed that windows were open. Going close up to one, she reeled from a foul odor. She ran home immediately and called the police. Upon entry, they found the uncovered, decomposing bodies of my son and my daughter-in-law, dead from bullets. Since the power had been cut off, their electric clocks had stopped at just past 1:45. The police at the scene estimated John and Nancy had been killed a week earlier, on August 12, at approximately two in the morning.

I was still holding the St. John Bosco book, and I was momentarily distracted. I started to shake. I had found that book among a pile of used books—on August 12. This seemed more than coincidental.

Sheriff Geldrich told me they had no suspects, and wondered if I had any idea who might have wanted to kill my kids. I think I went a little crazy at that moment.

Newspapers carried the story immediately. The *Bigfork Eagle* asked, "Was this a 'hit' carried out by a paid killer? Were the murders tied to past legal battles? Were the killings the work of a random madman? A jealous lover? None of the above? Sheriff Geldrich says he has no answers—at least not yet."

That lack of answers tormented me and my family, adding to the shattered peace that had taken over our lives. I was some twenty-four hundred miles away, but close enough to feel how the altering of my life had begun and to know that it would be permanent. Who would

I become as the case unfolded? I was consumed with anger that any one supposedly human could deliberately take the life of another. I desperately wanted to know who had done this terrible act, and why? My anger went into rage when I read the first report of the murders, in the *Daily Inter Lake,* a Kalispell, Montana, newspaper, quoting "an unidentified source," saying "Bosco indicated he 'would not mind' taking his own life." I was a newspaper editor at the time, and I called the editor of that paper, screaming at her that I would fire a reporter who included such a statement in a story when the bodies had only just been found and police had absolutely no comment yet as to what had happened. The intimation of murder-suicide from an "unidentified source" was beyond irresponsible. I received a sincere apology from the editor, saying she had not been at work that night, and so the story slipped by unedited. Later my anger escalated even more when rumors from Montana came back to me, telling me that people were saying, well, this was an execution-style murder, and John Bosco is Italian, so it must be Mafia related!

At that point all I knew was that Sheriff Geldrich had elicited help from the Criminal Investigation Bureau of the Montana Department of Justice, and two state investigators were assigned to the case, Ward McKay and Arlyn Greydanus. We simply had to endure the silence and the waiting.

I had my memories, of course, of the forty-one years I was blessed to have this son and the four years of joy in knowing Nancy—lovely as a model, the salutatorian of her 1979 class at the Lake Preston, South Dakota, high school, a cum laude graduate of Dakota State College. John was truly a man who lived by truth, who would give the shirt off his back for another, and was a staunch fighter for the individual rights of people. He was an artist with wood, a furniture maker, who played the violin and had a great sense of humor.

John was a great believer in children's rights and had once run for a seat on the Boulder Valley school board when he lived in Colorado. He put his stand in writing, saying, "Our society has become a harsh environment for the young, and *that* we can change if we commit ourselves individually to doing so. Loosen the reins, become more flexible. Learn to accept first, not criticize, those you don't understand. Cultivate an appreciation for the unusual among us and become able to love them. Their needs are the same as yours and mine. God bless us."

Now I reread his words and wondered, would he have considered a murderer "the unusual among us," and if so, would he be asking us to "become able to love" that person? His statement haunted me, as if I were getting a message from the grave.

As I waited to get snippets of news from Montana, I could only remember the great love John and Nancy, married in December 1990, had for each other, and I prayed . . . and prayed.

John and Nancy had expected me to come to Montana that fall to see the lovely place where they had decided to settle, with its great wide, open spaces, near a lake and a quaint town. They were nature lovers, and this was the location of their dreams. I had looked forward to coming to the home they had purchased from a man named Joseph Clark, a father of three and a furniture maker like John, being grabbed and hugged by my muscular son and tall daughter-in-law, sharing stories and having a great time. Instead, when I saw the house for the first time, I was greeted by the stench of death.

Actually, from the time John and Nancy, who then lived in Colorado, told me they had put a substantial down payment on a house in Bigfork, Montana, I don't know why, but I had an eerie feeling about this. Later, when they actually went to close on the house, they got some disturbing news. John had specifically wanted this property because it had another building on it, one that had been used by Joe Clark as a furniture-making facility called Frontier Furniture. My son felt the property was ideal because this building was partly set up already as a shop, and he felt he could get his business going right away. But just before completing the deal John found out that there had been a damaging fire in that building. Joe Clark had done some repairs and set up part of the building to look like a legitimate shop, but in fact, according to the state, he had violated state codes. On June 7, 1991, over a year before the sale of the property, the State Department of Commerce, Building Codes Division, filed a lawsuit against Joe Clark over the use of the shop where he manufactured furniture. The state's Building Codes Division had taken him to court and was attempting to get a court order to prevent Clark from making further additions to the place. Lon Maxwell, an attorney for the Division, said the case was not closed when the property was sold. My son inherited the problem.

When John was unable to go ahead with setting up his business, he accepted the setback, trying to work with the State of Montana to find out what he had to do to comply with the codes. While he was unhappy with this development, he never harbored any bad feelings toward Joe Clark, telling me, "He's a nice guy. He's being screwed by the system."

I remember this well, because while John kept telling me this was a temporary problem, I had a disturbing dream. I saw John dressed as a cave man, wielding a thick club, confident that he could overcome a kind of wormy monster that was in front of him. It was as if I were watching him on a screen. Behind him he was about to be attacked by a huge, very modern, destructive machine. He had no way of knowing the danger from behind, but I, watching, saw it and started screaming. He could not hear, of course, and as the machine destroyed him, I woke up, shaking. I became a bit fearful that some other calamity was facing John. With the news of the murders, within a month, I wondered if that had been a prophetic dream.

That dream was on my mind as I traveled to Montana with my sons Paul and Frank so we could pack up what belonged to John and Nancy, clean the place, and deal with all the matters that have to be taken care of when there is untimely death. The first thing my sons and I did was go up the stairs to the bedroom where our loved ones had been murdered. When we walked into that room of death, marked with remnants of their blood, we could feel the presence of evil. The three of us fell to our knees to pray and we asked the Lord to exorcise the evil from that room. When my eye went to the bullethole on the wall, I was suddenly attacked by a coldness and my body started to shake. It was as if I were being let into a new realm of knowledge where I could see a profound truth in a way I never had been able to see before. I was being shown the lasting pain that comes from unnatural death by the hands of another human being, and, in shock, realized that the One suffering this pain was the Father/Mother who had given birth to both, the killed and the killer. I knew in that moment that this was the evil of unnatural death, that it took away what rightfully belonged to the Parent who had loved so much and so had created those lives, all of them.

I was crying profusely, and the cold left, making way for a warmth that came over me. I prayed that I would cherish this message and honor life forever. I had always been a life person, opposed to abortion, the death penalty, and war, but the murder of my loved ones had shaken those beliefs. I had felt the anger that makes one crazy enough to kill, and at times I believed that if ever the murderer was caught, I would not know if I could want his life spared. Now I knew that I could never accept unnatural death at the hands of another again, not even when it is called legitimate, but more so, I knew why. Life and death are God's territory, not ours. I wanted the killer found, put away, and punished. I knew I would have to struggle a long time with my feelings, because the anger was still so fresh. But never would I be able to say, Kill the killer.

When we got back from Montana, my sister Jeannette Oppedisano, arranged to have a memorial service for John at her farmhouse in Castleton, New York, so that family and friends could get together to remember John. Nancy's parents had asked for her body so that her burial could be in Lake Preston, South Dakota, where they lived.

It was a very hot, very still September day, and Jeannette had set up a canopy with several photos of John, candles, and flowers on a table under the canopy. She had rows of seats, and soon all were filled. Two priests, John's old friends, were with us, and they, plus myself and my children, were all going to talk about John. We have several musicians in the family, and as they began to play, opening the service, suddenly a huge flock of small birds, it seemed to be a thousand of them, filled a tree next to the canopy. At that same time, a wind came up, which, as one and another of us talked about John, became stronger and stronger. Before the end of the service, the wind, increasingly gusty, blew down the canopy. As the final songs were played, the wind stopped, and we saw an amazing sight as the birds, as if on signal, left the tree in unison and flew away. The day returned to the stillness it had been and remained hot, without even a breeze, for the rest of the afternoon. We whispered among ourselves that we believed it was not wind and birds but John's spirit that had been there with us that day as we remembered him with love and tears.

The next few months were devastating for us since the case seemed to be full of dead ends. The murders remained a mystery, and when I would talk to the investigators, they were courteous and tried to be optimistic that they'd get a break in the case, but I could hear what they weren't saying, too, and I felt defeated. In desperation, I wanted to get in touch with Dannion Brinkley, a psychic I had met two years earlier after the death of my son Peter at the Alabama home of Dr. Raymond Moody, the psychiatrist who had written *Life after Life,* the first book documenting near-death experiences. Dannion had been declared "dead" after being struck by lightning in the neck and had two amazing near-death experiences of Christ and heaven. After a remarkable recovery, he was left with apparent psychic abilities. Sometime after I had met him he put his experiences into a book, *Saved by the Light,* later made into a movie starring Eric Roberts.

I saw that Dannion was giving a lecture in Maryland—it was now October—and I decided to go and talk to him about the murders. My sister Jeannette, a college professor, went with me. The three of us sat in my hotel room, and I told Dannion about the murders—the investigators at a dead end, no clues, no suspects. I was desperate for some help.

My sister took notes as Dannion, putting his hand on his forehead, closed his eyes and began to describe what he was seeing. Phrases started coming out: a young man ... "this is a kid" ... medium build, jeans and cowboy boots. He knew his way around the house. He had worked in the house. "Did John have an apprentice?" Dannion asked. I said no.

He went on, saying the killer had a connection to country music, that he could be a college student, out west. He said we would have a break in the case within two months. I asked if that meant December. He said, yes, early December.

I thanked him, and when he left, I told my sister, "Well, that was a waste of time." I couldn't make any sense out of what he had said. I could see no connection relating this brutal, terrible crime to a college kid out west. I had no way of knowing I was in for a surprise.

On December 7, I had been praying because it was the anniversary of Pearl Harbor. It got pretty late, and I almost absentmindedly turned on the TV to get the nightly news. Suddenly, I was appalled at what I was seeing. People were milling around at a railroad train stopped at a station on Long Island, all of them expressing shock. Unfolding before them was a tragic scene, with dead and wounded people being taken off the train. A man on the train apparently had brought a nine-millimeter gun with a fifteen-round magazine with him. He had suddenly opened fire, shooting people sitting peacefully on their way home from work.

By the time his fury was over, the man, later identified as Colin Ferguson, thirty-five, had killed five people and injured another twenty. It was a senseless massacre. All the bystanders, giving their reactions as television microphones were being shoved in their faces, expressed the same feelings—hate for the killer and desire for revenge.

I was undergoing an enormous emotional reaction as I watched, because I had been living for four months in terminal pain after getting the news that John and Nancy had been killed by someone wielding a nine-millimeter semi-automatic gun. All I knew to that point was that an intruder had, in the middle of the night, stolen into their home in Montana and blown them away. I was struggling with my anger and devastation and wrestling with the uncertainty of my own reaction if and when the murderer was ever found. Would I be filled with hate, like the people I was watching on TV, when that phantom killer became a face and a person?

I didn't have to contemplate that question very long. For just at that moment, as I was watching the Long Island Rail Road massacre, my phone rang. It was Sheriff Joe Geldrich. "I have some news for you," he said. "You're the first I'm calling. We got the person we think killed your son and daughter-in-law."

The news the sheriff gave me stunned me. The suspect was the eighteen-year-old son of Mr. and Mrs. Joe Clark, the people from whom John and Nancy had bought their house. As the story started getting pieced together, it was unbelievable. The young man's name was Joseph Shadow Clark, known to all by his middle name. He was a first-year student at George Fox, a Quaker college in Oregon. His parents, Fundamentalist Christians, were known to be "very religious," and Shadow himself had gone to Christian schools until his junior year, when he transferred to Bigfork High School, graduating in June 1993. He was an honor student, called "a nice boy" by most of his teachers, though some remembered him for being hooked on crime and blood-and-gore stories.

He might have gotten away with murder if he hadn't started talking to his college roommate. The student said that Shadow had started acting "weird," and so he asked what was wrong. Shadow looked at him and said, "I've done something worse than anybody's ever done before and I'm afraid I am going to get in trouble for it." It took some prodding before he finally put his hand in the shape of a gun, "said pchew," and pulled the imaginary trigger. The roommate asked him if he killed somebody. He answered that he'd had dreams of killing people, and one day it wasn't a dream. "I just did it."

His fellow student recalled how Shadow Clark had shown him a gun he kept under the front seat of his car. He also had told him that he used "Acid" and talked about drugs and getting drunk. He also knew of incidents where Shadow Clark was caught vandalizing. One was putting a stick figure that had x's for eyes and the word "death" on it on the door of their dormitory.

Believing that Shadow Clark might need professional help, his roommate went to school authorities. When the school security chief, Tim Commins, heard what he had to say, he contacted Montana authorities. Investigators McKay and Greydanus went immediately to George Fox College to question Shadow Clark. He admitted owning a gun and told them he had given it to Chris Dimler, a friend in Kalispell, to hold for him. It was a nine-millimeter Smith and Wesson semi-automatic. The pistol was retrieved by Sheriff Geldrich and tested at the state crime lab immediately. Tests showed it was indeed the gun that had been used to kill John and Nancy. When Joe Geldrich called me on that fateful December 7 evening, he knew the case would have an ending, assuring me, "We got the shooter."

I called my sister Jeannette to tell her, reminding her of what Dannion had said. She didn't need to be reminded; she had the notes she had taken. Neither of us was qualified to explain how the mind of a psychic works, or even what psychic power is. We just knew that somehow Dannion Brinkley had "seen" what none of us ever could have imagined. I called him to tell him that they had found "the shooter." He only answered, "I know."

The discovery of a murderer on the campus of a Quaker college, where love, justice, peace, nonviolence, and forgiveness are deep values, was traumatic for everyone associated with the school. George Fox President Edward Stevens, now deceased, issued a statement expressing the grief all were feeling because this situation had erupted on this campus. He spoke for all, saying, "We are grieved over the entire situation. We are deeply saddened for the family of the victims. We are concerned for Shadow and his family. Our hearts and prayers go out to all of them.... "

Within a week, feeling the pain that the college had been plunged into, I wrote to President Stevens: "I am writing this letter with a heart full of sadness over the tragedy that has fallen upon all of us.... Many reporters have called me to ask how I feel about the fact that the investigators in these nearly four-month-old murders apprehended the alleged murderer. My response to all of them is that I can feel no anger because of the overwhelming emotion of sadness that consumes me. So many lives have been wasted, so many hearts broken, so many loved ones left permanently altered.

"I wanted you and all the students at your college to know that my prayers are with you all. All my life I have had enormous respect for the Quaker way of life and it is more than ironic that a suspected murderer was in this nonviolent environment.... "

I enclosed three articles I had written since the murders "that show where my values lie, in peace, human rights, and hope for a global community to evolve in the future so that humanity, and not evil and discord, will prevail."

That letter initiated a long-distance relationship that developed between myself and President Stevens until his death a few years later. He answered my letter with thanks: "It blesses me that you have responded in a Christ-like manner to this incredible tragedy. Thank you also for your prayers.... We had no names, circumstances, etc. for the first two or three days, Antoinette, but I knew that lives had been shattered because of senseless violence—they always are....

"We called the entire George Fox community together for a special meeting of worship on December 10. I invited the students, faculty, and staff to respond by asking the Holy Spirit to examine each of our lives for bitterness, hatred, unforgiveness, and other sins that Jesus equated with murder in His sermon on the mount. We had a time of prayer and seeking God's direction for us as individuals, and as a community of believers.

"Thank you again for writing, Antoinette. . . . We would be honored to have you visit GFC. I would welcome the opportunity to get acquainted with you personally.

"In Faith and Friendship, Ed."

I never did get to George Fox College, but I shall always remember the consolation I felt in knowing that those of us who hold to the teachings of Jesus, our model of nonviolence, always find an instant fellowship. Ed Stevens and I certainly helped each other in those days after Shadow Clark's arrest. This fine man also told me "the Lord will be able to use your life" to do the work of opposing violence and affirming life. I never forgot that.

What became ever more important to me now was to get information about Shadow Clark, to find out what he did and why he did it. In the months since the murders I had made a good friend, William Simonsen, a reporter for the *Bigfork Eagle*, the weekly paper of what was to be John's hometown. Bill kept me posted on what was happening after Shadow Clark's arrest. Most of what I learned about what happened on that fateful night of August 12, 1993, came from Bill's caring, professional reporting and his personal calls that kept me informed.

Shadow Clark told investigators on that December 7 that he had been having a recurring nightmare about breaking into John and Nancy's home. This went on every night for three weeks, and then " . . . one night I woke up and did it." No motive was ever listed in the official records other than those statements about his haunting nightmares. He told the investigators that he bore no grudges against the Boscos. And he rambled on, "Well, you know, I realize that I have messed up. But I'm not a bad person, and anybody you talk to will tell you that. I think it's bad, but I don't think it's the end of the world for me, you know. . . .

"I shouldn't be condemned, you know, for doing one little, one thing. I've done a lot of good things and sure they don't make up for doing that bad thing."

Shadow Clark told how he parked in John and Nancy's driveway, took his flashlight and gun, and went to the house. He said he didn't remember shutting off the power and cutting the phone lines, but added, "It's probable." He got into the house through the window of a ground floor bathroom, and then went to the second floor bedroom where John and Nancy were sleeping. He remembered standing in the doorway to the room. He shot John first because he was "closest to the door. I just remember hearing or seeing the shot being shot. I just remember a point... sticking the gun out and shooting. I didn't aim or anything."

The autopsy on my son showed he died of one gunshot wound to the head. The bullet went through the back of his head and was found by the police under his head on the pillow. Shadow said that John never moved after he was shot.

Nancy awoke from the explosion and grabbed for her glasses, knocking the telephone off the bedside table. She screamed in terror. He fired at her three times. Two of the bullets hit Nancy. The autopsy report showed that one bullet entered her back, hit one of her ribs, her lung, and her shoulder blade before it left her shoulder, then went into her head below her jaw, hit bone and ricocheted out her eye, breaking the lens of her glasses. Autopsy studies show she must have been in a defensive crouch, similar to the fetal position, for the bullet to have traveled on its path. Clark said he left the room after the shootings, admitting, though, that he put a pillow over her head and he may have "touched her" after killing her.

Police checked the house to see if burglary had been part of his reason for breaking in. They determined that nothing was missing, except for a suspected handgun that John may have owned, since they found a gun box that was empty. They asked me endless questions about the gun, which I couldn't answer. I knew John had rifles, because he was a hunter. The rifles were still in a locked case in John's house, they said. I then put them in touch with one of John's friends, who said John had bought the handgun, a small pistol, about twenty years earlier. Sheriff Geldrich said John had not been killed with his own gun. They had retrieved the bullets and had a good idea of the kind of gun these were shot from. They definitely didn't come from a small pistol.

Investigators also said they found no money in the house, which I thought was strange, since John and Nancy were planning a trip to Colorado. I doubt they would have gone without money. Yet, police said there was no evidence of theft. Deputy county attorney Robert Long told me, "Clark said he went in to steal; the gun was missing.... He found himself in a position to shoot and then he did it.... This case doesn't have a beginning, a middle, or end, only a 'he done it.'"

Shadow Clark was charged with two counts of deliberate homicide and one count of aggravated burglary. The burglary charge was made not because items were found to be missing, Mr. Long said, but because the young man was alleged to have entered John and Nancy's house. "Burglary has nothing to do with theft," he said.

The more I heard about his breaking and entering, his sneaking up the stairs, his murderous fantasies, the more my emotions went on a roller coaster. I would cry as I thought about the terror Nancy must have felt as she saw, in the sanctity of her bedroom, what was coming. I would visualize Shadow Clark sneaking into that house where he had lived for most of his life. Did it still feel like it was his home? This was the bedroom where his parents had slept. Was he subconsciously killing them? I pondered his confession, and I could hear the subtle madness that had taken over his brain. It was a bad type, because it left him, I felt, amoral, unable to take responsibility for what he had done or to feel remorse. I would look often at the photo Bill Simonsen had taken of Shadow Clark and his mother, Brenda. The pain in her face cut into my heart. We both had lost sons. People would say to me that the worst thing that can happen to a mother had happened to me. I would think of that photo and respond, no. The worst thing would be to be the mother of the one who had killed another. Thinking of her pain, I knew that never, ever could I say I wanted to add to her pain by having her son die.

We knew that Shadow Clark was facing a death penalty because Montana was one of the states that had reinstated this final punishment for heinous murders. And there was no doubt that the killing of John and Nancy fit the description of premeditated, heinous killing. My children and I were in agreement that we did not want Shadow Clark to be in danger of getting the death penalty. I told Lake County Deputy Attorney Robert Long that we were opposed to the death penalty. In spite of that, he later told my daughter Mary vanValkenburg that he had informed the judge, the Honorable C. B. McNeil, that "as far as the family is concerned, no death could be slow enough for Shadow Clark."

We were so appalled that Mary wrote to Judge McNeil: "If that is indeed what Bob Long told you, the family's views were grossly misrepresented. The majority of John's bereaved family . . . oppose the death penalty. My mother communicated her opposition to the death penalty clearly in her conversation with Bob Long several weeks ago. In the 10 months that have passed since the horrifying, devastating events of August 12, 1993, we have all struggled, despite our complete heartache and aching grief, not to sink into any desire for vengeance. We made the decision early on that Shadow Clark would not destroy any more of our family by dragging us down into bloodthirsty hatred. Our focus is on healing. We feel terrible sadness when we think of how Shadow Clark, such a young man, has destroyed his own life along with the lives of others. This is very difficult, but we hope one day to understand what forgiveness in a case like this might mean. . . .

"Having said that, I also beg you to consider my views on the sentencing. Shadow Clark is young, Shadow Clark acted like a nice boy before the night he broke into my brother and sister-in-law's house to blow them away, and Shadow Clark confessed to the killings. None of that provides strong proof that he will never kill again if given the opportunity. I don't believe that human beings can forfeit their right to life, but I do believe they can forfeit their right to be part of society. . . .

"I urge you to consider imposing a sentence of true life imprisonment with no possibility of parole. . . . "

I was waiting to be informed of the trial date. It never came. Instead I got a call from Bill Simonsen telling me, somewhat in shock, that the case was over, done. There would be no trial. Shadow Clark had confessed to the murders in order to take a plea bargain that would give him a better deal.

It hit me that because there would be no trial, the evidence would never be put on the table. The news media would never have to report further on this horrible crime. It would be swept under the rug, and the people of Montana could forget about the infamous hour on August 12, 1993, when a Montana boy executed two fine people.

I remember calling Deputy Attorney Long attempting to find out if I could get more information about why Shadow Clark did what he did. He said no. Then I asked him if they had ever found John's gun. He said, yes, they found it a few days after Shadow Clark was arrested, back in December. I was shocked that after how they had questioned me about the gun, they hadn't told me that they found it so many months earlier. What was more shocking was how they found it. Shadow confessed that he had taken the gun and put it in a music case under his bed. Bob Long told me that Sheriff Geldrich had searched the house but hadn't found the gun. The gun was turned in to the authorities by Shadow Clark's lawyer a few days later. Apparently, Joe Clark had found the gun and given it to a friend of his from the Assembly of God church in Kalispell, who then turned the gun over to Mr. Nardi, Shadow's lawyer. When I

asked why Joe Clark had the gun, Mr. Long said he didn't know. "Didn't
you ask him?" I asked, surprised. He answered, no, he didn't have to
ask; he had the shooter.

I remained very disturbed because of two unanswered questions: Why
did my kids have to die? Shadow Clark never gave a motive. And why
did Shadow Clark's father find my son John's gun when a sheriff who
searched the house hadn't? I kept praying for answers so I could get
some peace of mind.

In a courtroom in Poulson, Montana, on July 27, 1994, Joseph
Shadow Clark, nineteen, was sentenced by District Judge C. B. McNeil
to 220 years in Montana State Prison, with no eligibility for parole until
he reaches the age of sixty. This sentence was the one agreed upon by
the prosecutor, Deputy Attorney Robert Long, and the lawyer for the
defendant, Steven Nardi, after the young man, simply called "Shadow"
by everyone, pleaded guilty to two counts of deliberate homicide and
one count of aggravated burglary in the murders of John and Nancy
Bosco on August 12, 1993.

Judge McNeil explained why the defendant would be ineligible for
parole or participation in the supervised release program until he had
attained the age of sixty: "The reasons for such restrictions are the defendant violated the sanctity of the victims' home at night without any
apparent motive, shot two totally innocent persons, John and Nancy
Bosco, to death. The court finds such restrictions against parole necessary
to protect this society from the heinous acts of this man. . . . "

The scene in the courtroom, Bill Simonsen told me, was grim. Nancy's
parents, who live in South Dakota, and John's father, who lived in Montana, were apparently close enough to Poulson to have been notified of
the court date, and, as would be expected, Shadow Clark's parents were
there. Bill reported that the relatives of both the victims and the murderer were wrestling with varying degrees of emotional frenzy. Shadow
Clark, clean-cut and calm, was emotionally frozen.

While there was an apparent "ending" to the case, a mystery remained
and still remains. Why did Shadow Clark do it? Why did he execute two
people and then close his mouth and say only that he doesn't know why
he did it? Doesn't an honor student and a "good" boy have a better memory—to say nothing of conscience—than that? These questions haunted
everyone after the trial. Even the editor of the *Bigfork Eagle* at the time,
Marc Wilson, had a problem with the secrecy. He wrote an editorial,
addressed to Judge McNeil: "We want to ask you a favor. . . . Please ask
him why he did it. Deputy County Attorney Bob Long says the piles of

evidence will be sealed from public scrutiny. Even you, your honor, will not see the evidence. . . .

"We who live in Bigfork don't understand what has happened. How could one of our town's children have killed two of our residents? Justice will not be served unless someone makes Joseph Shadow Clark explain why he murdered John and Nancy Bosco. He has to answer for his crimes."

I thanked Marc Wilson. We were both sorry that the judge didn't listen.

As a family, this is what we were left with—lives permanently shattered and altered, for no reason. Or if there is a reason, it remains sealed away. I will never be told the findings of the forensic psychiatric tests that were ordered done on Shadow Clark because that information belongs to the lawyer retained by Shadow Clark's family. All we were told is that Shadow Clark is not insane, nor is he mentally impaired. He knew what he was doing. It was deliberate murder.

The unanswered questions afflicted my journalist's intellect. I like information. I like analysis. I like answers. As a mother, I remained in torment over not knowing why my kids had to die. I remember back in the late 1960s when I was a reporter, doing a story on a Gold Star mother whose son had been killed in Vietnam. Billie Backer was her name.

Billie had taken her son's death insurance money given to her by the government, rented a store front, and set it up with photos and mementos of her son. She tried to get people to sign petitions to have a national holiday proclaimed in her son's name. Of course, as a noncelebrity, she couldn't begin to get the big news media interested in her appeal at all. Yet, as a mother myself of seven, I shall never forget what she said to me, words that cut into my soul as she explained her actions:

"My son was killed—*and the earth didn't shake!*"

Now I understood what she meant.

But understanding didn't bring me peace. John did, and his message came in a dream. I was in my kitchen and suddenly John was there, looking strong, smiling at me. I ran to him and threw my arms around him, saying, "I love you," over and over. I called out to my other children, telling them, "Come into the kitchen. John's here." And then I said to John, "Now, you've got to tell me. Why did he kill you? I've got to know." And John started to shrink away. I started to shout, "John, you've got to tell me. I've got to know." And he started to leave me. At that, I cried, "John, I love you. You mustn't go. I love you." And he came back, but with a message. He said, *"Mom, what seems so impor-*

tant down here is not important where I am now." My other children were now with us, all of us telling John how we love him. He seemed to be glowing.

When I woke up, I was at peace. John had helped me to understand that it is love, not answers, that is most important. Never since then did I allow myself to focus on the questions I had found so troubling, particularly the matter of why Shadow Clark's father had had John's gun.

After the sentencing I was interviewed by a reporter for the *Daily Inter Lake* about how I felt. I said Shadow Clark had to get a long sentence because nobody would want him back on the streets again. I repeated that my children and I adamantly opposed the death penalty for Shadow Clark, even though he killed our loved ones, and she quoted me saying, "We believe very strongly in the pricelessness of life."

I also told her that we refused to be destroyed or diminished by this tragedy, that we would strive to turn this into something positive, serving as a catalyst for spiritual growth, in spite of our pain, which we knew would never really be gone.

I had a yearning, though, so much like Billie Backer's. I wanted to tell the world what had happened to John and Nancy, so that people could know that once for a few decades, two beautiful people lived, worked, and brought love into this world. They would never know my son, a furniture maker, who would take a piece of wood and reverently show it to me, in awe of its beauty, remarking at the variety, the uniqueness, of the Creator's work. They wouldn't know my daughter-in-law, who collected, and wrote poetry, who spent the week before she was killed making raspberry jam to give us for presents when Christmas '93 arrived. And I promised them, they would not be forgotten.

Unexpectedly, a few months after Shadow Clark was sent away to Montana State Prison, I got a phone call from the famous television show *Unsolved Mysteries.* They were doing a program on Dannion Brinkley. The unsolved mystery was where and how he had received such powerful psychic gifts. They had asked him to recommend a "credible, recent witness" to be on the program and Dannion said, "Call Toni Bosco." They did. I told them my story of how Dannion had literally "seen" and described the young killer, adding that my sister Jeannette was there as a witness.

They brought me on to the program, and later, when it was aired, I was home alone. When they showed a full-screen photo, one taken at John and Nancy's wedding, I sobbed, but joy was mixed with my pain as I talked to my kids in heaven, telling them I had kept my word. They were not forgotten.

My family and I had been through an incredible period, one I would often think of as the twenty months from hell. But then I would wonder if, in some strange way that I had yet to discover, this could be transformed into a future where I would feel heaven. I was still overwhelmed by sadness at the tragedy of so many lives altered forever, and that included the young life of Shadow Clark. I had to ask myself back then, and over and over since then, do I have enough of God's love in me to pray for this young killer? Perhaps. Because I do pray for him, knowing in my soul that I must, for the sake of my own redemption.

I have related to a verse I read long ago by Henry van Dyke:

> Broken at last, I bowed my head,
> Forgetting all myself, and said,
> "Whatever comes, His will be done";
> And in that moment peace was won.

Chapter Two

BEGINNING THE
HEALING PROCESS

During all this time, from getting the news of the murders to the conviction of Shadow Clark, I had continued working at my job as executive editor of the *Litchfield County Times,* a weekly paper in Connecticut. I felt it was the healthiest thing I could do, to get up each morning, shower, get dressed, have coffee, and get out and drive the twelve miles to my office. At night, back home, I would get restless and sit at the computer putting down the feelings that kept welling up in me.

I would sometimes write about guns, violence, prisons, murder, and the death penalty, a few of my pieces appearing in my weekly column syndicated since 1974 by Catholic News Service in Washington and some published on the commentary page of my newspaper. I examined my own conscience to rediscover when, where, and why I had become opposed to the death penalty and found myself remembering scenes from my home when I was a very young child.

That was the time of the Lindbergh baby kidnapping, which became the celebrated crime of the decade. In March 1932 the two-year-old son of Charles and Anne Lindbergh was kidnapped from their home in New Jersey and later found to have been murdered. The terrible crime was on everybody's mind, and I remember how my parents and their friends talked frequently about this. When Bruno Richard Hauptmann was arrested and charged with the murder, he claimed he was innocent, but no one believed him. I can still hear my parents' friends saying without doubt that Hauptmann was the killer. When he was sentenced to die in the electric chair, everyone applauded, ghoulishly waiting for the day of the death.

I was a tot, but I could read and I could listen to what adults were saying. I still remember the April night in 1936 when the radio was turned on in my house, and probably in most houses, with people glued to it to hear all about the execution. I remember hearing someone say that Bruno Hauptmann's wife, Antoinette, was crying out that he was innocent. I felt related to her, since my name was Antoinette.

I was about to make my First Communion and had memorized the Ten Commandments. When the talk got frenzied about the execution, I started to cry and asked my mother why they were killing someone when God said, "Thou shalt not kill." She shrugged her shoulders and told me that when somebody kills another person, then they have to pay for that crime by going to death. I couldn't really understand that.

Shortly after, I read newspaper stories about another execution to come. This time it was a woman and her lover. I don't remember their names, but they were to be electrocuted for having successfully plotted to kill the woman's husband. What affected me, though, was the story I read that said all she asked for in her final time was to have a sewing machine and some fabric. She wanted to sew dresses for her children so they would have some new school clothes. I don't know if she ever got her request. Again I remember I kept asking my mother why they were killing a mother. The explanation that she had forfeited her life because of killing another didn't seem right to me. Even as a seven-year-old, I found it contradictory that killing was evil and wrong, unless one was killed in the electric chair.

This conviction became intense about ten years later when my Uncle Tony's wife was physically restrained one day and taken to what they then used to call "the insane asylum." I asked my mother why Aunt Margie went crazy, and she told me it was because her brother had been electrocuted when she was very young and she never got over it. The story I learned from my relatives was that back in 1926, Aunt Margie's brother, Charles Doran, then twenty-one, with two friends had robbed a store and in the process killed the owner. Of the three, Charles, Irish and poor, was sent to death row in Sing Sing, the notorious New York prison, and put to death in the electric chair in 1928, less than two years after the crime. My Aunt Thelma told me that Aunt Margie would talk about how she, then a teenager, and no other members of her family could even leave the house without a swarm of reporters after them. It left Margie traumatized.

I never knew any details of this story until I was compiling material for this book. I called Clare Regan, a board member of New Yorkers Against the Death Penalty who has been a longtime human rights activist in Rochester, New York, asking if she could help me get information about a man executed in New York in 1928. She told me to get in touch with

Scott Christianson, who had recently written a book about executions in New York State, *Condemned: Inside the Sing Sing Death House* (New York University Press). Hoping he could confirm the story about Charles Doran that had become family lore, I contacted him. Scott responded generously to my request and gave me details I never knew about this man, who was to be remembered by so many of us who were not yet born then—besides having such an influence on me as regards the death penalty.

Charles J. Doran, born December 29, 1903, killed as No. 79880 on January 5, 1928, in Sing Sing's electric chair, and some other young men, robbery in mind, targeted a gas station and confectionery store at 681 New Scotland Avenue in Albany, New York, on November 6, 1926. While one of them, allegedly Charles, held a pistol pointed at the owner, Raymond Jackson, a twenty-seven-year-old war veteran, an accomplice cleared the cash register of about $90. The men backed out the door, and the gun went off, killing Mr. Jackson. The lone eyewitness was an eleven-year-old boy, who gave a description of the getaway car. It didn't take long to find the car and the criminals. A front-page story in the *Albany Times Union* on November 28, 1926, reported the crime and the arrest.

Mr. Christianson told me that Charles, single, a cigarette-smoking chauffeur, had "no criminal record to speak of. He had been picked up once and let go." He was to be tried with his accomplice, Theodore "Chickie" Harrington, who "snitched" on his friend, cooperated with an interrogation, and pointed the finger at Charles, calling him the gunman. I followed up the information Mr. Christianson gave me, finding stories about the case in 1926–28 editions of the *Albany Times Union*. With no explanations given, Harrington was acquitted of the murder, with authorities even dropping the first degree robbery charge. Yet Charles was sentenced to death on May 9, 1927, after being convicted of murder in the State Supreme Court.

His two lawyers, Ben Holtz and Ransom Gillett, appealed, asking for a new trial, on the grounds that the verdict and sentence were "contrary to evidence, against the weight of evidence and against the law." They lost a final appeal on November 27 of that year. In prison, Charles received spiritual support from the Catholic chaplain, Father John P. McCaffery, who was with him when he walked to the death room, holding a large wooden crucifix. The priest was reported to be visibly shaken when Charles was strapped into the chair and put to death at 11 p.m., January 5, 1928, eight months after his sentencing.

His family, four sisters, a twenty-year-old brother, Henry, an auto mechanic, and his mother, Fanny, vigorously maintained that Charles was innocent to the end, as did Charles himself. "Charlie Boy never committed the crime. He is innocent," Fanny said, "old and feeble before her time, faithful to the end," as a reporter put it, "praying her rosary every day." Henry faithfully visited his brother; he was with him the entire last day of his life. He was active in the fight to save his older brother, and personally called Governor Al Smith the night before the execution to beg once more for clemency. Fanny insisted the governor "will save my boy. If the governor does not act, I will not be able to survive that sorrow, for my strength is slowly going."

Governor Smith denied clemency for Charles Doran, giving a statement that I have read over and over and find contradictory and immoral. "Upon a hearing on the application of Doran for executive clemency, it was urged that the other men engaged in the commission of this murder were either not punished at all or not punished equally with Doran. This is a matter with which I cannot deal; it is for the local authorities of Albany to handle...."

He goes on then to explain that "when one or more persons engage in robbery or any other felony and during the progress of such a crime, someone is killed, under the laws of our state, all those engaged in the commission of said crime are guilty of murder, first degree. In the case before me, it would make no difference whether or not Doran fired the fatal shot...."

How could this have happened—that Harrington and whoever else was there got off scot-free, while Charles Doran was murdered, not for a shooting, but simply for being there, as they were, while a crime was carried out? Equal justice under the law was apparently just as elusive in 1928 as it often is today! Mr. Christianson also asked the question that was on my mind, "I'd like to know why he was singled out."

I found myself crying when I read of the electrocution, with the first switch pulled by Robert Elliott, the executioner who put Sacco and Vanzetti to death earlier that decade. The Doran family claimed the body so Charles could have a decent burial. Reading all this, I began to better understand how seeds had been sown that one day would contribute to my Aunt Margie's breakdown.

As for why the family had become such a center of attention, Mr. Christianson said that at that time, "tremendous attention was focused on the death penalty." Charles Doran was in Sing Sing at the same time the prison held a woman on death row, Ruth Snyder. It was an infamous case of infidelity, with her accomplice in murder being a man named Judd Grey. Shortly after Charles Doran's execution, Ruth Snyder was also electrocuted in Sing Sing, and hers was the biggest story of the time. Another reason for death penalty attention was the fact that Sing Sing's warden, Lewis Lawes, was outspokenly opposed to the death penalty. Yet he had to carry out the law, and during his time there 303 executions were carried out. Charles Doran was the 266th person executed there.

My aunt never really got over the execution of her beloved brother, and when a second traumatic loss hit her—the death of her son, my cousin Tony, at age thirteen from kidney failure—she ended up mad. From that day on, the notion of the death penalty permanently appalled me. It also made me wonder why we never think of the condemned person's family and the punishment and torment meted out to these innocent relatives. Crime leaves victims on both sides in its wake.

Years later, when I was getting my master's degree and taking an ethics course, the death penalty question came up. I was a working single parent at the time, active in the causes I believed in, specifically interracial justice and protests against the Vietnam War. Never afraid to be outspoken about what I believed in, I told my professor in brash, convinced fashion that I was opposed to the death penalty. He looked at me and asked, "Do you have a daughter." "Yes," I answered, confused. "I have two daughters."

Then, piercingly staring directly at me, he asked, "Suppose someone raped and murdered one of your daughters. What would you say then?"

I was stunned. I hadn't ever expected such a crime to be a personal matter. Without thinking, I blurted out, "I'd say kill the bastard!"

I was deeply disturbed when I left the class. It struck me that I had been put in a new place with that question. I found myself struggling with what I knew was a position of phoniness if such a crucial sub-ject remained only something academic to study. True, I had always felt chilled at the thought of the death penalty, but that day I had been rad-ically more chilled by the thought of someone destroying my child. I knew now I had to delve deeply and honestly into the meaning of evil, and death by murder, as well as the meaning of life itself. I knew that only God is in charge of life's origins, and logically it should be only God who is in charge of its endings. I had come to see and believe that life and death belong to God, but now my emotions had been stripped naked, and, while I was still opposed to the death penalty, I prayed that I would never be tested in a way my professor had indicated. I still opposed the death penalty, but I admit, I truly did not know where I would stand if the death penalty question ever became personal.

I was to learn first hand the horror of unnatural death in 1991, when I had to survive the suicide of my youngest son, Peter. A delightful child, an honor student, a thoughtful sibling, and a devoted son, Peter suffered a radical change in his ability to relate to the world when he was in senior high school, and at age seventeen, he left me a suicide note. I was working at the State University of New York at Stony Brook on Long Island at the time, and the psychiatric unit at the new University Hospital had just opened. I was able to get Peter admitted and was told, almost immediately, that he was "hopelessly schizophrenic" and that when the onset is in adolescence, the illness is permanent. They told me he would spend all his days in an institution.

We didn't accept that. I found a psychiatrist who was an expert in adolescent psychiatry to work with Peter, and he made progress. He finished high school and went into the army, serving two years in Germany. He completed college, getting a cum laude teaching degree; taught math in a Catholic school in Guam; wrote three books for major publishers on war subjects—and then on March 18, 1991, he put a gun to his head and killed himself. He had struggled admirably with his illness, but never found a medication that really helped him. He would have periodic psychotic breakdowns that ultimately defeated him.

Peter left us several notes and a long tape explaining his pain and his defeat by life, in spite of his valiant struggle to have a life. The pain had become unendurable, he said, telling us the Gulf War had been the turning point. Once again, man's inhumanity to man would take over, as we killed not just soldiers, but innocent adults and children, all for oil. It was "time to go home," he said, quoting C. S. Lewis, as we had often done together, that "earth is not our permanent home." Truly, we could *hear* the illness, and we never judged him. We loved him too much even to try to understand his ultimate defeat. We wept for him, mourned his loss, and celebrated his life.

Now that I had to confront unnatural death in a devastating way, confusion vanished. It was so clear to me that death at the hand of anyone but God is always wrong. We must not get into the trap of concentrating on and trying to judge death at the hands of humans, giving ourselves permission to determine if that death is justified. I had always been disturbed by the thought of war. Now, empathizing with Peter's revulsion over the Gulf War, I knew that I would never, ever be able to accept or condone any war, unless it was clearly for our survival. I felt strongly that, except for self-defense, killing, no matter who does it, the country, the state, the individual, is wrong and diminishes all of us.

When I got the call from Sheriff Geldrich, telling me of the deaths of John and Nancy, I had already been confronting the wrongness of all death by human hands for two and a half years, trying to survive and emerge from the cauldron created by Peter's suicide. I was in a place where I had grown permanently strong in my conviction that life is God's business. When I got off the phone, I remembered the question my professor had asked, "What if someone raped and murdered your daughter?" Now someone had violated the bedroom of my son and daughter-in-law, the equivalent of rape, taking their lives. It was brutal, and it was wrong. The question was no longer academic, but intensely personal. Yet, even at that moment, remembering all I had come to understand about who's in charge of life from Peter's suicide, I felt an assurance that heavenly help would hold me up, even should I feel myself slipping into the pit of hate and vengeance. It was almost beyond belief to me to realize that it was Peter's suicide that would save me from despairing after the murders. God works in such mysterious ways.

After Peter's death I had thrown myself into a heavy work schedule, spending more time at my editing job, writing ever more features and Op-Ed pieces and still doing my weekly column. The house without Peter was like an empty tomb, and I was trying to fill that emptiness with busyness. One day I got a call from Emilie Cerar, editor of Resurrection Press, asking me if I would write a booklet for them. As we talked, we came up with doing it on the subject of faith, and I said yes.

Now I stayed at the computer even longer hours, but I found a strange thing happening. I would be writing something on faith, and then my thought pattern would change, and I would find myself writing something that I knew was coming straight from the depths of my soul. I was struggling with how to come to peace from my pain, and I would sense at times that Peter was encouraging me to "go deeper, Mom." Before long I had almost completed a book-length spiritual memoir. And then came the news of the murders. This intensified my need to find a path that would help me not get stuck in pain. With prayer and work I finished the book which was released as *The Pummeled Heart: Finding Peace through Pain*.

The response I received, mainly from parents suffering intense hurts after the loss of a child, was overwhelming. I was invited to be on several television interview shows, among them one put out by the radio and television network under the auspices of the Archdiocese of Hartford. They showed a repeat of that interview very early one morning, which strangely enough opened doors I had not at that point even thought about.

It was by coincidence that Wanda Rieger happened to see that program. She hadn't been able to sleep, a condition becoming familiar to her. Her only daughter, Melanie Ilene, a student at Naugatuck Valley Community College in Waterbury, Connecticut, had been murdered by her boyfriend. Wanda and her husband, Dr. Sam Rieger, then a chemistry professor at that same college, were devastated. In the early morning hours when Wanda saw me on that program, talking about my struggle to find peace from the pain of suicide and murder, she wanted to talk to me. I had been introduced as the executive editor of the *Litchfield County Times,* and the Riegers, who had a travel agency business in Litchfield County, knew the paper because they had run ads in it. That morning, shortly after I got to work, I received a call from the Riegers. When they told me their daughter had been murdered a few months earlier, in May of 1994, I got directions to their agency and was on my way.

Up to this point, I had not met other parents of murdered children, at least not personally, sitting with them, talking with them, sharing our stories, heart to heart. Sitting there with the Riegers that day, I heard what another family had gone through as Sam spoke, telling me that it was four years earlier that José Crespo had come into their lives, at Melanie's request:

"He came from a different background and we all helped to improve his life. Melanie helped him with his education and social awareness and cared for his two children from a previous relationship. Wanda and I constantly welcomed him into our home, took him out for dinner, brought him on a Caribbean cruise, and bought him clothes and furnishings. And how did José repay us? He killed our Melanie!

"He strangled her in our home on a day when we were away on a vacation. He stuffed her in plastic bags and then put her into our son Randy's hockey bag. He left her there while he pawned Melanie's jewelry. He then rented a storage locker, where he placed her body later that night with many personal articles and left her there to rot. During this day he still had time to pick up his children and take them to the beach as he had planned to do with Melanie.

"The next day he went with his brother-in-law to obtain parts to repair his car. When José asked him how he might store a car where he would not have to give his name, his brother-in-law became suspicious."

José then blurted out the story, and the brother-in-law advised him to see an attorney.

As Sam went on, I could see and understand the intensity of his anger. "Our family is devastated. Wanda cannot get out of the bed some mornings. I cannot remember things from one moment to the next. Even simple functions we used to take for granted are now sometimes almost impossible for us. And our lives will only get worse. We still have to live through a trial and all the inequities and inhumaneness it will bring. Our suffering will only continue. Laws and procedures cater to the criminal, not the victims or survivors. This must be changed now! This is not a political issue. This is about reclaiming our society from those who are destroying it. We need laws to be changed to favor the victims and survivors, not the criminals!"

I had had a little more time to confront my losses and was trying to move on without being overtaken by anger. I had prayed to be able to find forgiveness for Shadow Clark, and I truly felt that with God's help I was beginning to find peace. But hearing Sam and Wanda, I could sincerely relate to their anger and understand the devastation that made them want to do to José Crespo what he had done to Melanie.

We talked and cried, drank coffee and agreed to resolve that life would go on. Sam and Wanda had already contacted a nearly defunct group in Connecticut called Survivors of Homicide, founded some years earlier by people whose lives had been devastated by violence. Its purpose was to help each other cope with the grief and despair, the pain, rage, and even hopelessness that most survivors feel at times. It also was set up to help victims get practical advice about dealing with courts, compensation, and some of the frustrating details that are usually part of coping with this kind of loss.

I decided that day to join Survivors of Homicide specifically to work with Sam and Wanda to try to bring some good out of the evil that had invaded our lives. In the time since that first meeting, they have honored their daughter's memory by initiating an annual Melanie Ilene Rieger two-day conference against violence at the college she attended, along with setting up a scholarship. They have brought in outstanding speakers who have been shattered by crime, like David Kaczynski, whose brother Ted was convicted as the "Unabomber," a social worker who helps disadvantaged youth and now is an advocate against the death penalty; Maureen Kanka, whose seven-year-old daughter, Megan, was sexually abused and killed by a neighbor, a known sex offender, and who worked to get "Megan's Law" passed, to assure that people are informed when a sex offender released from prison moves into their neighborhood; Carole Carrington, whose daughter Carol Sund, grand-daughter Julie Sund, and her friend from South America were killed at Yosemite National Park, who has set up a fund, offering rewards for the safe return of missing persons; and Mark Klaas, whose daughter Polly was abducted from her California home and murdered, who now leads programs and speaks from coast to coast on effective ways of protecting our children. Dr. Henry Lee, the acclaimed forensic scientist who has investigated such high profile crimes as the O. J. Simpson and Jon Benet Ramsey cases, has been a frequent participant.

The conference also brings in high-level state officials involved with criminal justice, including Commissioner of Corrections John Armstrong, prosecutors, lawyers, defense attorneys, judges, and victims' advocates, among other professionals.

Shortly after Melanie's death, Sam and Wanda took on the leadership of SOH, committing the organization to educate legislators and professionals in the criminal justice system on the need to strengthen the rights of survivors and victims of violent crime, including such matters as informing victims about parole hearings, letting them make a statement in court about their loved one, bail and sentencing, allowing a photo of their loved one to be presented in a trial, getting transcripts of a trial and court proceedings without having to pay for these and to be notified if the convicted murderer comes up for early release for any reason.

During this time, the trial of José Crespo went on, and much to Sam and Wanda's dismay, he did not get life imprisonment, but was sentenced to sixty years. Because of the way the sentencing laws work, he will probably have as many as half those years shaved off because of what is called "good time," reduction in time served for behaving while in prison. Melanie won't have a life, but her murderer will, and this realization brings deep pain to her grieving parents. Because most murderers get out of prison and are back on the street after serving only a certain amount of time, the Riegers feel the death penalty makes sense. At least it guarantees that a killer won't get out to kill again. But then they acknowledge that if murderers got true life sentences, with no possibility of parole, they probably would not support the death penalty. A growing number of people in the country would agree with them. A Gallup poll in winter 2000 showed 71 percent of those polled favoring capital punishment, with 22 percent opposed and 7 percent with no opinion. Yet, when asked about the alternative, life in prison without parole, supporters of the death penalty dropped to 56 percent, with 38 percent preferring the option of prison without parole.

I respect the Riegers for their position, which points to the vagaries and failures of the criminal justice system, yet shows some willingness to consider life instead of death for a convicted murderer, in spite of their permanent pain of loss. Not all survivors of homicide can get to that place of compromise. You keep getting bombarded with what I call the comparison thoughts—the killer is living, breathing, talking, writing, being visited by family and other people—in other words, *having a life!* And your loved one is dead. You look at their pictures, and it hits you that they are frozen in time. You will never know what they would have looked like as they got older. A murderer has also cut your life line. Your dead child will never have children to pass on, beautiful young ones who would have been your grandchildren. No wonder the tears go on, year after year.

Perhaps the worst torment of all is if you never find out who actually took the life of your child away. We didn't know for four months who killed John and Nancy, and that is the closest I ever got to despair in my whole life. My children would agonize, as I did, and I learned that all too little attention is given to sibling pain when a brother or sister is taken from them. I remember my daughter Mary finally expressing her agony and anger, saying how it was unbearable to know that someone was out there who had murdered her brother and sister-in-law, who was in all likelihood having a fine time, eating, going on a high, having sex, enjoying life. The injustice of this heaps on so much more sorrow. When and if you do find out who did the killing, the sense of injustice remains, becoming even more intensified.

I would meet with other people coming to our meetings of Survivors of Homicide, and none of us really had to explain our feelings. We were all in the same place about loss. We also shared so many similar experiences about how others treat you after murder has shattered your life. So many simply walk away from you. They don't know what to say. Looking at us scares them because they have to face a frightening truth—that if a person did the unthinkable, killed someone we loved, perhaps that could happen to them, too. Most friends and relatives can't face that scenario.

We all learned that while we may look the same on the outside, we are not the people anyone used to know. We have been radically and permanently altered because of the way the life of someone we loved was taken away. This ghastly and horrendous crime has shattered our lives. We have been forced by this senseless act and devastating pain to recognize how vulnerable we are and to be filled with feelings of anger, rage and revenge that are frightening in their intensity. We have also been plunged into a new and scary role of having to deal with police, courts, and lawyers. All of us discover a new isolation—that social supports are inadequate and many one-time associates and friends are scared away. We come together as Survivors of Homicide because here we can have a heart-to-heart communication with others who understand what we've been through and where we are, because we've all been in the same cauldron. We also are honest enough to admit that healing is best achieved by turning our anger into activism, working specifically to shed light on all aspects of violence in hopes of finding ways to lessen this plague which pollutes our society.

I grew to love all these people who, like myself, are members of what I would call "the Fellowship of the Wounded." Yet, it was clear right from the beginning that I was in a different place than most of the others when it came to the question of punishment of a killer. I believe in punishment, definitely, but I believe just as strongly that prison, without the possibility of parole, is the way to go and not the death penalty. I was almost alone in that position. There were times when I would be enormously uncomfortable hearing some members talk, with such anger, describing how they would personally want to get "justice," which sounded at times more like vengeance. Some would say we should make killers suffer, let them have a cruel death. I remember the incident when the electric chair malfunctioned in Florida and a man died a slow and horrible death. It was an inhuman deed, yet one father of a murdered son laughed and remarked, "good," that's how it should be for a killer, "fry them slowly." A minority were in the same camp as murder victim survivors I had seen interviewed on television who said they would pull the switch if they had the chance, or inject the poison and watch the killer squirm and die.

I could understand these very human feelings. When a person has so destroyed your life, you can get plagued with urgings to "even the score," and the only way is to see to it that this person, too, loses his or her life. Yet I found it very disturbing when survivors would go in that direction. When I tried to present a different position, forgiveness and nonviolent punishment, a few would be confused by me, not able to understand how I could want anything but torture and death for the killer of my kids. Their reactions made me painfully uncomfortable, as did the escalating crowds on the death penalty bandwagons galloping from coast to coast. We were witnessing how "justified violence" was sweeping the country, interpreted as being right and needed "justice."

At the same time, seeing so many death penalty supporters to be good people, many of whom I loved, I would find myself wrestling with bouts of uncertainty about my own position. I would look inside myself and ask, am I so noble, so altruistic as to believe that the taker of innocent life deserves to live? When one member reacted to my anti–death penalty position with hostility, berating me for "judging" her and the others, telling me I thought I was better, holier than they were, I repeated what I had always said, that never could I judge another, especially one who had suffered the same agony that had crushed me. All I asked was that they would respect me for my position, and I have found that to be what has happened. Most members of Survivors of Homicide are angry about our criminal justice system, so flawed that many innocent people have been executed and so favorable to whites and the wealthy that an outrageous imbalance exists, with a majority of the thirty-six hundred people on death row in America's prisons being nonwhites, teenagers, or mentally retarded persons. My colleagues are not "revengeful," but we rather seek just punishment for a person truly, without doubt, known to be a murderer, which, as most of them see it, from their personal pain, has to be the death penalty. I disagree and I ask for their understanding, which most give me graciously.

I had worried in the first few weeks after the murders about myself. Who was I going to become as a result of this radical alteration of my being? Would I become hardened by this brutal crime? I had read something once in a column by Sidney J. Harris that I had cut out, so taken was I by what he said: "Nobody knows himself until he has come face to face with calamity. It is only in crises that we learn our true identity; . . . many have gone through life thinking they were strong when they were only safe." Who was I now that this calamity had struck with such force?

I was asking that question six months after the murders of John and Nancy when I had the opportunity to interview best-selling author Dominick Dunne, who had come to Connecticut to give a lecture to students at his alma mater, the Canterbury School in New Milford. I knew he had survived the murder of his daughter, Dominique, an actress who had played in the movie *The Poltergeist*. While I knew my interview had to be broad-based, covering the highlights of his life and career, I was most anxious to hear how he had survived the ultimate tragedy that can hit a parent, the murder of a child.

He told me his daughter had been strangled to death by a former boyfriend, a chef at a Los Angeles restaurant. The trial was devastating for the family—him, his ex-wife, and two sons—to live through. In the end, though the ex-boyfriend had choked Dominique for a full five minutes, he was, shockingly, convicted only of voluntary manslaughter and given a light sentence. He was back on the streets after serving only three and a half years for a crime that had so brutally stolen the life of a beautiful twenty-two-year-old woman.

"I had absolutely adored my daughter, and she, me," Mr. Dunne told me. The murder, "totally, completely, utterly changed my life. It was as if God had taken hold of my life and shaken it. I changed as a person, as anyone who knew me can attest to."

Still, when life deals you such a blow, "the fact of the matter is that you go on. You don't give up. If you gave up, you would do no honor to the person you have lost. And one day you find out that after a while, you can laugh again, and have a good time again. Yet, it's a wound that's never going to heal." Part of each day for him carries the reminder of his daughter's death.

A "great support" for him turned out to be the Catholic faith in which he had once been grounded. "I didn't ask, 'How can you believe in a God who would let such a terrible thing happen?' I never felt that way. I just kept saying, 'Help.' I had been sort of a lapsed Catholic," Mr. Dunne said in that February 1994 interview, but after his daughter's murder, he "returned to the church."

As a writer myself, who had recently completed a soul-searching book, I related to how he told me that part of his healing came from his work, his writing. "The first magazine piece I wrote after the murder was 'Justice.' It dealt with a lot of the feelings I had, like rage. It's important to deal with rage," he insisted.

Yet, when his daughter's murderer got such a light sentence and was so soon out of prison, his own rage "got worse. I hired a private detective and had him followed." Then he gradually understood that he was becoming obsessed with this injustice, spending so much of his time reading reports, stuck in his pain. He had worked with a group calling itself the National Victims Center and had spoken to and counseled families of homicide victims. "So many of them were living lives of revenge," he said, indicating his sadness at this. He looked at himself and "all of a sudden, I said, I don't want to live this way." He ended his obsession with the injustice done to them—when payment for a daughter's life was three and a half years of the murderer's time—to the great relief and joy of his family. "I have no idea where he [the murderer] is and I don't care," he said, adding that he had chosen to "deal in a positive way" with his trauma.

I could relate to all he said, because, thanks be to God, I had begun to find my direction after that mourning journey to John and Nancy's home in Bigfork. I had started to feel a heavenly assurance that if I reached out, the hand of the Lord would be there to hold mine. But I realized that for me "to deal in a positive way" with my heartache, I would have to work actively for what I believed in, for what I had been given to understand in that bedroom of death in Bigfork. As I heard and read more about the escalation of the death penalty, as I realized how almost everybody I talked to assumed I would be for it because murder had entered my personal space, I found myself seeking out people who were victims of crime or slander and yet had forgiven the one who hurt them. I began to understand that one thing I was to gain from the blow to our family was a new slant on forgiveness. The first insight was that if I let myself fall into the pit of letting this sword of sorrow erode my soul with hatred or a desire for revenge, I would no longer be able to call myself Christian. I reread the Gospels and saw that the major message of the Lord Jesus was *forgive*, over and over, forgive.

I saw clearly that what forgiveness is really about is putting the spotlight on ourselves to reveal who we really are when we become the victim of brutal evil. And it is, in some ways, very self-actualizing because forgiving doesn't mean to give in; it means to let go, and letting go is a precondition to becoming free. If you don't forgive you give the one who hurt you ever more control over you. If I didn't forgive Shadow Clark, I would be emotionally handcuffed to him, bound to him in a destructive way. Jesus said that he had come "to set us free," and he showed us the way. In a word—forgiveness. It was a contradictory path for his times, and has remained so in our time.

I learned shortly after the murders that I wasn't alone in my quest for forgiveness, that other people who had lost loved ones through murder were also on that path. My daughter Mary had called me to tell me about a magazine article she had seen telling about a man named Bill Pelke. He was working with a group called Murder Victims Families for Reconciliation, an organization for people who have had a family member murdered, but advocated the abolition of the death penalty.

I found out later that this group had begun small in 1976 with about ten members, founded by Marie Deans after the murder of her mother-in-law, specifically to provide a national forum for murder victims' family members—including family members of those executed by a state—who are opposed to the death penalty. Raised a Lutheran, Marie believed that killing those who kill "only takes us deeper into imitating and becoming what we despise." Maintaining that the death penalty "is a false God promising to bring justice and closure to victims' families," she concluded, "There is no justice for murder. . . . Instead we must put the vast resources we spend on killing a small percentage of murderers into preventing homicides." In founding MVFR, she created the opportunity for new voices to be heard—the too-long silenced ones of murder victims' families who wanted all killing to end—urging that "crime prevention, not retaliation, be our number one goal."

After reading about Bill Pelke, I wanted to talk to him, and somehow I managed to track down his phone number.

I reached him and we conversed a long while by phone. Bill told me his story began when his beloved grandmother was murdered by a fifteen-year-old named Paula Cooper in Indiana in 1983. This man also had to search his soul about where he stood as this teenage girl faced the death penalty. What he discovered, he said, was that vengeance, "an eye for an eye" response to this killing, would not heal the hurt of losing a relative to murder.

Bill Pelke then embarked upon an incredible journey, praying to his grandmother. He saw his "Nana's tears," and she was dictating to him that he had to pray for "love and compassion for Paula Cooper and her family." What happened then was a response that changed his life. "When God granted my request of love and compassion, the forgiveness was automatic. . . . I no longer wanted Paula to die." He reached out to her family, taking a basket of fruit to her grandfather's house and "spent several wonderful hours talking and looking through the old family albums." Seeing the photos of Paula, so young, so charming, he literally began to feel love for this very young girl and determined to communicate with her.

Bill Pelke then began a successful international campaign to overturn her death sentence, which got a boost when an Italian journalist, Anna Guaita, contacted him. She had found out in stories appearing in Italian newspapers that Paula had written to the pope, and that a grandson of the victim had forgiven Paula and sent her Bible verses. Anna told him that over forty thousand people, mostly Italian schoolchildren, had signed petitions to have Paula taken off death row. Bill was then invited to be on an Italian TV program. "I fasted about eleven days before I went to Italy, praying often about the opportunity I was about to have," he said.

The television program was called *Domencia In*. It aired on Sunday afternoon and had the reputation of being one of the most popular shows in Italy. To his surprise, he was on with an elderly Italian priest, a Father Gerganti, who was spearheading a drive by the organization "Don't Kill" to gather signatures on petitions to have Paula taken off death row. He also got to meet Father Vito Bracone, who later came to America to bring Governor Evan Bayh the petitions with the Italian signatures on them. Father Vito joined Bill for an Amnesty International Conference where the two of them led an anti–death penalty march and spoke on behalf of Paula, the thirty-two other juveniles, and two thousand others, then on death row.

The miracle came in the summer of 1989 when the Indiana Supreme Court overturned Paula's death sentence; she would now serve a sixty-year prison term. I found Bill Pelke's story amazing, especially how the "Italian connection," beginning with Paula's letter to the pope, seemed to figure so importantly in getting her off death row.

Bill was already working with MVFR, but now, after thirty years as a steelworker, he decided to retire and do more to find others, like himself and the members of MVFR, who would actively work against the death penalty. He began a very visible action in the fall of 1993, starting what has become an annual two-week tour in a different state each year called "Journey of Hope . . . from Violence to Healing, Inc." The goal has been public education in a very different and unusual way to get people to think about the wrongness of the death penalty while "spreading seeds of love and compassion, forgiveness and reconciliation."

On the tours to date Bill and MVFR members have described the experience of losing a loved one through murder and their eventual recognition, unique to each one, of how hatred and the desire for revenge is destructive to themselves and our society as a whole. According to a spokesperson, "Speakers tell stories of reconciliation and forgiveness; and all, for a variety of credible and compelling reasons, oppose the death penalty."

The bottom line, Bill Pelke told me, is that MVFR teaches that hatred and desire for revenge are deleterious and destructive "to themselves most of all." He explained, "They share their struggles to let go of vindictive feelings to move on and up to a healthier, more humane way of responding to the offender and dealing with their grief."

I could relate to what Bill Pelke was saying, yet at that time I wasn't thinking of joining any groups. But I was immersing myself whenever I got the chance in research about the death penalty, especially going back over the files I had kept and the many articles I had written in years past, long before my life had been shattered by murder. I found quotes that I had copied from newspaper stories and magazines in prior years, comforted by such comments as this one from Coretta Scott King, widow of one of America's most famous murder victims: "An evil deed is not redeemed by an evil deed of retaliation. Justice is never advanced in the taking of a human life. Morality is never upheld by a legalized murder." I'm sure Martin Luther King would have said the same.

I was shocked when I reread what I had written back in 1985 when the execution rate in the United States started escalating dramatically. From 1972, when the death penalty had been abolished, to 1976 when it was revived, there had been no legally sanctioned gassings, electrocutions, hangings, or firing squad murders. Then, from 1976 to 1983, eleven executions took place. In 1984, the pace stepped up, with twenty-one death row inmates put to death. Then, in the first thirty days of 1985, five men were executed. The rush to kill was on; the barbarous tool used by people and governments for as far back as we can go in history was now reigning in our land.

That was just the beginning. Since then legal killing has really taken off, with 98 executed in 1999. By August of 2000 we were already beyond a total of 650 men and women killed in the death chambers of more than thirty states since 1976.

Back in 1985, it was clear that as the executions were starting to take off in intensity, so was the approval, with little concern over the possibility that the convicted murderer might be innocent. As an example, on January 30 of that year, James David Raulerson, thirty-three, was executed in Florida, protesting to the end that a wild bullet and not his action was the killer of a Jacksonville police officer. The murder occurred during a 1975 gunfight during a restaurant robbery in which a waitress was raped. A crime? Yes, indeed. A bad one. But did this merit what happened outside the prison on the night he was executed? Police officers gathered to be there for the killing, some wearing T-shirts with a drawing of the electric chair and the words, "Crank up Old Sparky," the folksy name for Florida's electric chair. Newspaper reports said they "cheered and clapped" when the killing was over.

I became aware some fifteen years ago that a few of the people showing up to demonstrate their approval of the death penalty came because of their personal experience of pain. This was eight years before my kids were killed. How could I honestly know how survivors of murder victims really felt? I thought of this when I read that Vernon and Elizabeth Harvey and their fourteen-year-old daughter, Lizabeth, attended the execution of David Martin in the Louisiana electric chair on January 4 of that year, 1985. The Harveys had another daughter, raped and murdered by Robert Lee Willie, who was executed on December 28, 1984, in Louisiana. The Harveys witnessed Mr. Willie's death, promising to attend every execution they could in Louisiana to impress upon the public the suffering of crime victims. Later, to my surprise, I learned even more about the Harveys and their pain, when Sister Helen Prejean's book *Dead Man Walking* came out. Her "dead man" was a composite of killers, Robert Willie being one of them, and the Harveys were the people whose lives were devastated because of his brutal crime. By this time I had become one of them, a parent of murder victims, yet I was in a very different place. I wanted to forgive, and I kept praying to the Lord to help me hang on to the hope that I would not harden my heart.

Several years later, in 1998, I had a surprising encounter with a woman named Debbie Morris, who, in a tragic experience, had briefly known Robert Willie—and she spoke of forgiveness. Many are familiar with *Dead Man Walking*, especially after it was made into a movie starring Sean Penn. But few know that this convicted killer had another victim, a sixteen-year-old girl whom he kidnapped, brutalized, and then released. Her testimony aided the prosecution in getting him convicted. Yet, believing she wanted anonymity, Sister Helen Prejean never identified or mentioned Debbie in her book.

Debbie came out with her story in 1998, calling it *Forgiving the Dead Man Walking,* and I had the privilege of interviewing her, discovering a remarkably spiritual woman. She said she wrote the book to tell how she has forgiven her tormentor, with the hope of helping others find God's comfort in forgiveness, as she has.

I wondered where she found the courage to go on at all after what happened to her on a Friday night in 1980, when she and her boyfriend were parked in a car on a riverfront, sipping milkshakes. That's when Robert Willie and his sidekick Joseph Vaccaro put guns to their heads, kidnapped them, tortured and shot her boyfriend, leaving him for dead, raped her repeatedly and held her hostage for twenty-four hours. She had no way of knowing they had already raped and murdered another girl, Faith Halloway.

The aftershock of all this lasted for years. Debbie literally lost her taste for life and stopped seeing her boyfriend, who had miraculously survived. She began drinking heavily and became ever angrier at God, until she admitted her need for help. Though she had not been much of a churchgoer, she had prayed during her ordeal, and now she began to pray again. As she worked to heal, Debbie understood she'd never be healed if she couldn't forgive both Robert Willie—and God.

Then, when she heard about Sister Helen's book, she felt a bit angry, wondering how she could write this without having met Robert Willie's living victims. Debbie knew she should meet with Sister Helen. She did, and she found a woman she respected, full of love, doing what she believes God wants her to do in opposing the death penalty. Certainly, Sister Helen's work has initiated a major anti–death penalty movement in this country, and she deserves our everlasting gratitude for escalating the dialogue and action to end executions.

Encouraged by Sister Helen, Debbie told her story on television's *Frontline,* an experience, she said, which opened new opportunities for her to speak out, specifically on "forgiveness in a violent society." She then put her story into a book to let people know that, in spite of her horrible ordeal, by cooperating with the grace of God, she has been able to rebuild her life with the power of forgiveness. Debbie told me, "My life today is living proof not only that God does not abandon us, but that He has great things in store for us if we trust Him." She was referring to her husband, Brad, a pilot, their two children, her work as a special education teacher, their involvement in church, and her media appearances in which she speaks on forgiveness in a violent society.

When I read her book, the last two lines brought tears to my eyes: "Justice didn't do a thing to heal me. Forgiveness did." In our conversation, she elaborated on how she needed to forgive so that she herself could receive forgiveness. "I had to pray for Robert Willie," she said, "because he is a child of God and God loves him the same as God loves me."

As for the death penalty, she said at the time of our interview that she had not yet been given a "clear message" on that yet. "I keep the death penalty debate up to Sister Helen." But then, admitting that she slept better knowing Willie was dead and could never hurt her again, she reflected, "I don't know if that's reason enough to kill someone. . . . "

I liked her honesty, and I like this woman of courage who is cooperating with the Lord to be a witness to the Gospel message of forgiveness.

We need all the help we can get when it comes to holding on to forgiveness. It brings you to a place that's riddled with traps and setbacks. Forgiveness becomes fragile when birthdays and anniversaries of murdered loved ones come around, or when you hear a song unexpectedly on the radio that raises a memory. I was driving on a highway a few days before my son John's birthday, April 17, thinking of him, when suddenly the radio was playing the "Waltz" from Tchaikovsky's opera *Eugene Onegin.* The tears came suddenly. My son John had also played the violin, and I remembered the pride I had when he was with the Boulder Symphony one season, playing among other pieces that beautiful waltz. I cried and screamed at Shadow Clark before I was able to let him go, forgive him, and pray again, thanking God that I had had the gift of my son. Forgiveness is a tough call.

I find it hard to forgive the criminal justice system when I hear people say that we now kill most murderers "humanely," because we do it by lethal injection. With this kind of convoluted focus we can obscure the real issue of what we're doing—killing—by concentrating on methods, labeling them on some kind of scale, from "least humane" to "most humane." I still remember a *New York Times* editorial after the then New Jersey governor, William Kean, signed the death penalty back into law for his state. Commenting that the governor wanted to "civilize execution," the *Times* quoted him saying, "If ever I've seen a calm, pleasant death, it's an anesthetic death." Truly, hearing this unthinkable comment, you'd have to say, "Father, forgive him for he knows not what he's saying!"

I have concluded that forgiveness is a paradox: we cannot heal ourselves if we do not forgive others, but if we do forgive, it is we ourselves who benefit the most. If we let feelings of hatred and revenge consume us when we are devastatingly hurt, we cease to be the human being we were created to be. We condemn ourselves to live in anguish.

I think that's what Jesus meant when he told us we must overcome evil with good—that if we did not, we would erode our humanity, lessen the possibility of being able to love, and thus, sadly, alienate ourselves from the life-Source who loves us.

Good advice has come down from the ages: "Don't let the sun go down on your anger." We must forgive if we are to rise.

Chapter Three

RAISING MY VOICE

In the first year after the murders, I felt I was making some progress in my struggle to "find peace," a different peace, one that was being refashioned by my pain. I knew the key to this was forgiveness, the only balm that could help me let go of the emotions, confusions, and fears that would keep me engaged in a hidden, internal conflict that could turn into a private war preventing me from making any real progress on my life's journey. I had discovered how easy it was to deceive people about your inner state. On the surface, I could look terrific; I could do my newspaper work as if I were the same old person as before. People would comment on how remarkable I was, that I had "gotten over" the tragedies of losing loved ones so quickly. They knew nothing.

My task lay ahead and it was the difficult one of struggling to get the outer me and the inner me in sync. I read the Gospels endlessly, and, without conditions, said "yes" to Christ. I'd accept his contradictory blueprint, love my enemies, do good to those who hurt me, and forgive without counting the cost. But this wouldn't happen today, or overnight.

I felt that if I were to really heal, I had to put my body where my prayers were and so I began meeting with hurting people, mostly mothers who had lost a child by suicide or accident, or church groups, sharing my experiences and my faith. I even did some healing services with churches. I didn't know at this point that the Lord was waiting to challenge me to go in another direction, taking on the mission of being a voice for life.

It happened unexpectedly. In May 1995, Bill Simonsen, my reporter friend from Montana, sent me a clip from the *Daily Inter Lake* in Kalispell. The headline, in big letters, screamed "Justice Is Served." The story told of the execution of a murderer, Duncan McKenzie, on May 10. He had been on death row twenty-one years for killing a twenty-three-year-old teacher named Lana Harding. His death by lethal injection was the first in Montana since 1943 and the twentieth in the United States that year. Officials said he was cooperative and even joking with staff as the execution date neared, seemingly resigned to his fate.

At 12:02 a.m. execution witnesses had begun entering the chamber where they would watch the killing. By 12:06 all witnesses were seated and Corrections Director Rick Day asked Mr. McKenzie if he had any last words. He shook his head no. All he asked was to be able to listen to country music through head phones as he was being legally killed. He died in the middle of the night, breathing his last to a song by country singer Marc Robbins. Was justice served?

That question started to haunt me. Then I read an editorial in the *Bigfork Eagle* and knew by the headline, "Death Penalty Delays Cruel, Unusual Punishment for Victims' Families," that I was going to be disturbed by this piece.

It began, "The front page photographs of the table on which convicted murderer Duncan McKenzie Jr. is scheduled to die can send shivers down a person's back. That's good. The death penalty is supposed to be a deterrent.

"Behind the table—located in a trailer behind maximum security at the Montana State Prison—are two clocks. The clocks are symbolic that perhaps time may finally be running out for McKenzie, who was convicted of the brutal murder twenty-one years ago of Conrad-area teacher Lana Harding. That's right—twenty-one years ago. . . .

"Eight times McKenzie has been scheduled to die, and eight times his lawyers have found a legal loophole to delay his execution. Talk about cruel and unusual punishment—for the victim's family, that is. . . .

"Lana's mother Ethel is one of the dearest, kindest persons in the state. . . . She is a soft touch for anyone in need—almost anyone, that is. Not her daughter's killer. . . . She will attend a clemency hearing for McKenzie. . . . She will ask that no clemency be granted. 'It will be the first positive thing that I've been able to do for Lana in this whole ordeal,' she told the Associated Press."

Reading this, I felt such sorrow that this mother had carried thoughts of killing a man for twenty-one years. It had to be a terrible burden. I had no way of knowing if she had found comfort in the murder of Duncan McKenzie, but I thought of Shadow Clark, an inmate in that same prison, and I thanked God that this young man was still alive, that my children and I had never wanted to see him killed.

I was so affected by this execution in Montana that I wrote an opinion piece against the death penalty, sending it to Bill Williams, then the Op-Ed editor of the *Hartford Courant*. I had written, "I may be the only person in Connecticut who cares about an execution in Montana, but I do, and for good reason. For the past year and a half, my life has been dominated by the status of the death penalty in Montana. That's because my life was devastated by murder in that rolling state of *A River Runs Through It,* so tranquil, so beautiful, but also, for me and my family, so deadly. And I had to let the authorities know if I wanted the death penalty for the murderer. . . . "

I wrote the rest of the piece as a journalist, giving statistics and quoting others opposed to this deadly practice. Bill Williams called me. He didn't want the piece I had written. He wanted my personal story. That's what would be powerful, he said, the piece people would read, one that might make them uncomfortable enough to really consider what I had to say.

I took his advice, went back to the computer, and put my heart in charge. I remember struggling with how to end the piece, summarizing my feelings. Finally, I wrote, "The bottom line in my personal story may be that I opposed the death penalty for Shadow Clark for selfish reasons. I remember once reading of a rabbi who had lost his family in the Holocaust. *He forgave Adolf Hitler, because he did not want to bring Hitler to America with him.*

"It's hard to forgive. Not forgiving keeps us angry and anger makes us feel more powerful. But if we don't forgive, we stay emotionally handcuffed to the person who hurt us, as the rabbi understood. Now I am free enough to pray for Shadow Clark, hoping he will one day be able to respond to the touch of grace we are given by God, and find redemption. His act of killing reinforced my commitment to affirming life—and forever, my opposition to the death penalty."

My piece was published in the *Hartford Courant* on June 20, 1995, with a headline, "A Mother Comes to Terms with Her Son's Killer." Shortly after it ran, it was picked up by the Los Angeles Times Syndicate, and appeared in daily newspapers around the country. I started getting responses to what I had written. One letter especially touched me:

"Dear Ms. Bosco, I am writing to acknowledge the courage and faith you shared in writing 'A Mother Comes to Terms. . . .' You expressed emotions which we can all share, but tempered these human responses with an enlightened, sincerely held faith. I only hope that I would have the same courage of my convictions if faced with a similar dilemma. Sincerely, Richard Tulisano."

I knew his name. Mr. Tulisano is a state representative in Connecticut, openly outspoken against the death penalty. I didn't know then that he and I would be speakers on several pro-and-con death penalty forums to come.

But then there were the other letters, the unfriendly ones. One man wrote, "Shadow Clark should be executed by lethal injection and immediately after that, his donatable organs should be harvested and given to people whose lives would be saved by these organs. Shadow Clark will then somewhat have atoned for his deed...." That was a strange, new justification for the death penalty—the cannibalization of human parts—which could then become, I suppose, a profitable industry. It took me a while to stop shuddering after getting that "solution."

Another letter was from a man convinced that sacred Scriptures impose the death penalty. He wrote, "Even when Jesus entertained the thought of having his Father remove the cross that he had to bear, his words to the Father were 'Thy will be done.' It sure appears to me that the Good Lord imposed the death penalty." What? Had this man never listened to what Jesus said? In his own words, Jesus tells us he is One with the Father in heaven, come to earth to inform us and convince us that what the Father wants from all of us is love and forgiveness. No, the Good Lord did not impose the death penalty. Jesus' contemporaries, the law people of those times, were the ones who got Jesus, an innocent man, sentenced to death.

It was the letter from Patricia Garcia of Kansas City that touched me most, for she was a mother, like myself, who had been scourged with mega-pain. Thanking me for writing the article, she then wrote:

"On May 20, 1991, my husband, Lupe, father of our six children, died quite suddenly of a rare blood disorder we were unaware of. Then, on October 26, 1992, our youngest son, Robert, twenty-two, was murdered. He was shot down in a park here in Kansas City by two young men under the influence of alcohol and drugs. They were much younger than our Robert, who had become an unwed father in July that year and was planning marriage soon.

"Antoinette, my anger was not and never has been toward the two young men. I was angry at the society that has allowed our young people to become victims of all sorts of violence. I had to deal with family, friends and the authorities involved. I did not want the death penalty or even life imprisonment, because this would not bring Robert back. Also, he had served some time himself so I knew his feelings on jail and on prison. He was a gentle, loving, caring son when not involved in alcohol and drugs himself. So for these reasons, and the main one I learned from Lupe's fifty-three years of life and sudden death, I couldn't be for more death. Life is a very special gift from God that I treasure at whatever the price.

"Dear one, I want to say thank you as one mother to another for sharing your painful loss with me and many others. I know it is hard because I, too, share whenever I can in hopes that Robert's death will not be in vain. Antoinette, in spite of all my pain and sorrow, my Lord has been so good to me. Since I was forgiving, especially with Robert's death, I've been able to correspond my feelings and thoughts to Ernest and Rony [the killers] who are serving thirty years with a possible parole in eight to ten years. They have written me on several occasions and expressed sorrow about Robert's death and surprise about my attitude. They have both said they are getting close to God and doing their best so that when they get out, they can help others in similar situations as theirs.

"I pray this does happen for I believe it's what God may want, what I desire, and Robert would wish for, too! I pray daily that my children and grandchildren will understand my reasons for fighting against the death penalty, life in prison or any other forms that bring about a death to another person. I want them to always value life as a gift from God.

"Thank you again for your article and I'll keep you and yours in my daily prayers as I do all other families in situations such as ours. My Lupe's death was final, but each time another is murdered, I relive Robert's death over again. So perhaps our sharing and praying will help so that an end to senseless killing will come about.

"Peace, love and joy to you, Antoinette, and your family. Sincerely, Pat Garcia."

Her letter warmed my heart and pricked my conscience. I was not yet to the place where she was, able to correspond with the murderers of her son. I was aware that some members of Murder Victims Families for Reconciliation had reached out to connect with the killers of their loved one, and while I admired them, I didn't feel moved to contact Shadow Clark. I never felt that forgiveness required personal contact.

After getting news that Shadow Clark had cold-bloodedly killed John and Nancy, I would wonder for long periods what had turned an eighteen-year-old Fundamentalist Christian boy, who had gone to Christian schools, into a murderer. I wanted to talk to his pastor at the Assembly of God Church he and his family attended in Kalispell, Montana. It took a while for me to connect with him, but finally Rev. Brooks Baer took my phone call. He told me he had visited Shadow Clark some twenty to thirty times while he was in the jail, awaiting trial. He said, "The more you know, the less it computes. . . . He is just not saying. . . . He acted alone. . . . He's holding on to his faith."

Rev. Baer told me that an "incredible" range of psychiatric tests had been done on him, "but I'm unaware of the results." And then he added something that literally offended me. Commenting that Shadow has always been a really nice young man, he said, "If you meet him, you'll like him." I responded with sudden anger, saying something like, "Pardon me, but you're talking about the man who killed my kids!"

I was learning then, as I have continued to learn ever since, that no one really knows what you go through after a loved one is murdered, except those who have been in that pit. I could pray for Shadow Clark, asking God to help him seek forgiveness so he can find his own redemption. And I would visualize his mother's face, so mapped in pain, and feel her sorrow. My face, too, is mapped in pain. While I can't see my son any more, still I was, and am, glad for her, that she can see her son, and can have a hope that perhaps he will still make something of a life for himself. I could go this far, but no more.

Remembering my phone conversation with Rev. Baer, I reread Pat Garcia's letter, full of respect for her. I certainly didn't want to go to the Montana State Prison and try to hug Shadow Clark, but I did start to wonder if I was getting a message from the Lord that I was to do more writing about the death penalty, perhaps even become a voice against this monstrous punishment. Coincidentally, as I wondered, I got a telephone call from Mimi Klocko. She told me she was a member of Delaware Citizens Opposed to the Death Penalty and they were looking for a speaker to keynote their annual gathering to take place the following January. Their group, she said, was organized to seek abolition of state-sponsored killing in the name of justice in their state of Delaware, which had witnessed five executions in the previous three years, with many still waiting on death row.

"Many of us view our opposition to capital punishment as a form of ministry. Part of that ministry involves reaching out to victims of violence, particularly those who might differ with us on this topic," Mimi said, adding, "I found the editorial you authored that ran nationally to be very refreshing in this regard."

As we talked, I felt her conviction about the need to end the death penalty, which she said "continues to be used as a barbaric quick-fix solution to a very complicated problem." I agreed to do the talk, and I started to come up with titles for the program, like "Death by Lethal Injustice—

Our Nation's Shame"; "Man-made Death—A Mockery of Justice"; and then the one Mimi liked best, "Who Has the Right to Take a Life?"

January came, and when I went to Delaware, I was introduced to Kevin O'Connell, a lawyer, strongly opposed to executions, who was working on the conference. I asked him who had been the speaker the year before. He told me Sister Helen Prejean. "Wow, she's a hard act to follow," I responded spontaneously. He told me that wouldn't be the case. Many survivors of murder victims had come to her talk, and those who were parents, strongly for the death penalty, angrily rebutted her, saying she didn't know their pain, she had never been a parent and lost a child through human violence. "They can't do that to you," he said. I'd be talking from a gut-level position that gave me uncontested credibility. He was right. While many who came to the talk soundly disagreed with me, no one attacked me. Some could truly not understand my position, but they respected the fact that I had come to it honestly.

During the reception, I met Anne Coleman and heard her story. Her daughter Frances was shot to death in her car while driving through Los Angeles in 1985. No arrests were ever made for that crime. After the murder, her youngest son, Daniel, couldn't get over his anger and depression. Two years later, he died of cardiac arrest after taking antidepressant medications. Anne felt the same bullet that killed her daughter killed her twenty-five-year-old son. Then she surprised me, telling me she belonged to Murder Victims Families for Reconciliation, a group I seemed to be regularly running into.

She worked against capital punishment because this is "nothing more than vengeance, and vengeance is an evil unto itself. It's a disease. We are instructed to love both our friends and our enemies," she said. "The death of my daughter by murder caused my family a pain that I am unable sometimes to put into words. But the murder of her killer would not heal our pain. When the state kills, it does not help the victims. It creates more victims. We as a society must find a way to stop this senseless killing on both sides of the law. Don't kill for me in the name of justice, because the death penalty is not justice. It is legalized killing." We were in perfect agreement.

I felt great comfort in being with another mother who believed, as I did, that our pain is enough, that it won't go away by generating more pain to be suffered by more victims. Yet, we are the minority. Even people I have respected can surprise me by voicing opinions meant to support families of murder victims. I was in shock when I read a "viewpoint" piece in the *National Catholic Reporter* (July 2, 1999) by

Eugene Kennedy, professor emeritus of psychology at Loyola University in Chicago.

"There remains one argument, or, rather, uncontested testimony of human experience," he wrote, "that is not easy to track but is surely not easy to dismiss, either.

"That is the impact on and reaction of the victims' families—the spouses, children and siblings of those whose lives have been taken by the prisoners on death row. These human beings are often obscured by the shadows of the event that falls now this way and now that. There is so much else to see, and the focus on the prisoner and his moral rights is so intense, that those who have suffered losses that never fully heal are seldom interviewed, possess no lobbying group for their violated souls and are seldom if ever included as players in this high-stakes moral game.... The relatives of victims are witnesses to the destruction of their lives and bearers within themselves of spiritual wounds that weeping will not close."

I felt that Mr. Kennedy probably knew survivors of homicide and was expressing empathy for them, until I read on. "One thing does help them. Their inner peace is restored and some ending comes for their horrific experience when the murderer is executed. They get something of their lives back in that instant.... The peace that replaces intractable suffering after a killer is executed remains a potent but largely unexamined element in this discussion [of capital punishment]...."

I couldn't believe that the NCR had actually published this without a companion piece giving the other position, one that would be taken by members of MVFR. Thankfully, I wasn't the only one appalled at Eugene Kennedy's viewpoint. The NCR got more letters countering what he wrote than could be counted, and later Mr. Kennedy wrote another piece explaining that his motivation for writing the first one was to stimulate a dialogue. I wasn't convinced.

Truly there is a polarization of positions on the death penalty between those of us who are left survivors of murder victims. That was clearly brought out for me on February 3, 1998, when Karla Faye Tucker was executed in Texas, a killing that dramatically underscored how disunited we are when it comes to the issue of the death penalty.

Like many, I was riveted to the television set on that disturbing Tuesday, caught up in the emotional attention on Karla Faye Tucker, scheduled to die that night unless she got a stay of execution. I had seen clips showing Karla as gentle, caring, a lover of God. She had caught my attention in a very personal way before that fateful day. I had read about her complicity in a gruesome murder of two in 1983. Could the twenty-three-year-old drug-soaked prostitute who wielded an ax that day to steal the breath of two people be the same person as the thirty-eight-year-old woman I was seeing on television? No, no way.

I wasn't the only one who believed a new Karla had been born, but, sadly, the ones who could make a difference didn't. To them she was then, is now, and always would be a murderer. When the Supreme Court turned down her appeal on February 3 and the decision for a stay of execution was left to the governor, George W. Bush, I knew she was doomed. After all, he had his sights on the presidency, and he, like most of our politicians these days, wants to get a record for being "tough" on crime, a strong supporter of the death penalty. In Texas they're killing killers like popping popcorn.

So they killed her. Because Karla had been a murderer, they gave them-selves permission to murder, a contradiction that blights us no matter how we want to sanitize it. When the spokesman came out to give the news to the press that Karla was dead, I wasn't expecting the gleeful reaction I saw from so many people, many of them quite young. It was a dark circus—a strange dance of death, where people were whooping and hooting to celebrate the murder of a fellow Texan.

And then out came Richard Thornton, the husband of Deborah Thornton, the woman murdered by Karla and her companion, Daniel Ryan Garrett, who died in prison of natural causes in 1993. He had witnessed the execution and now came out to say, "Justice for Deborah Thornton is complete." And then he pronounced: "I want to say to every victim in this world, demand this. Demand this. This is your right."

His anger was now turned on Ronald Carlson, brother of his murdered wife, who had lobbied to spare Karla's life. He spouted ven-omously that he would never forgive his brother-in-law for forgiving Karla. On the NBC *Today* show the following morning, both men were interviewed. Ronald Carlson hardly got the chance to say a word about why, as a Christian, he had to forgive Karla. That's because Mr. Thorn-ton, in raging self-righteousness, came out speaking for victims, he said. And he repeated that we victims have a right to hate, demand death for the murderer, and call it "closure" when the death house deed is done. Loudly he berated his brother-in-law for what he called his betrayal of the family and said he would never, never be allowed into his house again, not ever.

I got immediately sick. He was speaking to me—but we weren't talk-ing the same language. I felt embarrassed and ashamed. I hoped that everyone listening would not assume that all victims of a murderous crime felt as he did—justified to remain in hate, wanting vengeance wearing the camouflaged name of "justice."

To my surprise, I learned that Ron Carlson was also a member of Murder Victims Families for Reconciliation. He admitted that after his only sister, Deborah, was murdered, he wanted her killers executed. His anger overtook him and he treated his pain with alcohol and drugs. But then something happened. I call it grace, welling to the surface. He turned his life "over to the Lord," became a Christian, forgave the killers, and worked to commute their death sentences.

"The world is not a better place because the state of Texas executed Karla Faye Tucker," said Mr. Carlson, who was invited by Karla to witness her execution as one of her representatives. "I was there to stand up for the Lord, for the strength of his love. Karla and I had both done a lot of wrong in our lives... but the love of Jesus Christ transformed us. We were able to forgive ourselves and each other."

As Karla was put to death, he knew that "God reached out of heaven to hold us in his hands and cradle us with his love and compassion. Karla died with a smile on her face. They took her body, but they didn't kill her spirit." I felt great respect for Ron Carlson, whose forgiveness was total.

Watching Mr. Thornton the night of the execution, I wanted to shout out to him that no one has the right to take away life, no one but the giver of life, the one some of us call God. Advocates of the death penalty say that a murderer forfeits his or her right to life. Maybe that's true, but I become ever more convinced that we can't be the ones to make that judgment. We have the right to punish—and I believe heinous murderers should be given life without parole—but we don't have the right to kill someone who can be confined and can perhaps even be redeemed and become, in effect, a new person, as we saw in Karla's case.

Richard Thornton told us victims to "demand" death for the murderers of our loved ones. I think harboring his anger for so many years had imprisoned him in a bad place. Sadly, he is probably in the majority when it comes to victims wanting the death penalty; many speak as he does. He was able to watch Karla's dying because Texas had authorized such witnessing by victims' survivors nearly three years earlier, joining six other states allowing this viewing. Texas had been pressured by victims rights groups to allow this.

The first survivors of murdered loved ones wanting to go to the death chamber to witness a Texas execution were Linda Kelley and her family.

In February 1996, they watched the execution of Leo Jenkins, who had killed two of Linda Kelley's children in 1988. He was a thirty-eight-year-old high school dropout who needed money for cocaine, decided to rob a pawn shop to get it and there killed Mark Kelley, twenty-five, and his sister, Kara Voss, twenty. "The best statement he can make is to go through with this," Mrs. Kelley said that day. "I'm not scared. He's taken my life away.... He's going out really nicely. There's nothing bad about it.... He's made his peace with God. I don't think I have. I'm still real angry with God about this. I just hope God doesn't forgive him."

Her words saddened me. She had lived through an abomination, losing two of her children at one time, brutally killed by a tattooed junkie. I felt she had been catapulted to a place where nothing would ever ease her pain, where perhaps nothing would ever make sense to her again, except to want that man who had stopped her life to have his life stopped, too. I understood! I know what it's like to lose two children. But could she really believe it was God's fault that they lost their lives? God had given them life, not taken it away. We can't blame God for what a flesh-and-blood person does.

I had been in her hell and through God's grace had escaped that despair. I was helped by the Lord, through my faith, to learn that never would I have to let a murderer determine who I would become, that never would I let a murderer make me forget the overpowering message of Jesus' Gospel—forgiveness and mercy.

I know the death penalty debate will continue to go on, with self-righteous arguments devoid of mercy getting center stage, particularly from those running for office. I know that most victims, like Richard Thornton, are vocal in their demands for the death penalty and feel justified in taking this position. Most of my fellow members of Survivors of Homicide—which does not take a position for or against the death penalty—would probably agree with Thornton. My friends in this support group now know that I have become ever more outspoken on the need to revere life—everybody's life—precisely because I don't want advocates for death to keep on assuming that all victims will be ready and anxious to jump on their bandwagon. Some of us learn a powerful lesson when murder enters our doors: unnatural death is an evil, no matter whose hand stops the breath.

Yet, I have great empathy for people who have had to deal with death by murder of a loved one, and if they believe there's some justification for the death penalty, I cannot judge them. I respect them for their position, even as I ask respect for mine. I have sat with so many, hugged them, cried with them as I heard their stories.

I think of Shirley and Larry Bostrom, whose daughter, Dr. Margaret Bostrom, was stabbed to death by her husband on August 16, 1996. Shirley and I often find ourselves talking about our beloved murdered ones and the tears flow easily.

Shirley says of the youngest of their three daughters, "Margie was my baby.... Losing her, a lot of the joy went out of our lives." Their daughter was a thirty-year-old, hardworking young woman who had earned her doctorate in clinical psychology specifically because her goal was to help others. At the time of her death, she was working with hardened criminals at Lewisburg Federal Penitentiary in Pennsylvania.

Margie had asked her husband of two years for a divorce, and since he was one who wanted always to be in control of his wife, he wasn't about to take this. He went for a butcher knife and when she got out of the shower stabbed her sixteen times in the chest, ending her life. The wounds she bore show that Margie tried to fight back, but she was no match for the strength of her husband.

When the Bostroms got the awful news, they felt "a certain numbness, a sense of unreality, a feeling that this can't be real and you're just waiting to wake up. We knew him, trusted him, and at some level loved him," Shirley said. "We feel so betrayed." It was an atrocious act of vehement violence. Here was a husband, a man who had pledged to love his wife. How could he pick up a butcher knife and plunge it over and over into her body, watching her blood spill and her life end? What kind of a defense would ever make sense other than to say this man, who acted so inhumanly, forfeited his freedom and should be put away for life.

That's what the Bostroms justifiably felt, that their son-in-law should be sentenced to life in prison without parole. Yet, he received a much lighter sentence. "He got thirty years and five months, which with good time would have been twenty-six years and five months. He appealed that sentence successfully and probably will be out in less than seventeen years," Shirley said.

Dealing with murder made the Bostroms confront their own feelings about the death penalty. "I've got some basic objections in how it is implemented. It shouldn't be all black, Hispanic, and the poor. But I really don't have any strong moral feelings about it. I would be very comfortable with life without parole, which would give murderers a long period of suffering. But I also think the death penalty should not be ruled out because it makes a good bargaining chip for a prosecutor to use," Shirley commented. She explained that in their case, since Margie's murderer wasn't facing the death penalty, that effectively ruled out a murder in the first degree charge, which would have been life imprisonment without parole. "Instead the prosecutor had to settle for murder two," she said, a much lighter sentence.

Margie's death, which almost coincided with Shirley's retirement after thirty-two years of teaching in public schools, launched her parents into an active life, different from what they had expected for their postemployment years. They work now for victims' rights, assisting the Riegers in projects undertaken by Survivors of Homicide. Shirley has also taken a further personal step. Using her teaching skills, she goes into schools, sometimes with other SOH members, to help youth understand and reject violence. And, wanting passionately to educate people about the danger signs of abusive relationships, she has created a workshop she titles "Funny—He Doesn't Look Like a Murderer" and has brought this to conferences, colleges, corrections officers, and inmates, among others.

"If one woman escapes an abusive relationship or one family becomes aware of the danger signals, Margaret's work will continue and her death will have meaning. My efforts will be worthwhile and our intense loss tempered," says Shirley, who has nearly completed a book about the crime and its causes that put her daughter in the grave.

Another friend from Survivors of Homicide, Rev. Dr. Stuart C. Brush, takes a solid position for supporting the death penalty. Having listened to him talk about the dual tragedy that befell him and his wife, Laura, I couldn't help but feel a deep empathy for these fine, caring people, even though I came to a different conclusion about a murderer's sentence. In early 1996, we found ourselves on the same panel, taking opposite sides on the death penalty.

This came about because we both were asked to speak at a symposium on the death penalty to be held at the Regional 7 High School in Winsted, Connecticut. Our invitations had come from the sponsors—the Bruderhof Foundation, an extended "family" of Christians who live in community, are exemplary in their interfaith outreach, work diligently for social justice, and are outspoken in their opposition to the death penalty. They wanted to bring a debate highlighting the pros and cons of the death penalty to high school students and had the full cooperation of principal Pat Llodra, who saw this as an "education event, designed to help you [students] form your opinion." The panel included some high-powered individuals, State Representative Richard Tulisano, who had written me that kind note after the *Hartford Courant* article, Assistant State Attorney Harry Weller, former legislator Anthony Nania, and Assistant Public Defender Ronald Gold.

I knew the Brushes to be outstanding people, caring for their neighbors and motivated in all their work by love for God. They had gone through a series of tragedies that Stuart had summarized in a sentence—"a son murdered, me without a job and fighting alcoholism, no income... then another son gone, and Laura in a severe automobile accident that left her hardly able to move, followed by a stroke...." In words befitting a preacher, he smiled and said some friends started calling them "Job and Jobette."

The initial trauma had been "the knock on the door at 12:30 at night back in 1983," when they were hit with the shocking news that their twenty-one-year-old son, Dean, a pre-med student working part-time as a pizza delivery man for Domino's Pizza in Bridgeport, Connecticut, was dead. He was found lying on a street, with gunshot wounds to his head, chest, right shoulder, and left leg. Three young men were quickly apprehended. Their motive for pulling a gun on Dean was to steal his money. For a total of $35, a young man, called "the glue that held the family together," was dead, and a family "would never be the same again," Stuart affirms.

"There's not a strong enough word to express the effect such news has on you. We ask, what do we do now? How do we get through this? I felt like Job on the garbage heap. My first response was to give up," said the minister, who had just begun to conquer his alcoholism with the help of Alcoholics Anonymous. "I had to let go and let God take over. There was no solution, except for the spiritual. We made a decision to turn our lives over to the care of God."

But more trauma was to hit the family. Not able to deal with Dean's death, a younger brother and sister turned to drugs and alcohol as escapes. Their daughter soon got her life together, but their young son, Jon, stayed mired in despair.

"He felt he had nowhere to turn. Dean was his best friend. His self-esteem was devastated. He just went off the wall," Stuart said, recalling that terrible day in June 1991, when Jon called them from Hawaii to say goodbye, telling them he "was going home to be with his brother, and he hanged himself."

Now they were left to deal not only with murder, but with suicide too. Again, the Brushes were determined not to be stuck in anger and not to be in denial about the dark place of pain they were in. Again, they turned to God. "You have to take your Higher Power with you into the darkness," Stuart said.

When it was time for the trial, in 1984, the Brushes learned that two of the young men involved in the killing, Charles Belcher and Jeffrey Tate, turned state's evidence, testifying that the shooter was Milton Green. They were given a light sentence, and Green, who was sixteen at the time of the murder, received thirty-eight years. But five years later, the State Supreme Court ordered a new trial, finding that the judge had erred in permitting the jury to hear incriminating statements made by Green before his arrest and before he was told of his right to counsel. Through a plea bargain for the much lesser crime of armed robbery, Green was sentenced to fifteen years but, astonishingly, was released from prison after serving only six years and nine months.

When Stuart Brush told this story at the Winsted symposium, emphasizing his firm belief in the death penalty, he asked, "If America values justice, what ought Green's sentence for murder have been? Until he brings back our son(s), should he not still be serving his sentence? Indeed, we are still serving our sentence, that of being without our boys, and will be in a state of loss for the rest of our lives.

"Why is Green free and we are bound, Laura and I, forever despairing for that of which Green eternally robbed us? Moreover, since Green cannot restore Dean and Jon to us, why should Green not pay with his own life?"

Stuart emphasized that there is justice in the death penalty. "It is often assumed that people in favor of the death penalty are simply acting from a 'getting back' approach, a 'let's kill the bastards, they're only human garbage' attitude. If so, this is a viewpoint of revenge, anger, hostility, and overall negative emotions. We look upon our approach and that of several others to come from a reasoned—not revengeful—point of view and a philosophy that justice must be done. The death penalty is included as an element of justice, not negative, vitriolic thinking."

He continued, "I don't find any difficulty with forgiving. It is mutually beneficial to forgive, but forgiveness does not take away whatever sentence results in justice. For the offended one to become a whole person again, forgiveness needs to be expressed—not forgiveness of the criminal act, but forgiveness of the person. Forgiveness has nothing to do with the sentence the person gets, only with the person."

The panel went on, three of us against the death penalty, three for it. Representative Tulisano said he understood that when friends and families of victims call for the death penalty they are motivated by an emotional need for retribution, and that makes sense, he acknowledged. "But there is a big difference between me acting with emotion and the state, which does not have a heart or brain, sanctioning the death penalty," he said, emphasizing that the state should not emulate the murders by itself legalizing murder. "Should we as a citizenry say that we should take as our mentor a murderer? We owe it to ourselves not to become part of the lowest common denominator."

I began my remarks by saying, spontaneously, that I believed the debate about the death penalty was going to become the most wrenching issue of the years to come. I commented on the death penalty mania that was sweeping the country, and how candidates for office now had to be for the death penalty or they couldn't get elected. I pointed out that the death penalty has become a simplistic answer to the terribly complicated problem of crime. When I talked about the murders of John and Nancy, I spoke honestly of what I knew in my heart and soul to be right—that taking a life is God's territory. Murderers must be punished, but their actions do not give us the right, in turn, to become killers.

With that, I walked right into the hands of Anthony Nania, a former state representative. He had come with a Bible in his hands and a determination to prove that all law is based on God's law and God's law demands the death penalty. He opened the Bible, citing passages which he read to convince us that we have a divine right "to expunge evil from our midst." God himself instituted the death penalty, he said, referring to Genesis 9:6, where God says to Noah, "Whoever sheds the life of a human, by a human shall that person's blood be shed."

He took this to prove that God gave to government the legitimate authority to use capital punishment to punish murders. I always felt that the passage meant whoever kills, initiates a cycle of killing that goes on and on. I wondered why he had ignored Genesis 4:9–15, where God confronts Cain for having murdered his brother Abel, telling him, "And now you are cursed from the ground, which has opened its mouth to receive your brother's blood from your hand." But God does not administer a death sentence. He banishes Cain, and then, responding to Cain's fear that someone he meets would kill him, God says, "Whoever kills Cain will suffer a sevenfold vengeance. And the Lord put a mark on Cain, so that no one who came upon him would kill him."

As Mr. Nania continued, flipping through pages of the Bible to prove his point that this inspired book authorizes the death penalty, he even went to the New Testament, interpreting Jesus' words, "for all who take the sword shall perish by the sword" (Matt. 26:52) to be a justification for the death penalty. That blew my mind. I have read the Gospels over and over, and I wanted to argue with him that there's no ambivalence in the New Testament about what God wants from us. It's forgiveness. Jesus spoke firmly and consistently about our need to forgive, of overcoming evil with good, and of putting away the sword so that we would not perish from weapons of destruction.

I sat there listening, getting fed up with this crazy game of Bible roulette to justify killing. I decided that in any talks I would be asked to give from then on, I would underscore that Jesus, who was executed, supposedly legitimately in his day, is our chief model for opposing the death penalty.

I didn't know that day how much in the months to come I was to find myself square in the anti–death penalty pulpit.

Chapter Four

PLUNGING INTO
THE DEBATE

❀❀❀❀❀❀❀❀❀❀❀❀❀❀

As I was becoming known as a mother of murder victims who is against the death penalty, I started getting calls from people who believe as I do, mostly hoping to enlist me for an abolitionist program or to request that I lend my name to a particular group. I was still a bit cautious, knowing how easy it is suddenly to find yourself in a complete state of overload. I needed to go slowly on this one, because every time I talked about the murders, my heart would break again. I was wounded and vulnerable, even as I was strong and dedicated.

One call I received touched me deeply. It was from Marietta Jaeger, a member of Murder Victims Families for Reconciliation and a woman I had heard a lot about. She was a mother who had dealt with the abduction and brutal murder of her seven-year-old daughter in a way that I felt could only be called saintly. Our stories had an eerie similarity, she said. Both our hearts had been broken because of a crime that took place in Montana. Marietta said she had read my *Hartford Courant* Op-Ed piece and was calling to encourage me to stay on the path of forgiveness and to invite me to think about joining MVFR.

When she told me her story, I went from being an emotional basket-case, to a humble, inspired "sister." It began in the early 1970s, when Bill and Marietta Jaeger went on a camping trip to Montana with their five children. It was to be a dream vacation, but at the first place they camped, in the middle of the night someone sliced a hole in the tent where they slept, silenced their youngest daughter, seven-year-old Susie, by choking her unconscious, pulled her through the rip in the tent and took off with her. The Jaegers never saw Susie again.

On the first-year anniversary of Susie's disappearance, the kidnapper called, "to taunt me," Marietta said. He told her Susie was alive, and he was teaching her to forget her family. What he didn't know was that this mother had been on a spiritual journey, struggling to balance her rage over the crime against her Christian belief that we are to forgive those who hurt us. She felt God had helped her and affirmed her struggle by giving her a vision six months after her child disappeared where she saw God holding Susie in his arms. As Marietta talked to this man who had called her, she heard his voice waver and, actually feeling compassion, asked him, "What can I do to help you?"

Somehow, the tone of compassion broke through his guard, and though it took a second phone call before he could be apprehended, the truth came out about who he was and what he had done. His name was David Meirhofer, twenty-six, a handyman and Vietnam veteran. He had kept Susie locked in a broom closet in an abandoned farmhouse, tortured her, raped her, and at the end of the week, strangled her and dismembered her body, eating some of her flesh. He committed suicide the day after he was arrested. The heinous crime and the killer who committed it became the basis for the 1991 horror film *The Silence of the Lambs*.

How, as a parent, do you live through something as horrible as that? "In the beginning, I would have been happy to kill the guy with my bare hands. . . . But I also knew it wasn't healthy, that it would destroy me," she said. Then, as a Christian, she knew her call was to forgive. "So I gave God permission to change my heart, to move it from fury to forgiveness." Then she moved to a point that is almost impossible for most parents of murdered children to reach, being able to regard the murderer with respect and dignity as a human being. She defined forgiveness, telling me it is "a letting go of the desire for punishment and, instead, taking up the idea of restoration, of putting things back in some good order, although it may not be the same order. . . . Forgiveness," she said, "means feeling concern, even love, for the offender." In all honesty, as Marietta talked to me and my admiration for her zoomed, I had to admit I wasn't yet that far along.

We were in utter agreement about the death penalty, though. "Loved ones, wrenched from our lives by violent crime, deserve more beautiful, noble, and honorable memorials than premeditated, state-sanctioned killings," she said. "The death penalty only creates more victims and more grieving families. By becoming that which we deplore—people who kill people—we insult the sacred memory of all our precious victims."

After talking to Marietta, I began to go back over notes and articles on the death penalty I had collected over the previous fifteen years. Among these was an Op-Ed piece which I accepted and published in the *Litch-*

field County Times back in February 1985, written by Charles Olivea, a schoolteacher who taught American history. I respected this man highly, and while I did not agree with him, I felt he had the right to say what he believed. I had already written an Op-Ed piece deploring the increase in executions that was now evident, for by 1985, only nine years after the Supreme Court lifted the moratorium on the death penalty, the number of people on death row had already jumped, from four hundred in 1976 to fourteen hundred by the end of 1984. Journalism always demands that both sides of an issue or story get equal treatment, and so I ran our two viewpoints side by side.

Mr. Olivea's main points centered on what he called the "social contract." He did not believe "the deterrence issue"—whether or not the death penalty deters criminal behavior—was the one on which the case for capital punishment should be argued. Instead he argued that "capital punishment is society's way of acting on the principle of self-defense that is part of the social contract. In return for the cooperative and lawful obedience of most of its members, the social order is *obligated* to defend the common interest and security of those same members. To do less by Government is to invite anarchy."

My friend insisted that the "supreme penalty is society's ultimate protection." He also maintained that actions and judgments must function on an impersonal level to insure that that the law and the courts operate justly, without favoritism or bias. While we debated many aspects of the issue, Mr. Olivea kept returning to his "chief justification"—that our society "is entitled to satisfy its moral outrage at heinous, offensive conduct. . . . Capital punishment is a safety measure taken by the state to protect the life, liberty, and the pursuit of happiness of its law-abiding citizens."

When I disagreed strongly and argued that I couldn't see how permission to kill could protect citizens, he quoted the decision written by Justice Potter Stewart in 1976 when the Supreme Court reinstated the death penalty: "This function may be unappealing to many, but it is essential in an ordered society that asks its citizens to rely on legal process rather than self-help to vindicate their wrongs."

I started playing dueling quotes, pulling out a statement I had just read from two Florida bishops, Roman Catholic Bishop John Snyder of St. Augustine and Episcopal Bishop Frank Cerveny of North Florida: "We hold that capital punishment is not necessary to any legitimate goal of the state and that its use threatens to undermine belief in the inherent worth of human life. We affirm the value of human life is not contingent on the moral rectitude of human beings and institutions. It is grounded in the sovereignty of God, Who alone vests his creatures with the dignity of personhood."

I knew, after that conversation, that lines for-and-against the death penalty were steel-strong and that we had a major conflict ahead of us, with people on both sides on this issue. I also began to see how our political scene was being affected by this new wave of wanting criminals killed. The pro–death penalty bandwagon was revved up, and it was beginning to look like candidates better be on board or they wouldn't get elected.

Case in point was New York State. Governor Mario Cuomo, a Catholic, was outspoken against the death penalty. I followed what he said because I felt something of a kinship with him. He lived in the governor's mansion in Albany, my hometown, and sometimes when I visited my family there, I would see him jogging around Lincoln Park, close to the house where I grew up. I found something he had written back in 1989 to express very much how I felt:

"I have spoken my opposition to the death penalty for more than thirty years. For all that time I have studied it, I have watched it, I have debated it, hundreds of times. I have heard all the arguments, analyzed the evidence I could find, measured public opinion when it was opposed, when it was indifferent, when it was passionately in favor.

"And always before, I have concluded the death penalty is wrong, that it lowers us all; that it is the surrender to the worst that is in us; that it uses a power—the official power to kill by execution—which has never elevated a society, never brought back a life, never inspired anything but hate."

Mario Cuomo lost the next election to Republican George Pataki, also a Catholic, but one adamantly for the death penalty. The campaign centered on the issue of bringing back the death penalty to New York. I heard people with a microphone in their face for a television news show blame Mr. Cuomo for all the murders committed in the state during his administration, simply because he opposed capital punishment. Mr. Pataki solidified this tack by going for more credibility—running an ad saying the same, but this time using a murder victim's mother in place of the person on the street. Mr. Pataki won the 1994 election and went straight for what he promised—that he would bring the death penalty back to New York. In September 1995, New York reinstated the death penalty. Six men are currently on death row in New York State.

As my awareness grew that the death penalty was in a galloping phase,

I got a phone call from a Methodist minister in Hartford, Rev. Walter Everett. He had heard that I was a murder victim's mother and opposed to the death penalty, and he wanted to meet with me for a specific reason. Pat Bane was coming to Connecticut, and he wanted me to meet her. I knew who Pat was. She had actually called me before Marietta Jaeger had reached me, telling me she was the executive director of Murder Victims Families for Reconciliation. Walt Everett said Pat was coming, hoping we could find enough people who believed as we did so that we could start a chapter of MVFR in Connecticut.

"I'm the father of a murder victim," he told me. I said he didn't have to tell me. I knew his story. I had seen it on a television show and read about it in the *New York Times*.

On July 26, 1987, Rev. Everett's twenty-four-year-old son, Scott, was killed by a man named Mike Carlucci. As he relates the story, Scott was out with friends and came home and found his apartment had been burglarized—"and he was off the wall," creating a commotion. He walked his friends down to their car and couldn't get back into the building because he had locked himself out. He started banging on the entrance door, calling for someone to open the door. It was late at night, and he was creating a scene. The noise brought Mike out, and he opened the door. He was high on cocaine, waving a gun and yelling to Scott to get out or he'd shoot. There was a confrontation between the two men, and Mike pulled the trigger. The gun—belonging to Mike's cousin—went off and Scott was killed, immediately.

Rev. Everett says honestly that he was filled with anger and bitterness. Mike was arrested but released the following day when an uncle raised the bond set at $50,000, putting his house up as collateral. Waiting for the case to come to court, Rev. Everett's anger escalated to the point where he could hardly feel grief, so consumed was he with the force of his rage. And then, the following May, the case was settled with a plea bargain, whereby Mike would plead guilty, receive a ten-year sentence, which would be suspended after five years. Rev. Everett was baffled and further enraged.

On July 1, he went to the court for the sentencing. It was the first time he had ever seen Mike Carlucci. To this day, Rev. Everett says, much of what happened that day is a blur, except for one thing. He was struck by what Mike said, recalling his words verbatim: "I'm sorry for what I did. I didn't mean to kill Scott Everett. I know these sound like empty words. I know they can't bring Scott back, but I'm truly sorry."

In the year after the murder of his son Rev. Everett talked with other parents of murdered children and felt the intense anger so many retained even years after the tragedy. He started to ask himself, "Is that what's going to happen to me?" At some point, he realized the destructive path he was on. He began to feel compelled to visit Mike Carlucci, and somehow knew that the only way he could end the rage within him was to forgive the murderer.

He wrote a letter to his son's killer, telling him what he had gone through since the murder and about his "pain, anger, bewilderment, confusion, denial, and frustration." But then he thanked Mike for what he had said in court, and he concluded, "As hard as these words are to write, I forgive you." As soon as he wrote that letter, Walt Everett says, he felt the burden he was carrying begin to lift. "By offering forgiveness, I freed myself from that hurt," he says today, acknowledging, however, that the healing is a slow, lifelong process which is still going on.

Never expecting a reply, the minister was surprised when he received a letter from Mike, about three weeks later. Mike told him he hadn't been able to open the letter at first, expecting it would be one accusing and harassing him. But when he did finally read it, he said it changed his life. He fell to his knees to pray for his own forgiveness. He told Rev. Everett that he had given him "the will to live."

A few months later the two met in prison, talking for an hour. This father went much beyond simple forgiveness. He offered, actually, friendship and love. This was essential, he said, because "it takes two for reconciliation to come about." Instinctively, when it was time to leave, the two men hugged each other, crying. Mike later said that what Rev. Everett did "blew me away. I never had anyone forgive me in my life. I started crying. He said he wouldn't be able to live his life the way he lives it if he didn't honestly forgive me for this."

The story then takes an amazing turn. The friendship between these two strangely related men grew. About a year after Mike was released from prison, he met a lovely woman and their relationship became serious. They asked Rev. Everett to marry them, and he did. This made national news, that the father of a murder victim could forgive enough to officiate at the wedding of his son's killer. The NBC *Today* show brought them on for a story, and Matt Lauer, the interviewer, asked Rev. Everett, "Can you ever look at this man and not think of what he did to your son?" The minister answered, "I can never forget what happened to Scott. I see someone who has been changed by God and I celebrate that."

Then Mr. Lauer asked Mike, "What have you learned from this

man?" I had tears in my eyes when I heard a one-time killer's immediate and direct answer: "unconditional love." Can a murderer be redeemed? Certainly here's one proof that the answer can be yes.

I got to meet Mike Carlucci in March 1999 when he, Rev. Everett, and I, along with Clementine Barfield—a Detroit mother who, after her son was murdered, founded Save Our Sons and Daughters, a group committed to healing the scars of violent homicide—were invited to speak at Boston College. The debate was raging over whether Massachusetts, one of the twelve states without the death penalty, would reinstate this punishment, and the college had arranged a series of six talks to bring "thoughtful discussion" to students and the community. Since we were survivors of homicide victims, we were asked to tell our stories and explain how we had come to know that healing the trauma of murder could occur only by forgiving. What made our panel especially noteworthy was that Mike was with us, a living witness to how forgiveness bears good fruit.

I wondered how it had come about that Mike was doing programs with Walt Everett, and he commented "it kind of evolved out of all the other stuff," the visits, the getting to know each other, and the reconciliation. While Mike was still in prison, he was getting furloughs every other weekend. "He would call me as soon as he got home. We would usually get together for breakfast on Saturday," Rev. Everett said. Then one Sunday, he was scheduled to give a talk at 6:30 p.m., and he thought it might have a better impact if Mike were there with him. They could be finished by 8:30, and he'd get Mike back to prison on time. "So I asked Mike if he'd be comfortable speaking with me at the church. He said, 'No, I won't be comfortable, but I'll do it.' He was nervous as a cat, convinced that the people were going to hate him.

"When I introduced Mike, a lot of mouths flew open, but afterward, everybody came up and embraced him." When they left, Mike said to Rev. Everett, "What a feeling!" and expressed awe that "this is what the church is like." Now a truck driver, Mike Carlucci still joins Walt Everett when he can to meet with groups and talk about forgiveness and his personal feelings on why we should end the death penalty. On that platform at Boston College, together with these two men, I experienced an understanding of forgiveness that can't really be expressed in writing. It was like viewing a masterpiece, where the hand of God was present and the face of God was smiling.

The Boston College program and meeting Walt and Mike together, learning more about their story, came long after the day I met with

Walt Everett and Pat Bane for a lunch meeting in Connecticut to talk about the group they both belonged to, Murder Victims Families for Reconciliation. Back on that day, Pat had come up from Virginia, where MVFR was then based, and arranged to meet with us to see if we had any ideas on how to start a chapter of MVFR here. Like us, Pat had learned first-hand what murder does to a family. Her uncle had been killed during a mugging in Syracuse, New York, and she and her family felt the pain, rage, and sorrow that follow the loss of a loved one by a violent act. Yet, she and her family, always opposed to the death penalty, remained strong in their rejection of this ultimate punishment.

We were in perfect agreement that the death penalty, which focuses on the crime, actually prevents families from grieving, that by encouraging families to hate, it prolongs their rage, that it is not a solution to violence, but an escalation of violence. Rev. Everett and I did not know if we could find other survivors of murder victims to join us in our state so that we could form a chapter, but membership in MVFR increased that day by one. I finally, formally, became a member.

I was at this time being formally challenged by many supporters of the death penalty to seriously consider the "valid" reasons why they believed in this "final solution." Someone gave me a list of quotes from people supporting executions, some dating back to the late 1920s, some more recent. This one, written by Charley Reese in the *Conservative Chronicle,* February 15, 1989, gave me the chills. "There are three good things about capital punishment. One, the killer gets to experience the same fear and agony he inflicted on others. Two, the recidivism rate for executed murderers is zero. Three, electricity (or rope or bullets or drugs) is cheaper than room and board.

"The average time served on a life sentence in the United States," he went on, "is about six years. Murderers can usually find ways to get out of prison. So far, none has gotten out of a grave."

Another quote, attributed to the *Cleveland Plain Dealer,* January 25, 1925, also had a vicious tone: "If we want order, we must stop being soft-headed sentimentalists when it comes to penalizing offenders. The murder rate in the United States rises to a scandalous figure. Of the many who kill, comparatively few are ever arrested, still fewer convicted, fewer yet ever see the inside of a felon's cell; only rarely is the murderer punished as the law says he shall be.

"A life term is commonly a short vacation at State expense with nothing to do but eat the fruit of others' industry. Americans are not a nation of murder lovers. We merely seem to be. We are made to seem to be by ill-prepared judges, woozy jurors, and a public opinion sentimentally inclined to sympathize more with the perpetrators than the victims of major crimes. This country needs a rededication to the everlasting truth that the fear of prompt and adequate punishment is the best deterrent for gentlemen tempted to slay."

At the same time that I was being selected to consider the reasons why one should be for the death penalty, I was receiving material from MVFR. The organization puts out a newsletter called *The Voice,* and reading the Winter 1995 issue, I learned more about why the founders had chosen to put the word "reconciliation" in their name. They quoted several definitions from the *Oxford English Dictionary* to explain the meaning of this word, among these: "to set (estranged persons or parties) at one again; to bring back to concord, to reunite (persons or things) in harmony"; "to bring (a person) again into friendly relations to or with (oneself or another) after an estrangement."

More important than these definitions was a thought on reconciliation written by a member, Teresa Mathis. She knew about surviving murder. Her brother Charlie was beaten to death with a baseball bat in 1983 at the age of twenty-one. She herself was the victim of rape and attempted murder in 1973. Her opposition to executions comes, she says, not from her head, "but from my gut. Now my opposition to the death penalty comes from outrage at killing, outrage that we're willing to settle for harsher punishments rather than changes that might actually reduce the rates of murder."

She wrote about those who belong to MVFR, acknowledging that "it's not surprising for some of us to begin discussing the meaning of reconciliation. The word is part of the name of our organization, but that doesn't mean we agree on what reconciliation is.

"All of us are family of murder victims. All of us oppose the death penalty. That's where we are similar. From that point on, our differences start coming out. Some believe that forgiveness is an important spiritual step toward healing, that forgiveness is an essential step toward recon-ciliation. For others, having contact with the individual who killed their loved one, or with others who have murdered, has led to healing and a sense of reconciliation. Others in the group speak more about being reconciled with the event, with the reality of murder. To them, recon-ciliation has something to do with accepting—rather than ignoring or hiding from—the hard reality that bad things have happened and will happen.

"If I had to choose a single definition, I might pick this one, from the

Vietnamese Zen master Thich Nhat Hanh: 'Reconciliation is to understand both sides, to go to one side and describe the suffering being endured by the other side; then to go to the other side and describe the suffering endured by the first side.'

"This definition reminds me of what I see over and over in MVFR members: a concern, not just for their own suffering, but for the suffering of others. While we know we can't ignore our own pain, we also want to know about—and prevent—the suffering that allows some people to become killers. And we are concerned about—and want to prevent—the suffering executions cause the children, parents, and friends of those on death rows. These attitudes are at the root of our opposition to the death penalty.

"This definition also reminds me of the need to be gentle with one another. While we have experienced the murders of our loved ones in ways that are often similar, our suffering is not identical. Just so, while our paths toward healing will be similar, we should not expect them to be identical."

Her last words consoled me because I still wasn't sure I could ever want any kind of personal contact with Shadow Clark. I wasn't at all sure that I cared if he were suffering or not. While I was happy to be a member of MVFR and agreed totally with their stand on forgiveness and the death penalty, I didn't yet know how I defined reconciliation when it came to the killer of my kids. I kept remembering the call I received from Bill Simonsen, the reporter for the *Bigfork Eagle,* who had become my friend. He had gone to the Montana State Prison six months after Shadow Clark began his sentence to do a story on what his life was now like, and hopefully to find out his motive for killing John and Nancy.

Because he was just nineteen, small built and somewhat innocent looking, they called him "the choir boy" at the prison. Shadow Clark was cool, unfeeling, unmoved, smiling sinisterly and declaring he was innocent, that he hadn't done the killing. He gave no reason for why he confessed or why his parents and his lawyer had allowed him to be sentenced for life. Bill felt the interview was more like a cat and mouse game for him. When he called me to tell me about his interview, he commented at the end, "He's got no conscience; he seems literally amoral. Toni, I think he's a serial killer who got caught after his first two victims."

I was left with a range of emotions and questions after getting this information. I could not believe that someone who had been given Christian teachings, such as he had received in his Fundamentalist school, could actually be "amoral," without conscience and unaware that he

had sinned. Yet, it stuck me that, yes, this could happen if he had developed a mental illness in his adolescent years. I remembered what the
doctors had said about my late son Peter, that the onset of his brain
malady had been adolescence. I also knew from much study that brain
maladies are not all of one kind. We know so little yet about the brain.
I also remembered reading about a man back in the 1800s who everybody cared for and respected because he was so very nice. Then he had
an accident. He fell on a metal stick that went through the front of his
head. He did not die, but he became a miserable, amoral person that no
one could stand to be around. Researchers used this incident as a case
study about how certain parts of the brain account for certain behaviors.
They concluded that the injury had destroyed the brain cells that allow
one to be human and kind. I thought of this, the mystery of how the
brain works, and wondered if it could be that Shadow Clark had had
a breakdown in the brain cells that allow one to be moral. That would
then explain how it came about that he could cold-bloodedly murder
two innocent people, never say he was sorry, and only smile about it, as
he denied he ever did it.

A few years later the February 2000 issue of the *Archives of General
Psychiatry* reported the results found by some researchers who had studied twenty-one men with antisocial personality disorder, a psychiatric
diagnosis often applied to people with a history of criminal behavior
and violence. They found subtle abnormalities in the structure of the
brain's frontal lobe. This made me wonder even more if the explanation for Shadow Clark's brutal murders lies in a malady in his brain. I
certainly do not know the answer, but the possibility of this being the
case, mellowed my attitude even more. I could now, in the new year of
2000, be concerned for his suffering, even if he did not recognize his
own malady.

All this thinking, all this wondering—that's what a survivor of a murdered loved one goes through, and I'm not sure it ever ends. I meditated
on Teresa Mathis's words on reconciliation and knew that I did not hate
Shadow Clark. I had already forgiven him, according to my own heart,
meaning that I would let go of any desire for vengeance, that I would
wish him to have a good and productive life even though he spends it
behind bars, that I would never wish or seek harm for him, that I would
pray for him, asking God to let him respond to the grace he was born
with so that he could ask forgiveness of God, be healed in soul, and find
his own redemption. I knew my redemption would always depend on
how truly I had sought redemption for Shadow Clark. Now, as I con-

templated that he might be mentally ill, I could also add to my prayers that he could be healed in body too. For the time being, this would have to be my definition of "reconciliation."

Thinking of Shadow Clark in his prison, I had begun to wonder a lot about life in a cage, behind bars, activities regulated, freedom gone. Unexpectedly I received a letter from a prisoner in Texas named Robert J. Zani. He had read one of my syndicated columns in *Catholic East Texas* and, since I answer all letters sent to me in response to my column, I responded. That began a long pen pal relationship that goes on to this day.

I became very curious about Robert, who was clearly educated, thoughtful, opinionated, strong, and independent, and, thus, he had been confined to a segregated solitary cell for a total so far of five years since his entry into Michael Unit in Tennessee Colony, Texas, on February 5, 1990, after serving at the Wynne Unit in Huntsville from 1982 to 1990 for a crime allegedly committed back in 1967. He answered my questions about his early years, writing, "I was raised in a single-parent household. In fact, the divorce case, 1947–50, *Zani v. Zani* appears in the *Northeastern Reporter* law books, a Massachusetts Supreme Court law case. Very short, I read it. I am fond of saying I made my first court appearance in 1949 (smile). My mother then became a single parent permanently.

"When I went to play Little League baseball, I was told I could not because you had to have a father who would help in some way. It was indeed like that in those days. Boys without present fathers faced a lack of—often zero—community support. It was something of a stigma attached by families with supposed 'family values.' However, as fate would have it, after sitting out the first year, I played all the rest....

"I did graduate from the University of Texas in Austin with a B.A. in 1967...," with major studies in English, history, Latin, and economics. Robert was witness to an execution he has never talked about at length, the shooting of forty-nine people, thirteen fatally, by Charles Whitman, who went with a gun to the clock tower at the University of Texas in Austin, in 1966 and killed those in the path of his bullets. That was done by a man who believed in the death penalty and that he could administer it, Robert says, making it clear that he didn't believe in executions—done by an individual or by the state—not then and doesn't now. As he once wrote to me, "The youth who killed your son and daughter-in-law believed in the death penalty. Crudely and directly put, he held court in a bedroom."

Since Robert had responded originally to a piece I had written against the death penalty, it is not surprising that all of our letters bring this subject up. He wrote, in honesty, "Although I consider your death penalty views nonradical, and they receive no play where they should, I think yours is a voice that should be heard. Whatever you do about the death penalty, it is the same as what everyone else who is actively involved does, dear soul. It is simply a matter of stacking straw on the back of a camel, one by one. That's what you do, I do, Sister Prejean does, no more, no less. . . . Anti–death penalty activists have been remarkably unsuccessful in this country for over two hundred years. It seems to me that when a strategy has been unsuccessful for two centuries, it is time to use another strategy . . . or you'll all be continuing to ram your heads into a brick wall. What would be your goal in your 'mission' to fight against the death penalty?

"Since I have dealt with the death penalty almost two decades, I know where the holes—the pitfalls—are. Why would anyone who is genuinely against the death penalty vote for any politician who supports it? That is the question."

It struck me that he had touched the core truth, that the death penalty will never be abolished in our country unless we elect leaders who will end it. Then I thought of Mario Cuomo and how his nonexecution position had cost him the election. This convinced me even more that we must get involved with the political climate if we want to reverse the death penalty mania. One of the best books I have read on this subject is *Against Capital Punishment: The Anti–Death Penalty Movement in America 1972–1994* by Herbert Haines. I have had the privilege of being a part of two conferences where we both were speakers, and I greatly respect what he has to say, specifically the following:

"If the future of capital punishment in America is in the hands of an anti–death penalty movement alone, then executions will most likely continue for a long time indeed. . . . New organizations will be needed, organizations that have as their goal reducing America's leadership of the industrialized world in violence." The fundamental issue, he says, is "America's habit of trying to solve problems through force. . . . Ridding ourselves of the death penalty may be a prerequisite to coming to grips with that deeper cultural problem, not its result."

Clearly, if this is to begin, we must have elected leaders who see this and have the political courage to say openly that they will work against the devastating position we've taken as a nation, that in the United States, we will solve rampant violence by escalating official violence. Years ago, back in 1927, a media giant of the times, William Randolph Hearst, wrote in the *Congressional Digest:* "There is no deterrent in the menace of the gallows. Cruelty and viciousness are not abolished by cruelty and viciousness—not even by legalized cruelty and viciousness. . . .

"Our penal system has broken down because it is built upon the sand—founded on the basis of force and violence—instead of on the basis of Christian care of our fellow men, of moral and mental human development, of the conscientious performance by the State of its duty to the citizen.

"We cannot cure murder by murder. We must adopt another and better system."

His words underscore a truth everlastingly valid that was ignored in his day and remains ignored in ours, except for the many—and growing—abolitionist groups nationally that are becoming more vocal and visible in their mission to call a halt to executions.

I credit Robert Zani, writing to me from his solitary cell in Texas, for helping me to see so many facets of the death penalty. In one of his early letters, he said: "Long ago I read a treatise by an obscure Mennonite Swiss nineteenth-century professor/philosopher who had developed a mental discipline of working with and applying the statement—'There is but one ethical standard for the state as well as the individual.' That comes from early Anabaptist doctrine, and at bottom it is what caused them most of the problems they faced. He understood the unique power of that statement when applied, which he considered the crux of philosophical Christianity. It sounds so simple and easy. It is so radical and revolutionary. Few thoughts run so deep. It took me some time to use that statement as a touchstone. What a powerful revelation," wrote Robert, who is a Catholic convert.

Later he wrote, "About the death penalty, much really comes down to that religious/ethical statement—'There is but one ethical standard for the state as well as the individual.' If one believes something is wrong for an individual to do, but right for many people (the state) to do, how do they explain the ethics of that? The bottom line is doubleminded, double-standard, doublethink, doublespeak. Psalm 12. The book of James, 1:8. Pure and simple. True enough, I've had halfwits tell me that it is wrong for an individual to take a life, but right for a collection of individuals (the state), for retaliation, protection, etc. That is merely a clever evasion of the one ethical standard statement and an admission/confession they do not believe in the one ethical standard."

Robert started telling me over and over shortly after our correspondence began, back in early 1996, that ending the death penalty hinges on "the innocence issue," not just the innocence of some of those on death row, but of all prisoners—"innocence across the board, not just death penalty innocence.... In any debate or in-depth discussion, a person who represents the anti–death penalty point of view needs to understand its ethical/moral link to the overall subject of innocence.

"I have spent fifteen years singing the same song. Same verse. One small voice. Over and over. 'Innocence is the key.' It is the key to the death penalty issue and it is the key to straightening out the entire criminal justice system, which is in a shambles, primarily because now it is in the grip and grasp of unfettered and uncontrolled capitalism. No money, no justice.... We now live in a time where social rank, class, position, and wealth places one above the law.... Innocence is no longer relevant in the criminal justice system because it is no longer relevant in the hearts and minds of Americans.... Law professors Fred Bennett of the Catholic University and Alan Raphael of Loyola University of Chicago went public and said: 'Death penalty opponents will not be successful until the focus is placed on innocent people.' Exactly, and amen."

As Robert says, the question of innocence is pivotal in seeking any reforms of the criminal justice system. When it is a death penalty case, a mistake is fatal. A fact sheet put out by the Judicial Process Commission in Rochester, New York, in April 2000 reports that more than eighty-eight innocent people had been released from death row since 1972. Since 1977, for every seven people executed, one was released from death row.

How do we feel about that ever present possibility that an innocent person is being put to death? Listen to this voice: "I am innocent, innocent. Make no mistake about this. I owe society nothing; I am an innocent man and something very wrong is taking place here tonight."

That was Leonel Herrera on Texas death row, convicted and sentenced to death for the 1982 murders of two police officers. Some years after his conviction, an attorney who had represented Mr. Herrera's brother Raul came forward with evidence that Raul and not Leonel had confessed to the murders. In addition, Raul's son, who was nine at the time of the killings, gave a sworn statement that he was an eyewitness to the crime and saw his father commit the murders.

Did this make a difference? No, because now we get into the area of the details of a state's laws. In Texas, any new evidence must be presented within thirty days of the conviction. And so, Mr. Herrera's motion for a new trial was denied. This denial was upheld by the U.S. Supreme Court. Mr. Herrera was executed on May 12, 1993. The reason may be seen in reading what Chief Justice William Rehnquist wrote in *Herrera v. Collins* 1993: "Few rulings would be more disruptive of our federal system than to provide for federal habeas review of free-standing claims of actual innocence. . . . The Constitution has no inherent protection against the execution of the innocent. Federal habeas courts sit to ensure that individuals are not imprisoned in violation of the Constitution, not to correct errors of fact. . . . 'Actual innocence' is not itself a constitutional claim."

That's a sad, frightening statement. I don't know the whole story in the Herrera case; I never thoroughly studied it, but I've read much about it. I don't know for sure if he was innocent or not. Yet, sufficient doubt was there to merit investigation of his innocence. But the verdict was simply, *case closed*. Was justice served? Have we become a people so bloodthirsty that we will kill even when evidence exists that a condemned person may be innocent? Doesn't it torment us to think that justice, which means to act in accordance with what is right, true, honest, fair, and equitable, is not the priority in the criminal *justice* system? We now have statistics showing that for every one hundred persons executed, one of the dead was innocent. We should reflect on what former Supreme Court Justice William Douglas noted: "A judge who denies a stay of execution in a capital case often wonders if an innocent man is going to his death."

Robert, writing from his solitary Texas cell a few years ago, had first clued me in to the innocence issue. "Although unpublicized, courts in this country have been moving toward declaring that 'innocence is irrelevant' in a criminal trial. The U.S. Supreme Court has inched closer and closer to that conclusion. Three justices on the Supreme Court have consistently held that 'innocence is not a constitutional issue' because the U.S. Constitution does not address it specifically! That makes the only question—If the Constitution does not protect the innocent, who, then, does it protect?"

Certainly as a nation that praises itself as a leader in guaranteeing human rights, we would have to shudder to think that we killed an innocent person to uphold a state's procedural grounds. A dramatic case that had to disturb us, but unfortunately did not bother those who could have made a difference, was the execution of Gary Graham in Texas on June 22, 2000. Substantial evidence existed that he did not commit the murder for which he received the death penalty, yet he was killed for this. True, he was not a good kid. At age seventeen, he went on a rampage with a gun, robbed people, and even raped a woman. He deserved long imprisonment for this. But he maintained, from the time of his arrest, that they had the wrong man when it came to who killed Bobby Lambert in 1981. He was convicted on the testimony of one person, period, a woman named Bernadine Skillern, who identified him unflinchingly as the killer, even though she saw him only through the windshield of her car from thirty or forty feet away. Other witnesses who disputed this identification were never called in, Mr. Graham's .22 caliber revolver did not match the murder weapon, and this youth—he was, after all, seventeen years old—insisted he didn't kill the man, repeating this even as the poison entered his body on that fateful night of June 22.

Gary Graham's death certainly raised the question of how reliable an eyewitness is. I would guess all of us have been misidentified at some point in our lives. I was an employee of a Catholic newspaper, and I'll never forget the embarrassment I had to endure when someone called the paper to say I had been in a questionable bar on a Saturday night in New York. I was at home sixty miles away, taking care of my children that night, but I was put in the mean position of having to defend myself on a person's "eyewitness" insistence. I was misidentified so many times in my life that at one point I wrote a column with the theme of "I have a universal face." When the misidentification involves someone accused of murder, as in Gary Graham's case, the mistake is a deadly one.

Charles Wilton, a volunteer with Amnesty International, has written eloquently on the issue of innocence. He writes about the statement he attributes to Attorney General Mary Sue Terry of Virginia: "Explaining why death row inmate Joseph O'Dell should not be allowed to have DNA tests performed—tests not available at the time of his conviction—she stated, 'Evidence of innocence is irrelevant.' O'Dell was executed in 1997."

Corresponding with Robert J. Zani became an eye-opener for me on the innocence issue. Some people have told me they wouldn't trust anything a prisoner writes. I can't buy into that cynicism, since some of my favorite people were prisoners, namely, Jesus, John the Baptist, Peter and Paul! When you have an active correspondence for nearly five years with a person, you get to know very well how that person thinks, or whether he has contradicted himself or changed his story. Robert has been utterly consistent, and I believe him to be an honest, thinking man and a friend. I asked him once to write down his reasons for finding the death penalty so wrong. This man, who has spent twenty years in prison, who faced the death penalty and spent endless years thinking about this ultimate penalty, sent me several reasons. They are well worth considering:

- I am opposed to the Holocaust. Without the death penalty there could have been no Holocaust. The only way to say "never again" and mean it is to ban permanently the death penalty. The perpetrators of the Holocaust believed in and advocated the death penalty. Banning the death penalty is insurance that no Holocaust can start up and occur.

- There is but one ethical standard for the state as well as the individual. If a person believes something is wrong for an individual to do, but right for many people (the state), how do they explain that? The bottom line here is double minded, double standard, double think, double speak. I don't remember how many people have told me that it is wrong for an individual to take a life but right for the state to do so for retaliation, protection, etc. That is merely an evasion of the One Ethical Standard axiom. By the state's double standard, which punishes a convicted killer by killing, they could give themselves permission to gang rape a convicted rapist. For shame. Once the one ethical standard for the state as well as the individual goes, anything goes.

- All guilty prisoners on death row at one time believed in the death penalty. They just held court in the street. If they hadn't (mentally) advocated the death penalty, they wouldn't be guilty and on death row. The assassins of John F. Kennedy, Martin Luther King, Abe Lincoln, etc. all believed in the death penalty. George Bernard Shaw put it this way: "It is the deed that teaches, not the name we give it. Murder and capital punishment are not opposites that cancel one another out, but similars that breed their kind."

- When point blank asked to support the death penalty (the woman taken in adultery), Jesus said: "Let he who is without sin cast the first stone at her." John 8. He did not equivocate or rely on excuses or pretexts. Stone-throwing Christians need to take a long, hard look in the mirror.

- The transparency of lying governors. Why are they lying? Time and again a governor will say, "I am personally opposed to the death penalty, but I must enforce the law." But the law gives a governor the direct or indirect power to commute a sentence or even pardon. Governors can always enforce that law.

- In the United States, only the poor are executed. Why is that? The death penalty is the ultimate tyranny of one man's domination over another. The death penalty is about being poor, and scapegoating.

- In 1982, I personally faced the death penalty in court. I won. But for those who have ever been in the position of defending against the death penalty, it is an awesome and terrifying experience. The mind tends to panic and/or numb. You are seeing first hand the State's ultimate and most permanent exercise of raw power. My innocence was totally irrelevant in what amounts to a psychological game, a deadly charade, a cruel hoax which is sardonically referred to as a "fair trial." We cannot expect the entrenched power structure to act ethically, fairly, honestly any time soon. But we can insure that there will never be a Holocaust and no execution of innocents by banning the death penalty. Simultaneously, we cannot forget that it is all a system which insures that people are not judged the same way. Judicial error is built into the system, and all judges have absolute immunity. Immunity corrupts and absolute immunity corrupts absolutely. It is the political authorities who create the law; they are not stupid and keep a way out for themselves.

I can't imagine what it must be like to know that whether you live or die is in the hands of human beings, sitting, listening to other human beings trying to build a case against you leading up to a climax proclaiming you must die and we must kill you. Robert knows that terror. He was there. I learned from him.

Chapter Five

A NEW DOOR OPENS—
AND PRISONERS BECOME KIN

ଓଓଓଓଓଓଓଓଓଓଓଓଓ

The letters I had been receiving from Robert J. Zani had more than raised my curiosity about prisons and prisoners in the United States today. Back in the 1970s I had done a lot of research on jails—which are the first stop, housing people arrested but not yet convicted of a crime—both as a reporter for the *Long Island Catholic*, the weekly publication of the Rockville Centre, New York, diocese and, later, as a human rights commissioner in Suffolk County, Long Island, appointed by the county executive. I became aware at the time of serious abuses in the criminal justice system, with people especially divided on the issue of whether jails and prisons should be institutions of punishment or of rehabilitation. Most opted for punishment.

I had one experience back in 1976 that I'd never forget. It taught me that anyone who works in a jail or prison, or visits one, knows this question of punishment vs. rehabilitation is an artificial one. How can you rehabilitate anyone who is living in a cage? I was in the Nassau County Jail to do some newspaper stories on their programs to "rehabilitate" inmates and was given a tour of the place by a lieutenant. When I got to one of the tiers, where the cells are lined up in a row, the officer asked me to step inside one of the cells. Immediately, the bars clanged closed, electronically, and I was locked inside. He stood there, laughing his head off. I was angry, disoriented, panicked, frustrated, and afraid—even though I knew my incarceration was only a demonstration that would last, I presumed, for a few minutes.

The officer left me there, as he walked away, down the tier, still laughing. Never before in my life had I been treated like a piece of garbage, and now I knew why prisons were not meant for anything but humiliation and punishment. When he finally let me out, I didn't say thank you.

Coincidentally, I had just returned from visiting my son John, who

93

then lived in Colorado, at the very time that the American Correctional Association was holding its 106th annual meeting that year—in August 1976—in Denver. Flanked by the beautiful mountains which frame the city, a few thousand corrections officers, wardens, parole officers, judges, prison chaplains, and others working in the criminal justice system had come together under the theme: "What Works in Corrections: A Search for Reality." The American Catholic Correctional Chaplains Association was holding its annual convention at the same time. Because I was there, I took a look at what was going on. It was difficult to find anything positive being said about the criminal justice system by anyone.

One of the speakers at that 1976 meeting was Norman Carlson, then the director of the U.S. Bureau of Prisons. He pointed out that the federal prison population had increased by four thousand in the previous year. Judges were also giving convicted criminals longer terms, he noted, adding that overpopulation remains one of the biggest problems, a ticking bomb, in a prison. And he emphasized that prisons "aren't equipped and never really have been to handle rehabilitation. That should be done outside the prison, in the community." This was exactly how I felt, after that terrible experience of being locked in that cage by a sadistic corrections officer—or was it just that he wanted to flaunt his power? I wondered how he treated the inmates.

I was beginning to feel that 1976 was a pivotal year for the criminal justice system. On July 2, 1976, the U.S. Supreme Court had cleared the way for resuming executions, which had been stopped with a ruling in 1972, after being judged to be unconstitutionally cruel. Probably to be expected, many Americans who wanted a death penalty were not happy over this, and polls showed a growing number to be concerned that eliminating executions would result in an increase in crime. Support for reinstating the death penalty thus grew stronger among the general public. According to Herbert Haines: "So why did the Supreme Court pull back from abolition? Why did it change course on the death penalty in 1976? The transition from a liberal Warren Court to a conservative Nixon/Burger Court was not the whole answer, because the shift was from five to four against capital punishment to seven to two for it. The most likely explanation for the Court's change of direction lies in public opinion." In other words, a vocal segment of the American public wanted the death penalty back and officials, both elected and appointed, were listening.

The decision didn't immediately attract much attention from the person in the street. But a month later, in August 1976, a prison riot erupted that did get people's attention. Inmates at a maximum security New York state prison staged a week-long strike that attracted the country's attention, not because of the strike itself, but because the action reopened a national wound.

The strike was at Attica—the place where forty-three persons died in a prison riot five years earlier, most of them by state police bullets during the retaking of the institution on September 13, 1971. This—the nation's bloodiest riot—will go down in the history books as the nation's "Hundred Hours of Shame." The riot began when more than 1,200 of Attica's then 2,243 inmates barricaded themselves inside D Yard, holding thirty-nine guards and prison employees hostage. They did this so their protests over poor medical care, unsanitary conditions, and the lack of other basic services would be heard and get attention.

It was a damp, dismal day. A small army of state police and guards stormed D Yard with guns in hand. Military helicopters poured out pepper gas, a tear gas variation, and troopers opened fire. Many of the inmates were forced to take off their clothes and crawl naked over broken glass while being beaten with nightsticks. Forty-three persons—eleven guards and thirty-two prisoners—died in the next hundred hours. In the August strike, five years later, Attica inmates complained that the promises for reform, including a promised overhaul in parole and sentencing procedures, never materialized. How could living conditions even come close to being human in this prison, which was built to house twelve hundred but held over two thousand, in double-occupied six by eight feet cells?

Lawyers for the tortured Attica inmates filed a class action suit three years later, but it took nearly thirty years before the case was settled. Finally, a federal judge, in February 2000, approved a settlement, mandating New York State to pay $8 million to the inmates tortured in that incident, described by a federal court as an "orgy of brutality."

Back at the conventions that were held in Denver that August of 1976, I had kept notes on a talk given by Bishop Andrew Grutka, of Gary, Indiana. He spoke of the ability man has to inflict pain on others in all relationships and applied this to the prison situation, asking, rhetorically, how much pain is added to the inmates' day by angry faces and voices of the men who hold the keys? The public must be protected from violent criminals, he said, and nonviolent people convicted of a crime must also be given a sentence of punishment. But, he asked, does a man ever lose his right to be treated humanly? And then he asked an even more thoughtful question: "What kind of a warden, corrections officer, chaplain, judge, etc., would Christ be?"

Funny how a variation of that question would haunt me seventeen years later, almost to the day, when I would wonder, "What kind of a mother of a murder victim would Christ be?" That question began then and continues to this day to define who it is I must become. I was to find out, little by little, that entering prisons would be stops along the way.

Soon after I joined Survivors of Homicide, Sam Rieger told me he had arranged with John Armstrong, the commissioner of corrections, for us to have a tour of the women's prisons, Niantic and York, in Connecticut. Several members of the group had already been to Northern, the maximum security prison for extremely violent offenders, including those on death row. These members felt they wanted to see the type of facility the murderers of loved ones were in and find out how they were treated, what benefits they had, how they were being given anger-management sessions. They found those convicted of the most serious crimes—serial rapists, child molesters, and a killer of a police officer—locked down for twenty-three hours, not getting much educational work and handcuffed every time they had to move out of the cell. In some ways, this helped the survivors, whose loved ones had been victims of heinous crimes, gain some comfort. If a prisoner was not a murderer or a security risk, Sam said most of the members wanted to see them have more freedom, just as long as they stayed behind bars.

I was very curious about women in prison. I was aware that the number of women in custody was escalating, doubling from 3 percent of the prison population in 1978 to 6.3 percent by 1997. Much of the reason for this rested in our punitive drug laws, which primarily came down hard on nonviolent, low-level offenders, especially people of color. This mainly accounted for the dramatic increase of women in prison, 80 percent of whom have children under eighteen. I had actually seen a statistic reporting that nearly seven million children have a parent in jail or prison or recently released on probation or parole—seven million children in jeopardy, who run a greater risk, experts say, of becoming juvenile delinquents or adult criminals. When it is the mother in prison, the children usually get shuffled around to be cared for by a relative or put into some kind of supervised foster care.

Because I wanted to see first hand what brought women to prison, I enthusiastically joined Sam and the others going to Niantic, a minimum security prison, and York, a maximum security one, located side by side. I wanted to know the reasons why more than a thousand women were confined here either in the one or the other. The warden was Eileen Higgens, a caring and competent professional. She gave me the story, and I came away thinking perhaps we all should have more compassion for women who get into so much trouble that they end up behind bars.

I learned that there's a significant difference between women and men in this state's prisons. Whereas many males are incarcerated for violent crimes, only 18 percent of women are in for violence, and these crimes are generally for armed robbery or risk of injury to a minor. Occasionally a woman is in for murder. Most of the women are imprisoned for substance abuse and crimes related to this.

Another surprising difference is age. Here the female population is older, with the majority of women between the ages of thirty and forty-five. A study of this phenomenon points to a bottom-line cause of later age crime. Most of the incarcerated women had a history of physical and sexual abuse at a young age. Studies have shown there is a very strong correlation between being the victim of physical violence as a child and growing up to be violent or self-destructive. After being abused by others, these women descend into self-abuse, via drugs, alcohol, prostitution or becoming the victim of a battering man. A strong issue was the lack of self-esteem, Warden Higgens told me. It is almost impossible for abused children to develop any sense of self-worth as they grow into adulthood.

Since the goal of this women's prison is to help inmates heal so that they can make a life for themselves outside the institution, the warden emphasized that those in charge focus on what matters most to these women, namely, their motherhood. About 75 percent were mothers, most often the primary caretaker of their child. When they come into the prison, they are emotionally and psychologically strung-out. But after de-tox in the prison, the first thing that hits them is that their babies are out there, being cared for by someone else, usually a grandmother.

They get very depressed, feel very guilty, and keep asking, "What did I do to my babies?" This prison is committed to "a heavy emphasis on parenting," said the warden, emphasizing that children were allowed to come in and even stay overnight in a private room with their mothers to try to reestablish the bonding between them.

Since most of the women coming in have a history of self-abuse, they come into the prison "very sick," Warden Higgens said, and so are given "a lot of medical and health services." On the average, 30 to 35 percent are pregnant, many of these high-risk, and 20 percent are HIV positive. Many of them have sexually transmitted diseases. Some have never seen a dentist. Here for the first time in their lives, they get full medical services, including breast and gynecological exams.

As might be expected, most have no job skills, making vocational training essential. Accountability is emphasized because the priority in a prison has to be public safety. And while no prison is 100 percent successful in rehabilitation—20 to 30 percent will be back—Warden Higgens said the signs of progress were increasing. "Some tell us they are happy to be here. One said it was a blessing for her because she had no place to go and she was tired of running." Now I had taken a human look at these prisoners, and I could see clearly that they needed compassion, never contempt. I was also aware that what I had seen in Connecticut's women's prisons was the cream of the crop, different from reports I had read about women in other prisons being sexually abused and shackled during childbirth.

I had also been reading almost every day about how prison construction was booming. In 1995 the Justice Department reported that 213 new state and federal prisons had been built in the first five years of this decade. As would be expected, prisons had become an even more thriving business for industries, with annual revenues for items needed by these institutions—everything from "maximum security toothpaste" that comes in a clear tube preventing hidden contraband, to better than ever weapons—reaching $26 billion by 1995. By the year 2000, the American Jail Association's annual Jail Expo, hawking everything needed for keeping inmates "in line and in style," held that year in the Sacramento Convention Center, had three hundred booths of new products, to be examined by two thousand sheriffs, wardens, and correctional officers.

There's big money involved here, as the annual convention of the American Correctional Association also shows. This is the world's largest prison trade show, with a recent one having "more than 600 booths touting the very latest in prison innovation and technology," the *New York Times* reported. So many are profiting!

One of the saddest stories of the 1990s will be how the United States dealt with the nation's fear of crime. We simply incarcerated more and more people, built more prisons, and never bothered to publicize the fact that close to two-thirds of these prisoners are doing time for crimes that involve no violence toward another. In fact, more than half of the people currently in prisons are there because they were convicted of a drug abuse crime. Fewer than 1 percent of inmates are there for murder. And here's one more statistic that needs reflection—an African-American man is seven times more likely to go to prison than a white man. Does this say something about race, or our criminal justice—or injustice—system?

People who were concerned about prison reform, the need for this underscored by the Attica disaster, hoped to see programs that would rehabilitate prisoners, that would reduce the recidivism rate, which remained high, and bring the prison population down. Instead, the opposite has happened. Since 1972, we've seen a fivefold increase in the number of people incarcerated in America's prisons, mainly for drug offenses, longer mandated sentences, elimination of "good time," which slices time off a sentence, and less willingness to parole nonviolent offenders.

As the new millennium began, it was reported over and over that the crime rate was down, yet the inmate population was climbing at an alarming rate, 645 per 100,000 people, more than double the rate of 313 per 100,000 only fifteen years ago, in 1985. Inmates in American prisons totaled 500,000 in 1978; that number, nearly quadrupled now, is expected to exceed 2 million in the year 2001.

The boom in prison building makes great PR for politicians. They can give speeches on how they are "hard on criminals" and are fighting crime by imprisoning more and more people. In New York State, after Governor George Pataki was elected, he proposed allocating over $600 million for new prison construction. At the same time, he wanted to make cuts in education, drug treatment, family support, mental health, child care services, and job training. No mention was made of funding programs for rehabilitation. By the fall of 1997, New York had built fourteen prisons, many of these in the Adirondack area, called by New Yorkers the "North Country," holding a total of nearly fifteen thousand inmates. Prisons had become the region's biggest employer.

The latest of Governor Pataki's prison proposals—to build a 750-cell maximum security institution, holding fifteen hundred violent offenders, costing $130 million—generated some opposition because it would be located in Tupper Lake, a valuable wilderness area of the Adirondacks. In spite of protests, the New York State Legislature approved the plan in September 1997. The *New York Times* had written editorials opposing the escalation of prison building, saying "Mr. Pataki does the state a double disservice, harming both the budget and the criminal justice system." Noting that State Senator Ronald B. Stafford, a Republican of Plattsburgh, had "waged a fierce fight in the Senate to bring the prison to his district," *Times* reporter James Dao wrote: "Mr. Stafford was among the first legislators to recognize the prison industry's economic potential. Since taking office in 1966, he has brought nine into a district that already had two.

"The Senator can speak from personal experience about prison town life; he grew up a stone's throw from Clinton Correctional Facility in

Dannemora, where his father was a guard. 'I feel fortunate to have grown up there,' he said. 'Prison towns are great communities.' "

I took quite an interest in the building of so many prisons in that area of New York State because I lived there for three years when I was young, just out of college, teaching in a town of nine hundred people named Cape Vincent. It was a job-poor place, very dependent on the summer visitors for any noticeable business to go on. They used to joke that they took the census by checking clotheslines. If there were diapers hung there, they would add one person to the population. There was an in-joke you heard right away if you were a newcomer, noticing the shutdown in town activity before fall began. They'd laugh and tell you, "In the summer we drink highballs, and in the winter, snowballs." Last I heard, everybody's employed now, thanks to the prisons. The important task Governor Pataki has now, I suppose, is to keep those cells occupied if he wants these upstate New York votes.

New York isn't the only state involved in prison building that boosts the economics of a rural area. So much prison construction has been going on to revive economically depressed areas that this became the soundest growth industry of the last decade. Someone showed me a T-shirt a few years ago proclaiming in big letters, "Corrections Capital of the World—Freemont County." This Colorado area now has thirteen prisons, including a maximum security prison where convicted Oklahoma bomber Timothy McVeigh sits in an isolation cell. This prison has a nickname, "Alcatraz of the Rockies." County officials comment, "We have a nice, non-polluting, recession-proof industry here." Never is there a mention of the human persons being warehoused in these prisons.

The booming prison industry is changing the face of formerly economically depressed small communities in other states, too, like Hobbs, New Mexico, South Bay, Florida and Beeville, Texas. It becomes clearer and clearer that little or nothing will be done to reduce the prison population in the United States, considering that prisoners are now the raw material needed to keep the industry going that has turned formerly depressed areas into booming towns.

I have in my hand a clip sent to me by Robert Zani. It's from the March 2000 issue of the *Texas Prison Echo* pointing out how, in truth, we have discovered a new way to bring revenues into "cash-strapped municipalities":

"Something isn't right. Texas has spent literally billions of dollars in the last ten years to cage its criminals. When the money spigot began gushing, a predictable thing happened—towns and cities reversed their universal disdain for prisons. City after city came begging in the '90s: 'Give us a prison unit.' And the state responded. Since 1990, at least 73 prisons have been built. Starlight glinting off razor wire is now a common sight throughout the Lone Star State, as are the white buses whizzing down scenic back roads, their shackled cargoes representing revenue for cash-strapped municipalities."

After George W. Bush took office as governor, this "compassionate conservative" expanded Texas prison slots from 41,000 to 150,000. The writer for the *Texas Prison Echo* concludes, poignantly, "Building cages is easy. More attention needs to be given to emptying them, unless there is truth to the charge that the system exists now merely as a money-making entity and serves only as a conveyor belt for the damned."

I know that this is a touchy subject for most people. Some, on reading this, will conclude I am a "liberal" and am "soft" on criminals. Not true. I've done much research on jails and prisons. I have been to many of these places, and I have met many prisoners. I correspond and visit with some serving time. I have seen they have sensitivities and feelings, and I believe many can learn from their mistakes—and be redeemed.

Nor am I "soft" on violent criminals. I want them punished. But we've seemed to gloss over the fact that the majority of convicts are not violent. Now, sadly, they are in a place where they can be subject to brutality and learn how to become violent themselves. As Ann Landers wrote a while back in one of her columns, "Many prisons not only do nothing to discourage crime; they are 'graduate schools' where neophytes learn the real tricks of the trade. I welcome suggestions on what can be done to cure this sick and costly problem."

We also have to ask what gets shut out when big money is allocated by a state for more prisons. When New York State's Governor George Pataki got his millions to build more prisons, where did this money come from? Probably from the cuts the state made in the needed human services area that might prevent young people from turning to crime—like education, drug treatment, family support, child care services, mental health, and job training. Doesn't anybody care?

Building more prisons does nothing to discourage crime. What we urgently need in our country is more concern and help for nonviolent people who get in trouble for using drugs and committing petty crimes. Our humanity demands that we must stop thinking of prisoners as "human garbage," a terrible term I have heard many times, for they, too, are children of God. We cannot simply "discard" them.

I now found myself focusing a great deal on prisoners, and I wondered if I was kidding myself. True, I had visited women's prisons and toured two men's prisons in Connecticut, but this was more as a researcher, not as a person who would be personally involved, one-to-one, with prisoners. I also had begun soul searching, wondering if all that I was writing against the death penalty and the prison system was truly from the heart. In my prayers, I would ask God where I was to go with this new "mission," not sure that was even the proper word for my concern. Certainly, I didn't want this concern to degenerate into being merely a cause.

Admittedly, my concern about prisoners wasn't winning me gold stars. Most of my friends would be confused, wondering why on earth I cared about these "lowest of the low" members of society, considering what one of them, Shadow Clark, had done to me and my family. Some warned me not to get involved in a personal way with any of them, citing tale after tale of prisoners who were con artists and had taken advantage of people, especially women, who had tried to befriend them. Few believed that a prisoner could be reformed or redeemed, and they tried to make me agree with them.

I wasn't naïve about criminals. In the 1970s when I was a human rights commissioner, an unpaid position of service and responsibility, the family of a child killed by a drunk driver had come to us for help in getting the man convicted. Truly they were victims of a tragedy stemming from the crime of driving after drinking. I felt such pain for them. Having to deal with this tragedy, I asked a Catholic jail chaplain whether the criminals he deals with ever thought about their victims.

"To them," he said, "the victim is an object. They don't deal with victims as persons. The victim has something they want and so they take it. Or the victim is someone who got in their way, and shouldn't have."

He went on to berate the criminal justice system itself, which is designed to keep the criminal separated from his victim—and thus, from any reminders of the consequences of his crime.

"When you consider crime, punishment, retribution, and rehabilitation, you see very clearly that the system makes the criminal responsible not to the victim, but to society. And impersonalism is built into the system. Once he's caught, the criminal becomes identified with categories—burglary, rape, assault, murder, and such. He never has to confront a person he has impoverished, injured, maimed, or murdered. Thus, he doesn't have to feel. If he should express remorse, it's usually only sorrow that he got caught."

The chaplain pointed out to me in that interview that about 5 percent of all crimes are labeled violent, and studies show that in most of these cases, the violence is triggered by something else—drugs, alcohol, mental imbalance, fear, anger. And the violent criminals have another set of victims no one ever thinks about, he added, "their families."

His personal feeling was that criminals should have to make direct retribution to their victims, but he said this would be a complicated change to initiate and enforce in a system with long established ways.

Little of what he told me back then has changed. I and my friends in Survivors of Homicide all have stories that fit that sad description— especially of being unable to have any contact with the criminal and of seeing denial and coldness in their faces.

Yet, perhaps because of my longstanding concern for human rights, my revulsion at the thought of the death penalty, my correspondence with prisoners, my disgust with the prison system, my need to believe that people can change for the better, I found myself standing just outside the prison bars. Putting everything together, I started to feel that I would have to prove to myself that all I was saying and writing was genuine.

Again I learned that God has ways of strewing clues for what we should do right in our path.

I was on this uncertain path in 1996, when I received a letter from a man named John McNamara responding to a column I had written about coincidences. I answer all the letters I get in writing, but this one impressed me so much that I decided to respond by phone instead. I didn't know then that this would be the beginning of a lovely friendship with John, his wife, Maureen, and, remotely, their eleven children. As we talked that first evening, John told me about the volunteer work he did. It was prison-ministry, through a program called Residents Encounter Christ. The heart of this is a retreat, where all inmates are welcome to come and be introduced to Christ and the Bible, to be shown how they can live the life of a Christian even behind bars.

I asked questions and John answered. The retreat heavily emphasizes what it means to experience "metanoia," or a change of heart. Prisoners are treated as individuals who are worthwhile and able to make choices about their present and future behavior. A symbolic and touching service is one that the REC leaders called a "paschal vigil." Slips of paper on which the prisoners have written their "sins" are burned, symbolizing that their sins are forgiven. The ashes then are placed on the inmates' foreheads, and each is given a candle to light from a central candle that symbolizes the light of Christ. The ashes are then wiped away as a sign of liberation from the burden of painful sins.

Prisoners are invited during the retreat to give testimonies. Some tell sad stories of abuse and neglect as children or how they became entangled in the web of drug addiction and subsequent crimes. It's not unusual to see a prisoner wipe away tears, John McNamara told me. Some will talk about the meaning they have found in their lives because they have found God.

I felt that the people who bring the love of Christ into prisons are noble, truly witnesses to the belief that all God's creatures are redeemable. Yet, I could hear the scoffing that would come from people cynical about prisoners, who could legitimately ask, are prisoners really willing to go straight because of REC?

I thanked John for telling me about this fine work and suggested we stay in touch. I didn't know then how soon we'd be getting together. It came with another phone call, this time from him. He told me that the REC program was ending on a Sunday, with the last talk being a "Peace talk." The people running the retreat were requesting that I come to the prison—a maximum security prison called the Greenhaven Correctional Center in Stormville, New York—on the first Sunday of October and give this talk to the inmates who would be completing their weekend. Thinking the ways of the Lord are strange—and that I was, indeed, being led, this time to the other side of the prison gates—I said yes.

I worked endless hours on that speech. I wanted it to be honest, to say exactly how I felt and why.

Arriving at the prison that Sunday, I learned what it meant to suddenly lose your freedom. Now I belonged to the prison guards, who checked everything I had on me, made me take off my shoes, watch, the medal of Mary on a gold neck chain, my late father's gift to me, besides having me walk through the metal detectors. My hand was stamped with an invisible ink that would show up under some kind of ultraviolet lights to allow me to pass from room to room. The entire passage from the entry to the chapel was wait, then clang, as the bars opened and closed. At times I found it hard to breathe. I passed a few men in prison-green jump suits cleaning the floors. They looked at me. I smiled. They smiled back. They were black. I was not surprised.

Fortunately, we had to walk along an outdoor path to get to the chapel, and I appreciated getting a breath of fresh air. I was astounded when I saw the chapel, appropriately named after St. Paul, who was often a prisoner himself. It was simply lovely, a semicircle floor plan and wood ceiling beams that converged over the altar to center on a simple, large cross. I was told it had been built back in the 1960s by inmates, after a determined effort by Msgr. Edward J. Donovan, who came as chaplain in 1961, succeeded. I was introduced to this deservedly highly respected priest, and I am honored still to call him my friend.

The Mass was beautiful, concelebrated by three priests, with several inmates as altar servers, and four others providing music, professionally done with keyboard, strings, and vocals. When it came time for me to give the talk, I went to the lectern and looked at the people in front of me, all men except for the women relatives and friends who had been invited to come for this gala spiritual day. I smiled at them and began:

"I have been asked to talk to you on 'Finding peace.' The reason has to do with the fact that life gave me some pretty hard blows in the past few years and I had to make a choice: I could cave in, or find the kind of peace that would let me get moving again. And I chose to find peace.

"I may be the most unusual speaker you've ever had here. You see, like yourselves, I have come up against the criminal justice system—though from the opposite side. In August 1993, my son and my daughter-in-law, John and Nancy Bosco, were murdered in the middle of the night in the home they had recently purchased in Montana. In addition to all the intense pain I was going through, I now had to deal with sheriffs, prosecutors, homicide detectives, and lawyers. None of this is a piece of cake.

"I was in a state of raw fury and obsessed with the horror of this evil. I didn't know for four months who had killed my kids. Then it turned out to be the eighteen-year-old son of the couple from whom John and Nancy had recently bought their home. His name was Shadow Clark, Shadow, if you can believe that. He stole into the house from a downstairs window—he had obviously done that many times when he lived in that house—crept up to the bedroom, carrying his nine-millimeter semi-automatic gun, and shot my son in the head, killing him instantly. My daughter-in-law woke from the explosion and groped for her glasses. She must have seen what was coming, because she curled into a fetal position, waiting for the bullet that would kill her. Shadow Clark never gave a motive. He is in prison now, with no parole until he's sixty.

"Here I was a woman who had always lived by faith, believing and accepting what Jesus had said about forgiveness. You know, over and over he said, "Forgive—seventy times seventy—Forgive."

"But now I was in a new place, facing a raw confrontation with my soul. My son and daughter-in-law had been brutally murdered. Could I ever forgive the killer—Shadow Clark? In gut honesty, now that the question of forgiveness was no longer simple, or academic, could I say, 'Father, forgive the murderer?'

"And then there was this human thing—anger was a comfort. I had been so mangled by the murders, I felt debilitated. It was only anger that made me feel more powerful.

"But then I started to realize that all I thought of day and night was Shadow Clark. My God, I was handcuffed to him. I knew that if I didn't free myself, I would be handcuffed to him forever. I'd know no peace. I'd never be able to do good work, and certainly not God's work.

"One thing I had long ago learned was the real meaning of peace. People get the wrong idea about peace. They think it means stillness, inactivity, being quiet. Wrong. Peace is the most active state you can have. And you get it when you find the power to let go of the hates and conflicts and wars that get into your life, from all kinds of assassins. And assassins have attacked everyone. Assassins are many things—like growing up in an abusive home, being rock-bottom poor, drugs and alcohol, being fired from a job, being made fun of by a bully, pride, arrogance, feeling sorry for yourself—or being struck with force of a bullet.

"All of these—and more, of course—are assassins that attack us and put us in a position where we face a moment of truth: will we let the assassins in our life rule us and keep the war inside us going, or will we choose to conquer these and find peace?

"That was the moment of truth that I was facing after the murders, and I will admit, it took some time before I could let go of my rage. I was falling into the terrible trap that so many of us do, of letting our hurts—which are really our assassins—take root in us. When we do this, think about what happens: we become what we hate. Just as an example, consider what's been going on endlessly between Israel and Palestine. One side throws a bomb, the other retaliates, people are killed. Hatred and war and revenge go on endlessly. There is no peace. Not only people, but nations, too, can become what they hate. We were raised on this 'eye for an eye' mentality. There was, of course, one person who said no to this. He said, enough of war and revenge. Overcome evil with good. Overcome hate with love. It is the blueprint that could change the world into a paradise. But who's listening?

"Thanks be to God, I found the grace to listen. My personal life had become a battleground, but I kept praying. I looked into my soul and found God's footprints there. We all have God's footprints on our souls. They have a name. It's called Grace. It made me remember a line—

actually it came from the women's movement. It said, "If you think you can, you're right!" In other words, the choice of where we're going to go with our lives—and I'm speaking of our lives from the inside out, what's in here—that's always our choice to make. We can stay locked in conflict and internal war, or we can choose to end it, by giving up the thing we're holding on to that keeps us at war inside—like anger, revenge, self-centeredness, feeling sorry for yourself, being jealous of those who have more earthly goods than you have, hatred. . . . You can fill in the rest.

"I came to peace when I least expected it. I had to go to Montana to take care of settling my son and daughter-in-law's belongings. I went with my sons, Paul and Frank. When we walked into that bedroom, so violated by Shadow Clark, the three of us fell to our knees and asked the Lord to exorcise the evil from that room. It was at that moment, realizing the horror of unnatural death, that I knew, really knew that Jesus was right. We cannot react to evil with more evil. We must, we must, overcome it by good. Shadow Clark was facing the death penalty. I could never, never accept unnatural death again, even under the cloak of the law. I, with the support of two sons and two daughters, notified the judge that while we strongly believed Shadow Clark must be punished for his heinous crime and we wanted him in prison for life, we did not want him to face a death penalty. It fell on deaf ears. It was only because Shadow Clark entered a plea bargain that he didn't have to face the ultimate penalty. I felt at peace with that.

"The murders of my beloved children altered me permanently, as I'm sure your experiences have altered you permanently. When I left Montana I knew I had a job to do. It was to pray every day that Shadow Clark would respond to the ignored and forgotten footprints on his soul given to him at birth by the God who loved him enough to give him life. I prayed that his heart will soften so that he can ask forgiveness—and find redemption.

"The strongest message Jesus left for us in the Gospels is that he longs for us to see that what's most important are mercy, forgiveness, and love.

"You think it's hard to get those? Oh, no. They're there for the asking. Just think about Jesus on the Cross, hanging between two criminals. When one asked for forgiveness, it was instant gratification for him. Jesus, I believe joyfully, said to him, 'This day'—think of the power of this—'this very day you will be with me in Paradise.' It is no different for us. All we have to do is ask—and be like Jesus toward everyone—even our enemies, and Paradise is waiting for us.

"To forgive is just what the word itself says—to offer a gift before it's been earned or even deserved. I wager many of us have never even given that gift to ourselves. Forgive yourself and others by letting go of the assassins that would keep you locked in conflict and internal war. And I promise you that you will find a peace that will give you a jump start on a new life. You can change your life and fill it with the joy that comes from finding peace."

At the end of the Mass I knew my words had touched the men. The ones who had made the retreat had just been on the altar, giving testimony to the joy they were feeling from having made the retreat. When the ceremonies were over, to great applause, we greeted the men. Never had I been hugged by so many men, of different ethnic backgrounds and ages. We had prayed together, received Holy Communion together, listened to each other, and now, even though briefly, we were one with each other. On that October Sunday afternoon, in no way did any of us think of what separates us, only what unites us, thanks to the wonderful people who had brought their ministry to the inmates, and thanks especially to Msgr. Donovan.

While I was aware that these men were only some sixty out of a population of some two thousand at Greenhaven, it didn't matter. I decided I would never change from thinking of all prisoners as children of God, becoming true in action to what I had often put into print. Again, I was to be surprised by a letter that arrived about six weeks later, three weeks before Christmas. It began:

"Dear Ms. Bosco,

"I was the altar boy serving the Mass with Father John here at Greenhaven. Your lecture that day was so heartbreaking to me, and so unbelievable that you have been a big inspiration to me. Msgr. Edward Donovan gave me the opportunity to work at Saint Paul's and it has been the best. These sixteen years past mean nothing. What counts is that God has come into my life. I say the rosary each day. I can't start the day unless I do. The Blessed Mother is my glory to God. Ms. Bosco, I can't say enough about the impact you had, not only on me, but for so many others here who feel you are a saint, if that is possible.

"I'm hoping that one day you return so we can meet again. But the main thing is that God watches over you and your family always. You will be in my prayers as long as I am alive. Thank you so much for being the impact person in my life. May the true spirit of Christmas bring you peace and happiness. God bless you.

"Charlie Grosso."

I was astounded. I remembered Charlie not just because he had been the altar boy, but because he looked like my sons and nephews, Italian boys like himself, and was probably the same age as the older ones. I felt a kinship with him immediately upon reading his letter and answered right away with a Christmas card and a long note, inviting him to stay in touch.

I didn't know then that I would discover a great friend in Charlie, who would keep me linked to Greenhaven and forever assured that nothing "bars" God, not even the metal ones in a prison.

I was to learn later that if and when one of the six men currently on death row in New York State makes it to the death house, he will be going to Greenhaven. It is in this prison that the deadly room is located. Certainly God is needed at Greenhaven, and the prisoners and I pray together that this place, where they have lived for so many years with more ahead, will be spared becoming a place of death.

Chapter Six

CALLS COME IN—
AND I AM THE LEARNER

Since the word had gotten around that I was the mother of murder victims opposed to the death penalty, I was not too surprised that calls started coming in, asking me to speak on this, always in a debate format. Clearly it was not yet time to touch this subject without presenting both sides. One call I got came from a Massachusetts television station. This is one of the states that has not reinstated the death penalty, but the subject keeps coming up because many residents want executions to resume in their state. I was told in that phone call that seven out of ten residents favored the death penalty and that Governor William Weld sought to reinstate this ultimate punishment. I said yes, I'd come to Massachusetts and be on their show.

The program was called *Case in Point,* and the interviewer, Joan Goodman, told me she would be talking to me first, and then the second part of the program would be with another mother of a murder victim, Ann Scavino, whose son, Michael, a police officer, was killed in the line of duty.

During the interview I talked about my loss and explained why I am opposed to "government-approved murder," which is how I described executions. I argued that we've given ourselves permission to do something which we really don't have the right to do, deliberately kill a human being. I acknowledged that it is logical for people to say a murderer should forfeit his or her life, but urged people to see that this deep, penetrating, difficult question should not be debated on the level of "an eye for an eye." It is a gut-level, moral issue, with links to God, and that puts the debate on a higher plane.

Then I listened to Ann Scavino, a mother hurting so deeply that her voice kept cracking. She remembered the day she lost her son so vividly. She had been cooking and wanted him to come home to eat, but he was covering for another officer and was going to be delayed getting home. She saved the meal, but he never got to eat it. He pulled a car over for a routine stop. As he approached the car, with a driver and a passenger, shots were fired, hitting him in the face. He dropped to the ground, dead. Mrs. Scavino said that the two men were brothers. One then committed suicide, and the other one is serving fifteen years.

This mother was strongly for the death penalty, saying "I believe the punishment should fit the crime," and insisting this would be a deterrent because "things would straighten out," reducing murders if the perpetrators knew they'd get the same treatment. "If Michael were looking into a gun and could say, 'Three months from now, it's you,' they'd think twice." Her belief was that killing will be ongoing so long as potential criminals believe their only punishment will be prison, "with air-conditioned cells and gyms so these prisoners can work out...spending holidays with parents."

I drove back to Connecticut wondering how residents watching this show would react to two mothers, both hurting permanently from a terrible loss, both in a different place when it comes to how to punish the ones who stole the lives of their sons.

Three years later, in March 1999, I was in Massachusetts again, speaking at an anti–death penalty program put on by students and staff at Boston College wanting to hear from survivors of homicide victims who oppose executions, striving, instead, to follow the Lord's way, believing that only with love and forgiveness will hatred and vengeance be overcome. It was the day after the state had once more defeated continuing efforts to reinstate the death penalty.

A few days earlier, hearings on the death penalty bill had been held at the Statehouse in Boston. One of the outstanding moments was when Cardinal Bernard Law testified. The *Catholic Free Press,* weekly publication of the Diocese of Worcester, reported the cardinal's position: "The base line of our opposition is the inviolable dignity and right to life of every human person."

I was especially touched when the paper reported that Bishop Daniel Reilly of Worcester said, "The hardest question is that of murder victims' families.... There's where we have to help people, to lead them through this time of grieving, this time of loss" when they feel so violated. The paper paraphrased his further comments: "The church and the faith are so important because there is a spiritual dimension to getting beyond grief. Being reconciled with the Lord, the perpetrators, and others involved is not easy, and takes openness from both victims' families and perpetrators." Supporting him, Cardinal Law stated his belief clearly that the death penalty "does not help victims' families."

Bishop Reilly perfectly expressed what we speakers at that Boston College program had learned. I was there with Rev. Walter Everett, the Methodist minister who had so forgiven Mike Carlucci, the murderer of his son, Scott, that they now spoke together as witnesses for Christ's healing power of forgiveness. Also with us was Clementine Barfield, a mother of a murdered son, who has refused to stay in personal mourning. In her state of Michigan she initiated and organized what has become a national movement to save our youth from violence.

Ms. Barfield calls her grassroots organization Save Our Sons and Daughters, a work that could be a model for communities across the nation. With about ten staff members, the organization provides grief counseling and support to survivors of homicide victims, training in violence prevention, crisis intervention, peer support, and something more—a peace program.

This hurting mother is creating "peace zones" in her city of De-troit. "A peace zone," she says, "is violence free, drug free, gun free. It is a place where peace activities are held and peacemaking training is conducted." When they can get these peace zones linked together—her goal—the entire city will be "a place of peace."

Her work to combat violence and Rev. Everett's work to promote forgiveness demonstrated loudly and clearly that much good can come out of the evil that causes such pain after the murder of a loved one. I was becoming more and more affirmed in what I knew—that life and death are to be left in God's hands; ours is the healing work.

Shortly after the *Case in Point* telecast, I was invited to participate in a high-level program being put on by an ad hoc group calling itself the "Death Penalty Forum Organizing Committee." The program was to be called "Vengeance Is Ours—A Moral Critique of the Death Penalty," to be presented live in a New Haven church, broadcast on WPKN, a Connecticut radio station, and later, in an edited version, aired over the National Public Radio Satellite System. The line-up of speakers included Detroit's Bishop Thomas Gumbleton, Richard Dieter, executive direc-tor of the Death Penalty Information Center in Washington, D.C., John Williams, an attorney representing Daniel Webb, a Connecticut death row inmate, Richard Tulisano, the state representative I so respected, and myself.

I spoke as a member of Murder Victims Families for Reconciliation and was followed by Bishop Gumbleton, who began by saying he has "rejected violence for any reason." I wrote down what he said after that and have repeated it often ever since. The bishop spoke of Jesus and said, "He taught us how to die—not how to kill. . . . He was a radical. . . . He taught us to die loving even those putting you to death."

Bishop Gumbleton spoke as a priest of the church should, emphasizing that we should not return violence for violence, hatred for hatred, but instead, respond with love. He reminded us of how this Christ-teaching was lived by the late Archbishop Oscar Romero, who said, anticipating that he might be killed, "I forgive and bless those who do it." And his belief in the Resurrection was affirmed in his promise, "I will rise again in the Salvadoran people." He was a murder victim, but nowhere did he speak of killing those who would take his life, only forgiveness.

Then Bishop Gumbleton said something I hadn't yet really focused on, the value and importance of *remembering* the harm we have experienced. He said that "what is forgotten cannot be healed. . . . An atrocity that is forgotten causes a [destructive] cutting off of the past." If we don't face the trauma and seek healing for both the victims and the perpetrators, "we imperil our future."

I had been listening to many people calling for the death penalty because they believed this was the only way a horrendous crime could be forgotten. The word that had become so popular was "closure," and it had become almost routine to say that only if a murderer is put to death could a victim's family find "closure." I detested that word, because I saw it as meaningless. What was it—a door slammed shut, the end of breathing, a body-filled box put into the ground, a heart permanently hardened? Now as I listened to Bishop Gumbleton, I understood what "closure" really meant when it was used to describe the benefit of the death penalty—that choosing such "closure" would keep all of us in a closed, fixed place, perpetually unhealed.

As I expected, the program that night attracted a good crowd, many of whom came to protest what we were saying and to offer their arguments for the death penalty. I was already getting used to being questioned about my position, with people saying they couldn't understand how I could forgive the murderer of my son and daughter-in-law. Some would actually accuse me of not loving my children if I didn't want the murderer to get the same fate that he had dished out. My answer was that, on the contrary, I was honoring my murdered children by raising my voice against killing, all killing. Most people would be courteous even as they turned away, saying they did not understand me.

Not long after this Sam Rieger called me and asked if I would join him and a few members of Survivors of Homicide for a call-in television show to be aired on a Connecticut station. The subject was to be the death penalty, and if I was there, the program could be somewhat "balanced," since I could present the opposing side. As I expected, Sam was eminently fair, telling listeners that Survivors of Homicide does not take a stand either for or against the death penalty. He introduced the program saying that all of us, survivors of a murdered loved one, "are tied together by this common bond," and that "we cherish these friendships." He also said that when it comes to the murder trial, "Nobody wins. Whatever high you might get for a maximum sentence dissipates," because when it's over, "you come back to the reality.... Your daughter [your loved one] will never come back again."

When I was asked to speak for a few minutes on why I was against the death penalty, the phone rang right away. The caller objected fiercely to what I said. Her suggestion was that "we should work to kill them faster." I felt sad about this reaction, which was becoming more and more familiar to me.

John Cluny, a fellow member of Survivors, spoke at length about his situation and feelings. I had gotten to know John quite well. He was for the death penalty for extreme cases, where the killing is so horrendous that all you can really see is the evil left in the wake of the crime. "If we don't execute killers like these, then we're saying that they have more value than their victims. That's sending the wrong message. The spirit of evil can dominate, like in the case of Hitler. We have to recognize that evil forces exist. That's why I believe in the death penalty. We have to make that distinction—that victims have more value than their killers."

Listening to his story, you can understand why he believes, albeit cautiously, in the death penalty. He goes home every day to a reminder of how he lost his wife, Elaine, and his young teen son, David. He sees the bullethole in the entertainment center of his living room, and the two bulletholes in the master bedroom, put there when a fifteen-year-old neighbor, Michael Bernier, went on a shooting spree.

It was supposed to be an ordinary, nice day that May 24 of 1993. David got home from school and went to his room, probably to put his books on his desk. He was shot from behind by Bernier, who was hiding behind the bedroom door, the gun poised ten inches from his head. The fifteen-year-old killer then dragged David's body, shoving it under the desk. Shortly later, Elaine, a language teacher, came home from school. Calling out for David and not getting a response, she went to his room, where she had no way of knowing Bernier was behind the door, holding a gun. She must have panicked, seeing David lying so strangely, and rushed over to him, bending down to see what had happened. At that moment, Bernier, standing six inches behind her, again pulled the trigger. The bullet went through her head, blowing out one of her eyes, and then went through the wall of David's bedroom, crossed the master bedroom and went out the exterior wall. The mother was now lying on her son's body, both of them dead. Downstairs, the Cluny family's dog was also silent, for Bernier had blown away this loved animal's head.

Normally, John would have been home from work before his wife, but this day he had stopped to do some shopping. He believes if he had been home, there would have been three murder victims. As he and the police later pieced the story together, it was clear that Michael Bernier was in a random killing mood that day. The viciousness of the crime would forever haunt John and anyone hearing the account of what Bernier had done that day.

The fifteen-year-old had left for school in the morning, but instead of going to class he managed to get into his neighbors' house. He simply took over occupancy, checking out the refrigerator, turning on the TV. Then he checked the bedrooms. In the master bedroom, he found keys that he no doubt was looking for. John Cluny had some guns, secured and with trigger locks. Now Bernier had the keys. He apparently fantasized, gun in hand, a good part of that day, killing the dog, perhaps for practice. When David came home, on this ordinary day, he became a target for Bernier, as did his mother. After the killings, Bernier took another set of keys, Elaine's car keys, and went off on a joyride in her car.

This was the beginning of a nightmare that John will live with for the rest of his life. I could relate. My nightmare goes on, too, as his does. That fifteen-year-old murderer "took my wife; he took my son. But he's not going to get me. You have two choices in life when you're faced with adversity—you can let it bury you or you can turn it around. I opted to turn it around," John said. It was an unbelievable challenge for him to move on. He faced a radical change in his life, and life-style, because he was also "plunged into financial ruin at age fifty-two." Everything came together, the loss of his wife's income, and a downturn in the economy radically affecting his job, along with loss of work time from having to deal with the criminal case. To have to cope with economic disaster while at the same time grieving for the loss of your family is a formula for despair. Fortunately, John was strong enough, and determined, to survive.

Understandably, this husband and father wanted a maximum sentence for the killer. Since Michael Bernier was only fifteen, it appeared that he would be tried as a juvenile, because the law in Connecticut was quite ambiguous, saying only that a juvenile "may" be tried as an adult. "That 'may' be would allow them to suppress his record, and he'd be out at age twenty-one. He could go to college, while I went to the cemetery," John said, adding that he was determined to do all he could to get his young murderous neighbor tried as an adult. Assisted by some members of Survivors of Homicide, John was instrumental in getting the ambiguous language changed so that teenagers charged with serious, sadistic crimes in Connecticut will be tried as adults. In these cases, it's now up to the adult court to argue whether there is merit in bringing the level down, so that the teen can be charged as a juvenile.

This change brought some satisfaction to John. Michael Bernier received two consecutive thirty-year sentences for the deaths of Elaine and David. With "good time," he could be released from prison in about forty-two years, when he is fifty-seven. As for why Michael Bernier went on the killing spree that forever would change John Cluny's life, who knows? John thinks the young killer did it to get a "high," an "adrenaline rush."

He believes the long sentence for Bernier is appropriate because "you can't cushion" the evil and the horror of a crime like this, and people must be accountable and undergo "the fullness of consequences" for their actions. This is essential for the preservation of a nation," John says, while he emphasizes that we must insist on having a criminal justice system that has safeguards and checks and balances, so that we have "real justice and not the illusion of justice." I agree fully with what John says. Amoral killers like Michael Bernier—and Shadow Clark—must be punished and removed from society to protect others, for when could we be absolutely sure that they would never kill again if they were back in the general population?

And yet, John Cluny's story always put me on the horns of a dilemma. I had long been concerned about the increasing push in our country to try children as adults. I considered anyone under the age of sixteen to be still a "child," meaning a person not experienced enough to have developed true concepts of what constitutes right and wrong, someone too immature to understand the wide-ranging, serious consequences of his or her actions. While I believed youths who commit atrocious crimes need to account for what they have done, I felt that putting them in a detention program where they could get adequate education, medical services, and mental health care was the way to go, certainly not confinement in an adult prison.

But then we have children like Michael Bernier, and I have to admit that my sympathies are with John Cluny. I, too, would want someone who murdered my spouse and my son put away for a very long time. For the good of society, I think children who are capable of doing such horrendous crimes should be properly confined, away from us, to guarantee that they will not kill again. Perhaps what we need is not the two poles, where a youth is tried either as a juvenile or as an adult, but something in between. Perhaps there should be a flexible system when it comes to juveniles, with the emphasis placed not on time to be served, but on treating them with the hope and goal of turning them into good and positively productive citizens. They could be released only when it is determined by officials, educators, clergy, counselors, and perhaps even family that this adult is now a mature person who will never again be a danger to others.

The tragic thing is that there are too many Michael Berniers in our country, troubled young people who get their hands on a gun and go on a murder spree. The nation is reacting by demanding they be tried as adults and, in far too many cases, be given the death sentence. Statistics released by the NAACP Legal Defense and Educational Fund show that sixty-seven juveniles, all male, have been sentenced to death and are currently on death row.

In a publication put out by the Judicial Process Commission, a group based in Rochester, New York, that is addressing the basic inequities in the criminal justice system, hoping to move toward creating a just, nonviolent society, editor Clare Regan wrote: "A Justice Department report released in late February 2000 revealed that in 1997 the number of youths seventeen or younger sentenced to adult prisons had more than doubled since 1985 (3,400 to 7,400)." This is in spite of the fact that, according to the Justice Policy Institute in Washington, D.C., in 94 percent of the cases, juveniles are arrested for a nonviolent offense.

Sadly, they would get another education in adult prisons, most likely lessons in brutality and how to become better criminals. Vincent Shiraldi, director of the Washington, D.C.–based Justice Policy Institute, wrote to the *New York Times:* "When children are imprisoned with adults, they are five times more likely to be sexually assaulted and eight times more likely to commit suicide than children in juvenile facilities." We have to ask, is this how a democratic society, which prides itself on its human rights record, should be treating its troubled youth?

The Justice Department statistic caught my attention because it was back in 1985 that I first began noting, and writing about, juveniles in the criminal justice system. In September of that year, Texas was scheduled to execute Charles Rumbaugh for a murder he had committed when he was seventeen. Reporters focused on this because it was newsworthy. If executed, Rumbaugh would be the first prisoner to be executed in more than two decades for a crime committed by someone under eighteen. Texas had held its last such execution on May 7, 1964, when James Andrew Echois was put to death for raping a white girl when he was seventeen. Suddenly in this fall of 1985 there was a spotlight on convicted murderers who had committed a crime when they were juveniles. What came to light was that there were thirty-two others, eighteen white, fourteen black, on the death rows of several states, all facing death for murders committed when they were young teens—three who killed at the age of fifteen. Texas had the largest number, nine at the time.

Rumbaugh had murdered Michael Fiorillo, an Amarillo jeweler, in a robbery in 1975. What came to light in the trial was how seriously abusive his childhood was, evidenced by the numerous scars he had on his body. He was six when he first got into trouble for breaking into a schoolhouse. He was twelve when he used a tire iron to rob a filling station, taking off on a stolen bike. He spent the next few years in reform school and mental hospitals. At seventeen, he murdered a man.

After ten years on death row, the appeals were done and Rumbaugh, now twenty-eight, was prepared to die by lethal injection. He said "goodbye" to his personal witnesses in the death chamber, and then to the others, said, "Even though you don't forgive me for my transgressions, I forgive you for yours against me. That's all I wish to say. I'm ready for my journey." He was killed on September 12, 1985, the forty-eighth person to be executed since the Supreme Court had allowed states to restore the death penalty in 1976.

The attention put on juvenile criminals because of this first execution brought out some disturbing information, namely, that sixteen states explicitly allowed executions for crimes committed by youths under eighteen, with minimum ages set anywhere from seventeen down to fourteen. Indiana actually allowed execution for a crime committed at age ten. Three states, Delaware, Oklahoma, and South Dakota didn't specify age as a mitigating factor, making it possible, theoretically, for a child of any age to be sentenced there. Anti–death penalty groups publicized that in executing juvenile offenders, the United States held hands with Iran,

Pakistan, Nigeria, and Saudi Arabia, the only other countries that also defy the international prohibition on executing youths. The House of Delegates of the American Bar Association had adopted a resolution in 1983 opposing the death penalty for crimes committed under age eighteen. The prohibition against imposing a death sentence on youths under eighteen is also contained in the International Covenant on Civil and Political Rights and the American Convention on Human Rights. None of this stopped the death penalty bandwagon carrying juveniles to the death houses. Thirteen juvenile offenders have been executed since 1976, eight of them in Texas, making this state the worldwide leader in putting juvenile offenders to death. At least one Texas legislator felt the "message to our kids that they can't do this kind of crime" wasn't strong enough. State Representative Jim Pitts, in 1998, proposed a bill that would allow his state to impose the death penalty on murderers as young as eleven. Fortunately, his proposal appears to be stalled.

The mood in the country is certainly changing when it comes to youth crime. We are getting hardened by the all too frequent news reports of yet another shooting by a juvenile. Our death penalty mentality has become so entrenched that it is no longer surprising to hear people say that a child who kills, even one as young as six years of age, should be put on trial as an adult. In November 1999, when Nathaniel Abraham, thirteen, was convicted of murder by a Michigan jury after being charged as an adult for shooting and killing an eighteen-year-old man when he was eleven, the verdict was applauded by many. Apparently the jury believed Nathaniel was well versed in right and wrong and fully understood the consequences when he pulled the trigger. Could it be that the real cause of the shooting was that a child of eleven was able to get his hands on a loaded gun and then did what came naturally—pull the trigger—without even giving a thought to the consequences?

It is astounding that adults in the last year of the twentieth century suddenly seemed to become aware that juveniles in our country are an armed force. It may have taken the killing spree at Columbine High School in Colorado to open eyes, or perhaps the killings in schools in a half dozen other states to get us to focus attention on what is probably the greatest problem with youth that we have not yet dealt with, and that is their ability to get weapons of destruction and use them. After the Rumbaugh execution, I started researching youth and guns. I didn't know back in the late 1980s that a teenager in Montana was able to purchase a nine-millimeter semi-automatic gun from an individual, and because it was a private sale, it was legal. At least that's what the authorities told me when I questioned how it was that Shadow Clark was able to buy a lethal weapon and use it to kill my children.

I discovered in the late 1980s that we were going to have to modify our old notions of youthful innocence. The famous "three R's" had been changed to "reading, 'riting, and revolvers." Newspapers carried stories like this: a five-year-old showing up at school in the Bronx with a loaded .25 caliber pistol; a sixteen-year-old in New York City carrying a loaded .38 caliber revolver to school; a thirteen-year-old Dade County, Florida, schoolboy threatening to "torture and kill" his social studies teacher for giving him a bad grade, and then showing up at school with a nine-millimeter semi-automatic gun, a box of shells, and a .22 caliber pistol loaded with ten rounds of ammunition.

Statistics, beginning in 1986, were starting to paint a picture that showed schools had clearly lost their innocence. A study funded by the U.S. Department of Health and Human Services found that over one-third of eighth to tenth graders polled said they had been victims of serious crimes at school, with one-third of those crimes involving weapons. Of those polled, 41 percent of boys and 24 percent of girls said they could obtain a handgun if they wanted one. One percent of the boys surveyed said they carried a handgun to school every day. The tragic fact becoming clear was that guns, other weapons, and violence had become a young person's game. Such weapons were simply all too available. A government-sponsored study in 1984 found that 44 million Americans owned 192 million guns, with 54 percent of the gun owners saying their firearms were unlocked. Sixty-five million of these were handguns. As these facts started coming to light in the second half of the 1980s, I was writing Op-Ed pieces, joining a few other voices pleading, "It is time for us to support forceful policies to discourage—if we can't prevent—the acquisition and use of guns by youngsters who haven't yet developed the moral backbone that's essential for the responsible use of a weapon."

But that was the 1980s, and who was listening? Never did I dream that one of my sons would become the victim I was trying to protect with words. It took the slaughter at Columbine High in Colorado at the end of the century to get the issue of guns way out front, only to start a new battle, a million moms marching to Washington to appeal for more effective gun legislation versus the National Rifle Association.

Now we have found a new way to deal with the alarming problem of children toting and using guns and other weapons. We give them hard "justice," the same as we do adults. I was to have a disturbing experience in the fall of 1999 that showed me the road we have taken when it comes to kids committing crime, that people no longer and in no way want to focus on their youth, but only on their destructive deed. It came from an invitation to appear on the nationally televised *Leeza* show, which, according to the information given to me by phone, was to be a program on the death penalty, featuring two parents of murder victims, one for and one against executions.

The *Leeza* show producers had heard about me from Renny Cushing, the new executive director of Murder Victims Families for Reconciliation, who had replaced Pat Bane. I had talked to Renny, a former New Hampshire state representative, several times and met him when I spoke at Boston College's anti–death penalty conference. His story is another heartbreaking tale of murder. His father, Robert Cushing Sr., a retired schoolteacher and father of seven, had spent June 1, 1988, planting a garden with his wife, Marie. "In mid-evening, I stopped off for a visit, some quick tales, some smiles, some laughs with my dad....A while after I left, a stranger knocked on the front door. My father got up to answer. Two shotgun blasts were fired through the screen, lifting him up and hurling him backward, the shrapnel tearing the life out of him before my mother's eyes," Renny wrote in the *Concord Monitor.*

The shooter was Hampton police officer Robert McLaughlin, who committed the murder apparently over a longstanding disagreement involving him and the Cushings. His then-wife Susan was an accomplice to the crime, and both are now serving life sentences without parole. Renny speaks honestly and painfully about the trauma he and his six brothers and sisters experienced. "The most difficult thing I have ever had to ask anyone was to help me clean my father's blood off the floor and walls," he said. I related so intimately to that pain, remembering the bedroom in Montana, with the blood of my loved ones on the floor.

He then tells of a man who came up to him after the arrest and said, "I hope they fry them so you people can get some peace." For Renny, that was "the most horrible thing he could have said at the moment. Before my father's murder I had evolved a set of values that included a respect for life and an opposition to the death penalty. Although I am of the Irish Catholic tradition, whose religious teachings include 'Thou shalt not kill,' that's not all of it. It is more how I want to live my life and the vision I have for the society I want to live in.

"For me to change my beliefs because my father was murdered would only give over more power to the killers, for they would take not just my father's life but also my values. The same is true for society. If we let those who murder turn us to murder, it gives more power to those who do evil. We become what we say we abhor....

"Every day I think about murder. When I hear my children's laughter, I hear the sound of my father. I miss him. I wish I could bring him back....I can't bring him back. What I can do is honor his life and try to lead my life upholding the ideals he instilled in me." His words reflected exactly what I believed.

Those of us in MVFR were delighted when Renny Cushing became the new director and a new central office was established in Boston. Every conversation I've had with him is an energizer, reinforcing my conviction that, as he says, we, the families of murder victims who are appalled at state-sanctioned killings, must not be invisible. Rather, we must find the courage to be visible, to speak out how we feel about the death penalty, underscoring especially how "it coarsens us as a society and makes us what we abhor," as Renny Cushing puts it.

With my respect for Renny and MVFR in high gear, I responded cooperatively to the call I received from Eliza Schwartz, an associate producer of the *Leeza* show. She asked me many questions about the murders of my son and daughter-in-law and why I was opposed to the death penalty. She was very empathetic and asked me to send her newspaper clips about the crime and photos of John and Nancy by Federal Express. I did and almost immediately I received another call, on Tuesday, October 12, saying they wanted to fly me to the Hollywood studio where the show would be taped on Thursday morning. I took a deep breath and said I'd drop everything and come. That's how important I felt the subject to be.

I was there, in sunny Beverly Hills, on that Thursday morning, as they had requested. When the limo dropped me off at the studio, I was welcomed by Eliza and other people involved with the production and taping of this daytime one-hour show. They had their beauty experts fix my face and hair. Everything seemed professional and cordial. I finally was introduced to Leeza Gibbons, who asked me a few questions and said she was impressed with my answers. I was then brought to a tiny room, with a couple of chairs and a television set, and told to watch the show being taped, adding that when they wanted me to come on, someone would come and get me.

When the taping began, Leeza, facing the audience, explained that they were going to hear about one of the most horrendous murders imaginable, the stabbing of nine-year-old Matthew Cecchi by teenager Brandon Wilson, who had been convicted in this California murder and now said he wanted to die. They played a tape showing Brandon saying,

"I feel no remorse....I'd do it again....Execute me." Leeza then, commenting on the arrogance of this teen, who killed "this darling, innocent little boy," asked her audience to vote, by sitting or standing, on whether he should be given what he wants or sent to prison for the rest of his life. The vote was 60 percent yes, 40 percent no for the death penalty. To her left was a smaller group of people. She explained they were undecided about the death penalty, but by the end of the program she would poll them to see if any then had come to a pro or con position.

Her main guest was there by satellite. He was Lou Cecchi, the father of young Matthew, who had recently had cancer surgery and was on chemotherapy. His anger was fierce, and it came through. Chris Mc-Donough, an investigator on the case and a major guest on the program, said Brandon admitted the murder idea had been brewing for a while before he actually did it on November 16, 1998. "He fits the profile of a thrill killer," he said.

The deed was cruel. Matthew, his mother, aunt, uncle, and some others had gone to a beach. At one point he had to go to the bathroom and his aunt took him, waiting outside. He never walked out. Brandon was in the bathroom, knife in hand, waiting to kill someone. When he saw Matthew, he said, "This is it," and he stabbed the child to death. "He got a rush, didn't he?" Leeza said, asking Mr. Cecchi. "What do you want to happen to Brandon Wilson?" "Nothing can be too bad....We don't have enough penalties in this state to take care of his ass....He's just lucky the authorities have him, not me."

At this point, Leeza reminded her audience that "our focus today is, should he get the sentence he wants. Is that justice for little Matthew?" Then she told them that what they would see next was the "most chilling thing I've ever seen. It will get you right at the core. What do we do with people like this?...[We'll see] the nature of sheer evil." And she said they'd poll the audience again at the end of the program to "see how much minds are changed" about the death penalty.

I was beginning to get the idea of what this show was all about. It was not to be an equal presentation of both sides of the death penalty. It was a sensational entry, whether planned or unplanned, in how murder has become entertainment, a ghoulish, popular pastime, so upsetting to the national organization of Parents of Murdered Children that they promote a campaign to stop this, which they call "Murder Is Not Entertainment." Shown next was a tape of Brandon reenacting the way he stabbed and killed his victim, with Chris McDonough taking Matthew's place as the victim and the murderer talking about the killing, in a very agitated voice. Leeza asked Mr. McDonough, "How did you get him to say so much?" He answered that he had had "the opportunity to interview a serial killer of children" and he "learned a lot." Brandon was "really up.... Our focus was to keep him 'up.'" This, after all, was the tape to be presented to the jury, so they could see Brandon reliving the event, so they could see the truthfulness of his evil side, the investigator said, adding, "He was a predator searching for a victim."

Gene Wagner, the foreman of the jury was also a guest. He affirmed that the tape was so shocking and deliberations were so difficult that "at one point, we had to stop."

A woman from the audience spoke up, saying it was almost impossible to watch. He had to be put to death, she said. "How could you give him the chance to get out by some fluke. Kill the guy!" Mr. Cecchi responded, "Amen to that." I was appalled that this tape had been released to the media. It may have been appropriate for a jury to see, but not an audience, who could only be stirred to anger and hate by seeing and hearing this very disturbed teenager talk of his excitement at killing a child.

The show went on like that, with people getting more and more vocal about killing Brandon Wilson, agreeing with the one who said, "Do it. Get it over with."

It was now the halfway point of the program, and I thought they had forgotten about me. Then Leeza said, "We have a mother here. She wants to challenge your view." A few moments before, someone had come to get me, instructing me that I was to walk on, stand in front of the undecided group, hold up a picture of John and Nancy and say I was against the death penalty. When I walked out, I looked at the group of people sitting there and told them that we had just seen a crime so heinous that I was crying, like we all were. I told them I knew the pain of the Cecchi family because my heart is cut out, too, showing them the picture of John and Nancy. "But I can't say we should kill.... The question that haunts me is what turns an eighteen-year-old into a killer, and why are we not doing anything in our society to help prevent such crimes from happening?" A few people clapped. It was commercial time.

Leeza opened the next segment by addressing me. While everybody else was introduced by their name and profession, I was simply called "Toni Bosco, a mother," not even given the courtesy of being introduced as Antoinette, let alone as a Ph.D. professional and an author. She began by saying she understood that I am so opposed to the death penalty that I even wrote to the judge telling him we didn't want the murderer to face this. I answered yes, but said I wanted to make one very important point first. We cannot argue the pros and cons of the death penalty on one horrendous case, like the brutal murder of young Matthew Cecchi. Because our human and natural emotions surface so strongly in the face of horrendous sin, we are stirred to want "an eye for an eye." Then I spoke for about two minutes about why I don't want executions. That was the end of my role on this show. I was even effectively blocked from the camera range. I had become the invisible person.

The rest of the show went back and forth about what had happened to Brandon. Interviews with teachers, fellow students, his mother, and people who knew him presented him to be a person with high SAT scores, in the 98th percentile, a shy boy, extremely intelligent, who read a lot of books, easily cruised through high school, and never had a history of violence. Apparently, at age sixteen, a lot of anger started to surface, and he had taken some drugs, marijuana and hallucinogens. None of the show's guests would even suggest that Brandon Wilson had had an onset of chemical deterioration in his brain, that he was in any way mentally impaired. In fact, Mr. McDonough maintained, "he knew the nature and quality of his act, knew it was morally and legally wrong." I did not disagree with that, but I wondered if Brandon had any idea what had happened to his thinking, why he had suddenly changed from being a productive, bright student to a sadistic killer.

The professionals felt that now, at that point in his life, he was so delusional and antisocial that there was no hope for him. No one even mentioned the possibility of a professional psychiatric drug treatment that might control the distortions in his brain. Then there was something else that was brought up and dropped. In the video, Brandon said that he first thought about killing, first held a knife in his hand, when he bought and listened to his first Marilyn Manson CD. Nothing was said on the *Leeza* show about the influence of media violence on adolescents. I recalled at that moment what a father, Raymond Kuntz of Burlington, North Dakota, had told a Senate committee exploring the effects of music on teens a few years ago. He said his fifteen-year-old son had killed himself after listening to songs about death in the album *Antichrist Superstar* by Marilyn Manson. Media violence is just another way of poisoning our kids. When you have a teenager, suddenly beset in adolescence with a brain malady, from natural causes or drugs, listening to death lyrics from a popular CD, you have all the ingredients for madness.

Leeza then asked Mr. Cecchi about a letter that Brandon's mother had written to him and his wife. He answered that he never read it. "I had no interest in it." Leeza read from it. The mother said there were no words to express their deep sorrow, and how they were all devastated. "We have lost Brandon as well.... Your loving Matthew is in the loving arms of Jesus, and we hope Brandon will be one day, too." Mr. Cecchi's comment was terse: "I don't think they let demons into heaven."

Matthew's father had some final words, expressing the possibility that Brandon could get killed in prison. "Nothing could be better than for him to be taken care of in California State Prison.... His hell is just beginning, and we're looking forward to it."

Well, now it was time for the final tally on how many people wanted the death penalty after hearing about Brandon Wilson. "We've had a lot of movement," Leeza said, as the figures showed that 73 percent were for executions at the end of the program as opposed to 60 percent at the beginning. Her concluding remarks were about how as a society, we have to look at these issues—"not to scare you, but evil's out there, like Brandon Wilson."

The show was over, and suddenly I was whisked out of the studio and pointed in the direction of the door, where a limo driver was waiting to take me to the airport. My plane was not due to leave for nearly three hours. As I was about to exit, Eliza Schwartz came running up to me. She took my hand and thanked me, telling me I did a great job. She was gracious and sincere, and I appreciated that. I never had the opportunity to say goodbye to Leeza Gibbons.

I called Renny Cushing when I got home to tell him what had happened. I said I had just undergone an absolutely miserable experience. If I had been given more information about what they had in mind for this show, I never would have taken three days out of my life for an appearance of three minutes on television. My motivation for being on the program was to present the MVFR position. I never had the chance to mention that some seven hundred people across the nation, like myself, who have lost loved ones to murder, plead to end the same kind of violence that has deprived us of a loved one. We want no more death by the hands of humans. Renny consoled me, telling me that two members of MVFR had been in that audience and that it was good that I was there for them and the few people in the audience who needed to be assured that there is another way to believe.

I found myself in the days following thinking a lot about how media can influence the way we feel about almost anything. The *Leeza* audience was groomed to feel revulsion and hate for the young killer. After seeing those tapes of a boy apparently reexcited by reenacting how he killed a child, anyone would be justified in feeling disgust and wanting him taken off the face of the earth. I was reminded of a movie released in early 1996 called *An Eye for an Eye,* starring Sally Field, playing a mother whose daughter is raped and murdered. The system fails her by letting the murderer get off on a technicality. The mother then goes for revenge, getting a gun and learning to shoot so she can kill the man. Those responsible for this film had one thing in mind, to push the hate buttons in all of us, and it worked. At the end of the movie, when the mother pumped bullets into the rapist, everybody—and most of the audience were young people—was hooting and hollering and clapping for the mother, who had now become a murderess herself.

I later saw Ms. Field on the *Oprah* show, where the hostess asked the actress if she came to empathize with the mother. Ms. Field said no. The mother, she said, goes down into herself and touches the dark places there, the latent evil that could always haunt us. She descends to become what the killer is. I admired Ms. Field for her insightful understanding of the evil of revenge. But I don't think the audience got it. Media had force-fed them the false power of "an eye for an eye," and, to no one's surprise, the majority of the audience walked right into doing what they were expected to do, cheer for violence.

I kept thinking of Lou Cecchi, a father in torment over losing his nine-year-old son in such a horrible way. I understood his pain and had great empathy for him and his family. But it saddened me to see how he had fixed himself into this place of pain by his anger and inability to feel any mercy, if not for Brandon Wilson, at least for his parents. Shakespeare's *Merchant of Venice,* which we all had to read in high school, kept coming to mind and I found myself quoting, "The quality of mercy is not strained; it droppeth as the gentle rain from heaven upon the place beneath. It is twice blessed—it blesseth him that gives and him that takes." When we had to read and maybe memorize that soliloquy, we were probably too young to understand what mercy really means. When we get older, we get too jaded to respect the idea of mercy, relegating it to the weak-spined. Jesus had said, "Blessed are the merciful, for they shall obtain mercy." Murder Victims Families for Reconciliation, who take that beatitude seriously, are clearly holding a minority position.

I went back to Shakespeare's play to reread again the exquisitely beautiful speech following those often quoted lines that captures the essence of mercy. Shakespeare first speaks about the strength of kings and fear of their earthly power; he goes on to explain that mercy—which originates with God—is a quality from a level above worldly power; it is the level to which humankind should aspire.

But the deepest wisdom comes through when Shakespeare talks about the relationship between justice and mercy. In effect, what he brings out is that there are many times in life when we are justified in proving someone else wrong and in retaliating against that person or punishing a wrongdoer. We can and do legislate human justice, and no one can deny our right to see justice done. Yet, above the level of human justice, we always have the option of exercising mercy, and when we do, "Earthly power doth then show likest God's when mercy seasons justice."

The play's most important message of all is blunt, that it is a tragedy when the justice we would have would violate God's mercy, and have the worst outcome—"that in the course of justice, none of us should see salvation." Shakespeare is making the point, poetically, that we may have a right to see justice accomplished, but what do we call "justice"? And he emphasizes that seeking that kind of earthbound satisfaction will never save our souls or bring us closer to heaven.

In rereading that play, I began to see mercy in a different way, as the most noble of teachings given to us by the Lord. Yet, beginning with myself, I had learned that so often for most of us mercy and compassion are fine in theory, but in practice, the moment we are faced with a question of justice versus mercy, our egos and fears take over. Real situations are always full of doubts and complications. We often feel a need to teach a lesson, punish, and prove our point or our power. We are afraid that if we don't retaliate whenever our rights are infringed upon, we will appear weak. As human beings, struggling with fears and insecurities in everything we do from our personal relationships to international politics, we are always craving what we perceive to be justice and satisfaction. It is from this place that we respond when our lives are shattered by the evil deed of another. No wonder it becomes a natural reaction to seek "an eye for an eye," to destroy criminals for having brought destruction into our lives.

If Shakespeare were around today, I don't know if he'd be preaching his mercy-wisdom and seeking the end to the death penalty. But I propose we learn from him and accept that at some point, as individuals and a people, the climb toward higher truth and goodness must begin. We can't keep opting for revenge in the name of human justice for the sake of perceived justice or gaining security by being hard—to the death—on criminals. Mercy is needed, for it has everything to do with rising toward God, letting hatred go so that we never sink to a level of distortion that generated the hatred in us to begin with. It's a tough call, given our human nature that always wants to "even the score."

If we want to be one with God, we must be merciful. Bruce Ledewitz, quoted in *The Voice,* the MVFR newsletter, expressed this so well: "The point is that an embittered heart cannot pray in a way that communicates to God. Vengeance cannot utter any kind of prayer."

Chapter Seven

BEHIND THE BARS, SERIOUSLY FLAWED PRISON SYSTEM

One of the saddest stories of the first decade of the new millennium will be how the United States dealt with the nation's fear of crime. We simply incarcerated more and more people, built more prisons, and never bothered to publicize the fact that more than half of these prisoners are doing time for crimes that involve no violence toward another. The majority of inmates in prison have been convicted for drug abuse; fewer than 1 percent of inmates are there for murder. And here's one more statistic that needs reflection: an African-American man is seven times more likely to go to prison than a white man for a comparable crime. Does this say something about our criminal justice—or injustice—system?

A National Crime Survey in 1997 compiled data showing there had been no significant increase in crime in the past twenty years, yet the incarceration rate in our nation's 1,500 prisons had quadrupled! Of these prisons, 168 of them were new state facilities and 45 of them federal institutions built in the first half of the 1990s. Naturally, the boom in prison building is great for politicians. They can give speeches on how hard they are on criminals, a sure way to get more votes. By focusing on how locking away lawbreakers, somehow including the nonviolent ones, protects society, we can forget about them, even though, sadly, they are now locked away in places where they can be subjected to a smorgasbord of inhuman conditions and, in the process, learn how to become violent themselves.

Whenever I have written a column on the need for prison reform, I usually hear from a few people who want to make prison harder, not more human. But then I may get one or two letters from readers who have had to come up against the criminal justice system, and they thank me, almost always asking me not ever to use their name should I write again about prisons. There's a sense of fear that comes across. We are all so intimidated, understandably, by laws, uniforms, and bars.

One mother wrote to me to "commend me" on my article asking people to care for prisoners and not think of them as "human garbage": saying, "I'm sure yours isn't a very popular viewpoint, but I totally agree with you."

She has had to brush against the prison system first hand after her twenty-four-year-old son, who, like all her children, had attended twelve years of Catholic school, was arrested for drunk driving, and then spent twenty-seven months in prison. She wrote, "I have never known or hoped to know anyone in prison and was completely dev-astated and scared to death for him. He was a gentle soul and never hurt anyone.... Now I certainly do not condone drinking and driving and do think you should be accountable for your actions even if caused by a disease. But, at different periods of time, my son shared a cell with an arsonist, a child rapist and a murderer, along with various other sick people. My son called it the land of the walking dead because of the look of fright and despair on the faces of the less violent. How can you put nonviolent people in an 8x10 cell with violent offenders and expect these people to leave there unaffected and normal?

"I understand there is more drug use in prison than on the street. If there is a strip search each time they go out in the yard for air or have a visiting day, how do the drugs get in? How else? Three guesses. They also must purchase everything from the commissary, which charges more than outside. Where does that money go? Many of the inmates don't have any outside financial source and so they are at the mercy of those who do.

"I do believe nonviolent offenders should be fined and given probation and other types of repayment such as community service in hospitals and mental wards so that it might make more of an impression on them and also help the patients, as well as build their own self-esteem, instead of being demoralized and mentally destroyed by being surrounded by some truly harmful individuals.

"Why not spend all this money on research to end alcohol and drug abuse and thus eliminate much of the crime caused by their needs. We don't need more guards or prisons, but as long as there are people profiting, why would they want to eliminate it?

"I cannot tell you how comforting it was to read that I am not alone.... Thank you again for your insight. I hope that someday we can change all this."

This mother's pain is shared by all caring families of inmates in our prisons. Scott Christianson, author of *With Liberty for Some: 500 Years of Imprisonment in America,* writes of the "intergenerational impact" and the "long-range consequences of imprisonment," which "may actually strengthen ties to criminals, inculcate a criminal code, promote antisocial behavior and teach criminal skills. Whether or not by design, imprisonment can injure an inmate's physical health and reduce life expectancy. It can damage psychological well being and impair an individual's ability to function independently, spawning all kinds of post-traumatic stress disorders. . . . And it can shatter personal relationships, dissolve friendships, and disconnect and distress fragile families."

Whenever I talk about prison conditions, I expect that I will get a negative, if not a hostile, response. Polls taken have shown that people think prisons are too easy. They want punishment for anyone in prison, not educational opportunities, gyms, barbells, television sets, or computers. I spoke about this with Scott Christianson, who has done the research. He writes, "Prison education programs, vocational assistance programs, recreational programs, job training programs, drug treatment programs, therapy for sex offenders, and programs to address domestic violence and other problems usually accounted for an *infinitesimal* share of the corrections budget. Moreover, in many prisons, they hardly existed at all. . . . Despite their image as 'country clubs,' most prisons remained stripped down to the basic necessities of life, except for the cable television and weight-lifting equipment that right-wingers liked to complain about—programs that corrections officials retained because they were such a cheap and effective tool for occupying inmates."

I have often been told by people who work in corrections that prisoners are manipulative and conniving, and that lying is their way of life. I have heard stories of how guards must protect themselves from physical harm that some prisoners would inflict on them. I don't dispute that the prison population includes some very bad apples and that the job of being a corrections officer, which is a difficult one, can also be a dangerous one at times.

Yet, strictly from the human point of view, I find it very difficult to understand how anyone could feel that prisoners, who live in cages, have it easy. These are people who are deprived of their freedom, the most essential ingredient we must have to be well-functioning persons; they are continually depersonalized, unable to receive mail or have a visitor unless they are identified, not by name, but by a number; they are always made to feel powerless in a place where the authorities have utter control of every facet of their lives; they can never for a moment forget they are trapped behind bars; they can be subject to humiliating searches or lockdowns at any time, sometimes at particularly punishing times. As an example, just before Christmas 1999, there was a lockdown at Greenhaven, and I was concerned about the men I know there, hoping they could still have their special Christmas Mass. I also read that other prisons in New York State were also in lockdown.

A few weeks later, a story came out explaining why there was a lockdown at the very same time at the Sing Sing Correctional Facility at Ossining, New York. A corrections officer, Hanser Hernandez, had filed a report saying he had discovered five rounds of nine-millimeter ammunition hidden in a firehose box accessible to inmates. Immediately, the twenty-one hundred inmates were put in lockdown. An investigation discovered that it was Officer Hernandez himself who had planted the ammunition and then filed a false report. Somehow, I concluded, there seemed to be a spillover effect in Greenhaven, with the lockdown there getting two lines in news stories saying this was necessary to control prisoners who were planning a strike.

Would anybody want to spend Christmas this way, locked in a cell twenty-three hours out of twenty-four, because of rumors spread that affected a number of prisons in the state? Prison means never to have control of your life. This is what I have seen time after time when I go into the prisons. The marvel to me is that prisoners survive, and some even manage to create a new and better life for themselves.

With the escalating prison industry bringing a ghoulish prosperity to the nation, it's hard to imagine that we'll see any real reform in the causes leading to the ever-increasing prison population. It's no mystery why prisons are booming. The major reasons are the "hard on crime" approaches, which have resulted in longer sentences, a tightening of parole, a "three strikes and you're out" law under which someone is sentenced to life in prison after three convictions, even if these crimes are non-violent or minor, and, the predominant cause, mandatory sentencing for drug offenses.

Attention is now being placed on the "draconian" drug laws enacted under Governor Nelson Rockefeller of New York in 1973. People back then believed that if you put drug pushers into prison for very long sentences, the drug traffic would be sabotaged. Scores of first-time offenders were sentenced to fifteen years, or twenty years to life, including many women being used by boyfriends to buy or sell drugs. The law still in

effect imposes a mandatory sentence of fifteen years for first-time offenders convicted of selling two ounces or more of cocaine or heroin, or
possessing four ounces or more. The Correctional Association of New
York states: "These penalties apply without regard to the circumstances
of the offense or the individual's character or background. Whether the
person is a first-time or repeat offender, for instance, is irrelevant."

Consider what happened to Hernando Méndez, a fine young man
I call a friend. I heard about "Nando," as he is called, from Charlie
Grosso at Greenhaven. Both prisoners, they had met when Charlie was
moved to Honor Block, the housing unit where Nando was assigned.
He was from Colombia, spoke little English and, sentenced under New
York's mandatory minimum laws, was serving fifteen years to life for
drug possession.

As it happened, when Charlie moved in, their friendship really took
off, and one day Nando asked Charlie if he'd read his case. Nando had
noticed that Charlie was going to the law library almost every night,
wanting to learn so he could "fight for" his freedom, and he desperately
wanted help because he maintained he was innocent. When Charlie read
the case, he was appalled, convinced that Nando should never have gone
to prison. The young Colombian had been working later than usual that
day and missed his ride home. A co-worker, as a favor, asked two friends
of his to take Nando home. The driver, unfortunately, did not completely
stop at a stop sign and was pulled over by police. The men were ordered
out and the police searched the car. Inside the glove compartment, they
found two ounces of cocaine. The two men told the police that Nando
had nothing to do with the drugs, that he was just getting a lift back
from work. He was arrested anyway.

Because of multiple complications, the case went to trial and the fact
that Nando was just getting a ride home got lost in the legal arguments. The jury never heard the truth, and Nando was convicted and
sentenced.

After Charlie read everything about the case, he became tremendously
empathetic toward Nando. He started working on the case, hoping to
find a way to get Nando back in court. "Nando and I became insepa-
rable. I met his family; he met my children; we all had visits together
like one family. And then the worst news came. Immigration was going
to deport him as soon as he completed his sentence. I couldn't believe
it. I felt sad, especially for his mother, Lucy. She worked so hard to get
her children one by one to this country without being a burden with
handouts. Would this country break up a good family like that?"

Nando's family came for a visit, and they were quiet and depressed. At that, Charlie just tried to convince them they would beat the immigration ruling. Nando didn't believe it. Somehow Charlie found himself saying, "You have to believe me. My birthday's coming and the [immigration] judge will give me this for a present." That night and many to follow, he knelt and prayed the rosary, always asking the Lord to let his birthday be joyful—by getting the news that Nando would not be deported. On November 9, his birthday, the judge's order came through, with the good news Charlie had prayed for! Finally all the papers were in order, showing that Nando had a perfect institutional record; letters of support came from the civilian staff, his family, and, of course, Charlie.

"Within a few weeks after the judge's decision," Charlie said, "we applied for clemency to Governor George Pataki. Then one year later, on December 25, 1996—the Joyful Mystery of the birth of Jesus—Governor Pataki granted pardons to seven inmates. One of those seven was Hernando Méndez. Nando is now a free man. All I can add to this story is while I continue to be confined, a blanket of happiness covers me. In time, a sign will appear for me to go free. I will join my friend Nando when that happens. But if no sign ever appears, well, the events that did happen will carry me until I come face to face with God."

Nando has been working for the past few years; he has now completed his parole requirements and so is a completely free man. As for how he feels about having spent twelve years in prison for a crime he never committed, when he had an absolutely clean record, no evidence ever of violence, a family that cared for him, this handsome, soft-spoken young man only smiles and says, "God bless Charlie."

This is a true story from a prison that I have encountered first hand. I believe it underscores the unjustness of mandatory minimum sentences for some drug involvements, while it highlights how goodness and friendships can thrive behind prison bars.

Some high-profile people, like actor Charles Grodin, several legislators and clergy, columnists, and the *New York Times* have spoken out about these inhumane laws, pointing out that we now have effective drug treatment programs which should be an option to imprisonment. The late Cardinal John J. O'Connor, as the leader of the New York Archdiocese, was outspoken in pointing out the injustice of the Rockefeller drug laws. Writing in *Catholic New York,* the cardinal stated his belief strongly that "the Rockefeller drug laws need a major overhaul." He said he wanted to "raise awareness" because justice appears to be "made murky" for the great number of people "caught up in a web of laws and regulations that at least on the surface seem to result in things which do not always make a lot of sense." His statement affirmed that of the Bishops of the State of New York. In June 1999, they called for a reform of these laws, seeking a more humane approach for the penalties, which apply without regard to the circumstances of the offense or the individual's character or background.

Rockefeller wasn't alone in passing these bizarre laws. In the 1970s and 1980s state and federal lawmakers passed mandatory sentencing laws that took judgment out of the hands of local judges, who since then have been forced to sentence nonviolent, low-level drug offenders to incredibly long prison terms—far longer than those given for manslaughter, assault, and sexual abuse.

Mandatory drug laws completely changed the prison landscape in our country, making prisons a huge, booming, profitable industry, expanding mainly because of drug users caught in the mandatory sentencing trap. The *New York Times* commented in June 2000 that primarily because of these "pointlessly rigid mandatory sentences ... much has changed in the past quarter century." A fact sheet from the Correctional Association of New York shows that since 1981, this state has added over 46,000 prison beds at a capital cost of more than $4.5 billion. There are now more than 71,000 inmates in the system, up from 12,500 in 1973. In 1999 about 45 percent of the people sent to state prison were drug offenders. Nearly 80 percent of them were never convicted of a violent felony. African Americans, who make up 12.4 percent of the state's population, make up 51 percent of the prison population. In 1980, 33 percent of those sent to New York's prisons were nonviolent; in 1999 that had escalated to 60.8 percent nonviolent.

Similar statistics can be found in many states. The cost to the taxpayer is enormous. Taxpayers spend four times more to incarcerate one nonviolent drug offender ($21,837 and up) than to educate one child ($5,421 and up), according to 1998 figures from the Bureau of Prisons and the Department of Education. The National Center on Addiction and Substance Abuse estimated that in this first year of the new millennium taxpayers would be spending $100 million a day, not for drug treatment, but to incarcerate inmates with drug and alcohol problems.

A momentum is gathering now across the country to end what has gotten to be called "drug war prisoners." Vigils are being held throughout the country, spearheaded by groups called Families Against Mandatory Minimums, the November Coalition, and Common Sense for Drug Policy, which explains its purpose: " ... to show that the injustice of the drug war is not only impacting those incarcerated but also their friends and families. People gathering in public to highlight the harms of the drug war policies is a visible way to urge an end to the drug war."

Much can be done on the local level to mobilize people to join groups like Families Against Mandatory Minimums, asking for reform of "mandatory sentencing laws that remove a judge's discretion to consider the facts of a case before sentencing." One good example of this is what Father John Fitzgerald, a longtime friend of mine, told me had been done in his parish of St. James in Setauket, New York. They invited Sister Marion Defeis, a Sister of St. Joseph of Brentwood who is a chaplain at Rikers Island, a New York prison, to come and speak, opening the meeting to other parishes. She gave astounding statistics and stories to this large gathering of people.

Pointing out that some 80 percent of incarcerated drug offenders were never convicted of a violent felony, she also stated that 25 percent of the drug offenders were locked up for drug possession as opposed to drug selling. She spoke of injustices "that abound which entrap the inmates," such as money, drugs, and drug paraphernalia "being planted to make the charges stick." She also told heartbreaking stories of women caught in this web, while the actual drug dealers are rarely pursued or arrested. One story, published in the parish's journal, *Tidings,* which is edited by Father Fitzgerald, told of Janet, who was returning to Boston after visiting her family in Nigeria. As Sister Defeis related, "Her boyfriend tricked her into bringing three containers of his deodorant indicating that he had no room in his suitcase and would take a later flight. When Janet's bags were searched at Kennedy Airport, heroin was found in the containers. Janet was charged with A-1 felony. She had two choices: she could go to trial and lose, in which case she could be sentenced to fifteen to twenty-five years to life, or she could plead down to an A-11 felony and go to prison for five to fifteen years. Terrified of spending a minimum of fifteen years in prison, she lied and said that she was guilty of transporting drugs, although in fact she was innocent. Janet was sentenced to five to fifteen years."

The people attending that informative talk decided to take action. The leaders presented letters to be signed and sent to the governor and several influential state legislators. Father Fitzgerald related that they obtained 144 letters that night and on the Sunday following, gathered another 150 signatures "of our wonderful parishioners who took the time and effort to help on behalf of those who are our brothers and sisters."

What was done at St. James could be a model for other organizations concerned about the legal, civil, and human rights implications of mandatory sentences, wanting to change quickly what has become an abomination of injustice in our criminal justice system. For as Cardinal O'Connor wrote, "Justice deferred is justice denied."

Is prison the answer? Not according to what Rolando Martínez, executive director of the Hispanic Health Council in Hartford, Connecticut, was reported to say: "Institutionalizing young men of color for a long period of time for nonviolent crimes is more destructive than productive. If a young man spends ten years in jail, he'll wither away. His spirit will die."

It will take courage on the part of elected officials to come out into the open and abolish the draconian drug laws because they will then have to answer to their constituencies, many of whom believe we need to counter the destructive drug taking in our country with strong, punitive measures. When I write about the need to end mandatory sentencing, I get opposition letters, some by thoughtful people, like this one:

" . . . Concerning your recent column on mandatory drug laws, I hope you will consider another point of view. The way some Americans are being enslaved by drugs is a national disgrace. I'm sure that if someone I love were serving a mandatory sentence for possessing a small quantity of marijuana my point of view might be somewhat different. But when it comes to importing, producing, transporting for sale, and distributing hard drugs, the kind that quickly hook the user and do tremendous damage, I think the laws should be much harder than they are now.

"In your column you mention that 'Some 1.8 million men and women are in prisons, triple the numbers in 1980, even though crime is down.' I would have written that sentence, 'Some 1.8 million drug dealers and other criminals are in prisons, triple the numbers in 1980, and *therefore* crime is down!'

"Granted, we have all heard of people serving unconscionably long sentences for possession of small amounts of marijuana. But for every person serving such an overly harsh sentence, there are scores of people, ranging from petty street dealers to those who brazenly import drugs by the ton, who are willing to ply their trade because they feel the chance of doing any serious prison time is almost nil.

"Let me give you an example of something that happened right in our area that left a deep impression on many people here.... A young man was convicted of beating an eighty-year-old woman to death....

Although he received a lengthy prison term...after just a few years he was paroled. He migrated to [another state] where he enrolled in college. Although theoretically he was under the jurisdiction of parole authorities, neither his college nor his employer nor his fellow students were told of his horrible past.

"An unsuspecting coed befriended him and he raped and murdered her. Had the state kept him locked up forever, or at least for the full term to which he was sentenced, the second woman would not have died.

"Similar examples are legion.

"I, too, am troubled by the disparity between sentences given to drug dealers and those who are guilty of manslaughter, assault, and sexual abuse, not to mention fraud, swindling, robbery, and so on. But going easier on members of the drug culture is not the answer.

"What is the answer? I wish I had it. Until someone comes up with a way of really rehabilitating criminals, I say keep them locked up where they can do less harm...."

I believe the man writing this was most sincere. But what he says, I have heard over and over. It is the argument that makes sense to people. Keep criminals locked away, and they won't be out in the streets to hurt another person. The real problem, however, is that we're not really in disagreement. I say keep the violent ones, especially the heinous murderers, put away for the protection of others. But should we be looking at the nonviolent offenders through the same lenses?

I don't believe so. Why, I wonder, is a good man I know still in prison? He never carried weapons, had no record of violent crime. He was apprehended for dealing four and a half ounces of heroin—ounces, not pounds. For this, he was sentenced to "twenty-five years to life." He was never able to even say goodbye to his family in Puerto Rico. "He wasn't a big drug dealer. He was a little guy on the street," but Puerto Rican, not white and wealthy, said his wife, noting he has already served over thirteen years, but still was turned down on appeals. Does this make sense? Not an iota. When citizens complain about the cost of keeping people in prison, they ought to look at the people like this man, denied the healing they need and warehoused behind bars for years on end for dealing in a few ounces of a drug.

I also feel we must question why prisons have become so punitive. Should anyone question this, a look at the escalating growth of what is now known as "supermax prisons," better known as "special housing units" or "SHUs," will explain what's happening. They are the cells within a prison, or a facility specially built to have only SHUs, where prisoners are kept in solitary confinement for up to twenty-three hours a day in tiny cells, sometimes alone, sometimes doubly occupied. Father George Anderson, associate editor of *America* magazine, writing of these "maximum control" units, points out that "as the name suggests, what they have in common is extreme isolation, with inmates cut off from the outside world to a far greater degree than prisoners in general prison populations . . . sometimes there for years—with virtually nothing in the way of educational, religious or other programs."

Father Anderson, pointing out the extremely harsh conditions in these isolation cells, continues: "Human rights advocates increasingly see aspects of it as violations of international conventions against torture, as well as of the eighth amendment to the U.S. Constitution, which forbids cruel and unusual punishment. Thus, in its 1998 report, . . . Amnesty International USA claims that a number of the conditions prevailing in supermax prisons 'are a flagrant breech of minimum international standards for the treatment of prisoners.' "

Long before I had seen Father Anderson's article, I had become aware of the move to put increasing numbers of prisoners in solitary. I had sent a small article I had read in the *New York Times* about this growing tendency in the prison system to Robert Zani, my "pen pal" in a Texas prison, asking how bad it was in Texas. Until I received his reply, I had not realized that he was in, and had spent many years in, solitary confinement. He wrote:

"I could tell by your clipping comment that—perhaps fortunately—you have no idea what it's like here. My fault. But when you said, 'Did you see the enclosed?' I had to laugh! There are 3,100 prisoners here and 925 employees. Approximately 550 prisoners are in solitary confinement. Prison systems everywhere do not want the public to know how many large numbers of prisoners they are holding in solitary, so they use different euphemisms . . . like 'Administrative Segregation.' That is now a common term within the criminal justice system. [In this cell] there is no electricity; light, but that's it. So, no radio, no fan, no TV, zip. Twenty-four hours a day in cell. Probably three hours of recreation a week. No library. No dessert. No deodorant. No shampoo. No typewriters. No. No. No. A whole list of no's. One roll of toilet paper a week, if you're awake when it is delivered! The worst scenario you can fathom. God's truth. . . .

"I am not allowed to participate in any Roman Catholic programs, including Mass at present, nor have I ever been allowed to attend educational programs while in prison. The warden abolished Mass for

'Close Custody' prisoners—another euphemism for solitary confinement—some time back. And due to the fact that (1) I came into the state prison system with a fair educational background, and (2) I have been a court witness against the state and the prison system, as part of their retaliation, I have been denied any/all educational opportunities. When I bought my own personal library, the prison 'authorities' came in, seized it, destroyed it—and admitted it. You are no doubt familiar with the reputation of the Texas prison system as the most retrograde and sadistic in America. No system has received more bad publicity, or deserved it. If it were not for a few good people in the system, they would replicate Nazi Germany. Consider—what state leads America by a wide margin in executions? Why is that?"

Robert quoted Dan Pens, a writer for *Prison Legal News,* reporting "Today's 'supermax' prisoners are entombed in concrete boxes with solid steel doors—totally isolated from human contact; their meals are shoved through a food slot; and they spend 23 to 23 and 1/2 hours per day alone in their cells—allowed out only for showers 3–5 times a week or to spend a half hour alone in a tiny outdoor dog cage (often given the choice of 'shower or yard'). When being moved to the shower or yard prisoners are handcuffed, shackled, often with a dog leash attached, and are escorted by two 'ninja suited' guards carrying batons and electric stun devices."

Can this be America, the nation that prides itself as a champion of human rights? Why do we justify such a blatant violation of human rights when it comes to certain prisoners? Paul Grondahl, a reporter for the *Times Union* in Albany, New York, investigated why growing numbers of inmates were being removed from human society in specially designed SHU cells that prisoners call "The Box." My sister, Rosemary Grieco, who lives in Albany, sent me his eight-page story, published March 26, 2000, with the comment, "the inhuman treatment is unbelievable."

It so happened that Paul Grondahl and I were acquaintances, going back about five years when he interviewed me after one of my books came out. The first facts to hit me in his story were that nearly fifty-seven hundred prisoners in New York are now held in extreme isolation—roughly 8 percent of the state's inmates, four times the national average of about 2 percent—in prisons located in isolated regions of the state, with access by the press or prison watchdog groups generally blocked. I called Paul, wanting to know what had gotten him interested in investigating "The Box." He credited Bishop Howard Hubbard, leader of the Albany Roman Catholic Diocese, and a group of interdenominational clergy, "who had become aware of the growing numbers of people in 'The Box.'" Four days after Paul's story appeared, Bishop Hubbard, Bishop Susan Morrison of the United Methodist Church in Troy, two senators, and clergy representing eight denominations spoke out denouncing these twenty-three-hour-a-day disciplinary lockdowns and urged a review of corrections policy.

Paul Grondahl didn't have an easy time of it trying to get a thorough and honest report. "They block access...no contact with the prisoners other than mail," he said, telling me he got some information through families, secret visits, and clandestine correspondence. "I heard from a lot of mothers." Prison officials justify putting ever-growing numbers of inmates in these "prefabricated, high-tech cell blocks, operated from a central console station," saying these keep rule-breakers out of the general prison population and, therefore, reduce violence. "They claim they're all bad apples and bad actors. But you can't get access to any files or reports....A huge number of prisoners are confined for fairly dubious reasons. Some clearly show behavior that might warrant that treatment for a time," said Paul. "They are a silent, forgotten group. It's hard for them to have a voice."

While the time a prisoner spends in solitary is supposed to be limited to six months, most are in for up to a year, with others confined in isolation from one to five years. Paul reported that 154 inmates have been in this confinement for over five years. Prison officials "keep finding things to add to time," something as innocuous as "mouthing off to a guard. There's a whole book of rules on life in The Box."

He quoted Sol Wachtler, a former chief judge in New York who served time, convicted of harassing his ex-mistress, and was confined to an isolation cell for "mental health observation." "I saw guys put in the hole for making fun of a guard, for having a radio with someone else's initials in their locker and a lot of minor infractions....If you're in the hole and complain, they'll double your time in the hole." Now a teacher at a law college, Wachtler told Paul Grondahl that two inmates in a single isolation cell is "totally inappropriate," that long isolation constitutes "cruel and unusual punishment" and that "after a long period of isolation, these people come out ten times worse than when they went in."

Most touching was the interview with Father Joe Romano, a retired prison chaplain. He worked with young inmates, between sixteen and nineteen years of age, at Greene, a medium security prison in Coxsackie, New York. What he witnessed caused him "deep despair." He spoke of "scared kids who cried and cried," "human wreckage," much of which he blamed on The Box. While there was "an angry, loud vitality in the general inmate population . . . after a few weeks in The Box, that life force seeped out from the inmates as inevitably as air from a punctured balloon." Some of the things he saw were attempted suicides, sexual assaults, self-mutilation, inmates unresponsive and catatonic, in psychotic rages, inmates sleeping naked on cement floors to combat sweltering summer heat without air conditioning.

In the end, Father Romano said, he "couldn't take it any more. I was burned out and it was time to go. . . . I'm a priest and we're in the forgiveness business. . . . The SHU is only about punishment and breaking down these guys. There's nothing about forgiveness or rehabilitation."

Paul Grondahl said he learned a lot from this experience, mainly that everyone involved is "living their own kind of hell. It's an awfully diseased system and everybody's going to be damaged by it." He felt "sadness and pity" for everybody, "for the corrections people and administration, too. New York is not unique. The prison system has grown too big and too fast. There are no programs, no chance for rehabilitation. Those in charge don't have a good rapport with inmates any more. There's a lot of antagonism, and 'cracking down' by the administration. I'm afraid it's going to backfire. I worry about the whole thing exploding."

The corrections administration wrote a rebuttal to Paul Grondahl's thorough and professional report. The *Times Union* reporter said he "got quite a bit of response" to what he wrote. Sadly, "a huge contingent showed no mercy, saying The Box is too good and 'execute them right off.'"

Five weeks after the *Times Union*'s published report, Amnesty International issued a news release "condemning increasing institutionalized cruelty in the United States." Noting the "spiraling prison and jail population," the report stated: "From the use of long-term isolation in supermaximum security units, through the routine employment of chemical sprays to subdue suspects and prisoners and the incarceration of asylum-seekers in cruel and degrading conditions, to the use of electro-shock weapons in local jails and courts, the USA is standardizing practices which undermine the aim of the Convention Against Torture [which the United States ratified in October 1994] to eradicate state torture and ill-treatment from the planet.

"The U.S. Government, which so often labels itself as champion of human rights, must take serious steps to ensure that international standards are respected throughout the country."

The question of the human rights of prisoners must be considered as more states, faced with more convicted persons than their institutions can handle, are now sending inmates to privately run prisons-for-profit. By 1999, a private prison industry was well underway in many states around the country, having grown from 2 institutions in 1984 to 163 in twenty-six states, with over 200,000 inmates, up from 85,000 in early 1998. This raises questions, namely, should the profit motive have a place in corrections, and what regulations and protections are in force at these prisons?

The early news out was not encouraging about whether privately run prisons, built with capital provided by investors, will be better or worse than state-run institutions. A *New York Times* report stated, "There is often no contract outlining the prison's responsibilities to that city or its state; the prison's only contract is with the supplier of inmates. And if there are not enough inmates to fill up the prison, the company may bring in out-of-state inmates, who might misbehave because they are unhappy about being away from home. Some states exporting inmates, including Idaho and Montana, have been so dissatisfied after violence and escapes that they canceled contracts with private prisons in Louisiana and Texas."

The most alarming news came in spring 2000, when horror stories from a privately run prison for teenagers in Louisiana came out. The prison was located in Jena, operated by the Wackenhut Corrections Corporation, the world's largest for-profit prison operator. Judge Mark Doherty took action, removing six teenage boys from this juvenile prison "after finding they had been brutalized by guards, kept in solitary confinement for months for no reason and deprived of shoes, blankets, education and medical care," according to *New York Times* correspondent Fox Butterfield, "partly caused by Wackenhut's efforts to cut costs."

Juvenile justice officials said that while this prison had been built to provide treatment for juveniles with drug addictions, they found no such programs, only that this was "a dangerous place to be, with a quarter of the inmates traumatically injured in a two-month period, many by untrained guards... who routinely threw the inmates against the walls, twisted their arms or shoved them to the ground.... A quarter of the inmates had I.Q.'s of less than 70... but no special education" was provided for them. A month after this news broke, the Wackenhut Corrections Corporation announced it was abandoning the contract to run the juvenile prison in Jena. The tragic situation here underscores the importance that justice departments in all states monitor privately run prisons to make sure that the profit motivation doesn't become more important than safeguarding the human rights of prisoners.

Again Pope John Paul II has shown his human concern for prisoners. Besides his leadership in seeking a global end to the death penalty, in early summer 2000 he released a document pointing out the situation of prisoners around the world to underscore that he had declared a Jubilee for Prisoners, to be celebrated on the coming July 9. A Vatican statement said the new document confronted "the theme of the condition of prisons around the world, from the human, social and pastoral points of view, but above all it will provide some ideas about facing the problems and not only through the use of clemency." The pope clearly seeks pervasive reform of prison conditions, while supporting the need for just punishment. We should all follow his lead.

Another area of needed reform in the criminal justice system is openness and compassion for the families of inmates. Scott Christianson has written forcefully on how imprisonment affects a family, economically and socially: "There has been little attention given to the extent to which imprisonment may contribute to poverty, delinquency and criminality on the part of family members in addition to the imprisoned offender. Clearly, the family left behind can become an incubator of social problems. . . . Imprisonment punishes the family as well as the prisoner, but there has been little attention paid to the results."

It is undeniable, however, that when loved ones can remain close to their incarcerated son, husband, wife, father, mother, relative, chances for rehabilitation and a renewed life for all are greatly improved. I have seen love in action at the Greenhaven prison each year when the chaplain is able to have a family picnic day and "Celebration" for the inmates and their loved ones, under the umbrella of their prison Holy Name Society, a very human occasion launched years ago by the then chaplain, Msgr. Edward Donovan.

I met an extraordinary mother at one of these family gatherings. I knew her son to be a fine man, having talked to him many times. I found out that his mother had visited him faithfully and frequently— sometimes every other day—over the past twenty years. She said the picnic celebration was a special occasion because it was one of the rare times when families can get up and walk around together, eat with each other and find things to laugh about. "Family ties are so important, and just being here with him makes us so happy," she said, commenting on how little people on the outside know about prisons. "They complain that prisoners have it easy, with TVs and gyms. But they still have four walls. People just don't know what their life is like. They make remarks that they're animals, monkeys in a cage," said this mother, whose strength comes across and who has gifted her son with a similar strength.

Her son was only eighteen when he was sentenced for thirty-five years-plus for being one of three involved in a robbery in which someone was shot and killed. He has already served twenty years and has made these as good as he can, staying busy, getting his high school diploma, being involved with church, going to chapel almost every day. Ask him why his life is on a positive track, and he points to his mother and relatives. "You have to have family ties," he answers directly and simply.

Unfortunately, correctional systems have not taken this need for family contact into consideration as any kind of priority. Prisons are being built in the sticks, miles and miles away from families, often in areas lacking public transportation so that relatives who don't have cars are effectively removed from their husband, son, brother, uncle. In Connecticut, Governor John Rowland and the General Assembly looked at overcrowding in the prisons and decided to enter into a contract with Wallens Ridge State Prison in Big Stone Gap, Virginia. The deal is that up to five hundred of Connecticut's high security and maximum security sentenced inmates would be sent to that prison for a period not to exceed a year to ease overcrowding in the Nutmeg State's prisons. The main reason for the overcrowding is, says the Department of Corrections, "the continually rising offender population," an increase of 24 percent since 1995. According to the department, "The prime pressures of the increasing prison population we face today are the result of deliberate, progressive steps taken to hold criminals more accountable for the consequences of their acts.... [Because of these steps:] percent of time served behind bars has increased; shift toward determinate sentencing; minimized opportunities for early release; truth in sentencing requirements; federal task forces; local and state police efforts."

While saving money was not "a motive for transfers, there is a bonus, nevertheless," says Corrections, pointing out that to house a prisoner in Virginia costs $62 a day as compared to the $66 to $156 a day that it costs in Connecticut. In defense of why 480 of their prisoners have been sent to Virginia, the department says, legitimately, that the state needs more prisons, but nobody wants these in their communities. Connecticut towns and cities aren't looking for employment via the prison industry and the word is state officials will continue to face an uphill battle when it comes to trying to convince a town here to expand a prison or build a new one. Some say a better answer would be to get the nonviolent inmates who need drug treatment out of the prisons and into treatment programs. That would immediately reduce the numbers significantly.

Families of the inmates sent to Virginia immediately protested this action, pointing out to the Department of Corrections how devastating this separation was to families. One mother of an inmate explained, "Some of us can't afford to go down there and visit. They need our support. They're down there, snatched away from us."

Criticism of this decision escalated in April, when a twenty-year-old inmate, serving a two-and-a-half-year sentence for the sale of drugs, committed suicide by making a noose out of bedsheets and jumping off his bunk bed. This followed an incident where three Connecticut prisoners were shot with rubber bullets, and other complaints surfaced, such as reporting an inmate having cuts on his ankles from tight shackles and having Mace sprayed in his face. Then, three months later, a fifty-year-old man, Lawrence James Frazier, died of an apparent heart attack. Now criticism of the decision to send inmates to Virginia became more intense as questions surfaced about whether the state was sending people with medical problems to Virginia and about the kind of medical care and emergency response treatments available to inmates there.

The friends and families of the transferred inmates, from the beginning, brought their concerns to the Department of Corrections. They said the move had added unfairly to their punishment. They told of sons becoming depressed and suicidal, being deprived of religious materials, and agitated over not being able to have visits with their loved ones. Their complaints and worries were more than justified considering that the FBI had been requested to do an investigation of Wallens Ridge for alleged inmate abuse. An Associated Press story of January 15, 2000, said the probe was requested by New Mexico Attorney General Patricia Madrid after many of the 150 inmates that state had sent to Virginia complained of beatings, misuse of stun guns, and the lack of medical attention. By summer of 2000, families of Connecticut inmates in that Virginia prison could make the same complaints.

When you begin to study what life is like for a person whose wrong actions land them in prison, you discover that the prison system, just about everywhere, could be said to be notoriously unconcerned about the long-term rehabilitation of imprisoned people. I believe the best chance an inmate has of wanting to return to society as a useful citizen is to stay

connected to family and friends. Unfortunately, prisons have become
very good at breaking up families.

An important way of staying in touch with a loved one in prison is
via telephone, but prisons, in a money-making arrangement with phone
companies, have effectively made this another way of keeping bars between families and inmates. I discovered this because many times I have
picked up my ringing phone to speak with the MCI operator. My calls
often came from Charlie Grosso at Greenhaven, whom I have come
to know and respect. The operator tells me the cost of the call will
"not exceed" $3.33 for the first minute, and the charge will be $.33
for each additional minute after that, plus a tax charge of 8.2 percent.
Outrageous? You bet!

When I started to wonder "what's going on here?" I looked into this
arrangement and found out that prisons and telephone companies have
developed a very effective system for exploiting the families and friends
of prisoners. Artificially high rates are charged, and prisons and phone
companies split the profits. And "profit" is the word. As one example,
New York State projected that it would receive $21.5 million in com-
missions from the telephone calls in fiscal 2000. In total, the states, over
thirty-two of them, that have profit arrangements with phone companies nationally collected $180,422,264 in one year, according to research
done by a new organization called Equitable Telephone Charges (eTc),
based in Kalamazoo, Michigan, directed by Kay Perry.

Sadly, that money comes mainly from the pockets of poor people,
because the rich don't usually go to prison. They go to lawyers. The
only way prisoners can stay in touch by phone with their families is by
making collect calls.

After the *New York Times* report, some letter writers responded with
the nasty self-righteousness I have come to expect when the subject is
prisoners. One said prisoners have no right to phone calls, because "telephone service is a privilege. . . . " I encounter it often—the attitude that
prisoners are scum, not human beings, and certainly not redeemable. It's
a sad commentary on us. In answer to the right-versus-privilege argument, eTc responds: "It is a privilege—one that should not be abused
by any party, not the prisons, phone companies, families of prisoners or
prisoners. It is also worth noting that studies have demonstrated that
prisoners who have a strong social support system are more likely to be
successful upon release. Loved ones who agree to pay these exorbitant
charges are performing a public service and should be given a break!

Further, we are convinced that prisoner telephone systems enhance the security of any prison. Prisoners who maintain family ties have much more to lose than those who are cut off from all outside contact. They have much more incentive to obey rules."

I found out about eTc after I wrote a column for Catholic News Service about this abominable practice of further punishing inmates and got a letter from Sister Dorothy Briggs, a Dominican sister from Massachusetts who is one of the coordinators of the eTc campaign "to end the immoral charges inflicted on innocent families and friends of prisoners by the prisons and phone companies. We know that taking on the Department of Corrections is a nearly impossible task. But we feel the families have suffered for years, and now enough is enough," Sister Dorothy wrote.

I also received other letters, one from a family member of a prisoner who thanked me, but did not give her name, "fearing retribution, I suppose," she wrote. Commenting that she is fortunate because she lives close enough to be able to visit her loved one often, she nevertheless was "upset about this injustice regarding folks who have few or no advocates. So when I read your article, I was surprised and thrilled to see so many facts made public.... Please continue to write such columns and perhaps give us suggestions as to what we can do to help." And she added, "I have seen real Christianity on the hottest days in summer and coldest days in winter with other visitors to our loved ones in prison."

Her letter made me think of Matthew 25, where Christ gives us a blueprint for how we should live and treat one another, beginning with, "I was hungry...." All I have learned—and am still learning—about the prison system in America makes me ask, Where's the compassion this world so badly needs? And when Jesus asks, "Why didn't you visit me when I was in prison," what will be the response?

Chapter Eight

THE OTHER VICTIMS

More than once I have been the recipient of sympathy from people who, hearing about the murder of my son and daughter-in-law, tell me that "the worst thing that can happen to a mother" has happened to me. I tell them, no. The worst thing would be if it had been a son of mine using a gun to snuff out the life of another person, and I express sadness and concern for Brenda Clark, the mother of the eighteen-year-old who killed John and Nancy. On two occasions, mothers of murder victims challenged me on this. Their argument was that she was much better off than we were because her son was still alive, and she could visit him, see him, hug him.

I would think about that and I would be happy for her that at least she was spared the terrible pain of having to bury a son, his life ended by a person or the state. This was another reason why I detested the death penalty, which could cause such ultimate pain for mothers who had already been plunged into hell. I never would want to be part of a system that could bring such torment to a mother.

The memory of my Aunt Margie being taken away in a straightjacket when the agony of her brother's death in the electric chair finally consumed her brain had always made me feel tremendous sorrow for the families of those who commit the crime. I'm not denying that in all too many cases, the families are among the factors that make a person turn into a criminal, a lawbreaker, a murderer. But this does not justify judging all members of a crime perpetrator's family as unworthy of concern. As Christ said in the Gospel of John, when the scribes and Pharisees were about to exercise the death penalty on the woman caught in adultery, "Let anyone among you who is without sin be the first to throw a stone at her." I believe the message here is that judging is God's territory; ours is compassion, without boundaries.

A woman who puts this belief into action is the remarkable Anne

150

Coleman of Dover, Delaware. I met Anne and her friend Barbara Lewis in January 1996 when I addressed the Delaware Citizens Opposed to the Death Penalty. Anne's daughter Frances was shot to death in her car while driving through south Los Angeles in 1985. They never caught the murderer. Barbara is from the group I call "the other victims." Her son Robert is on death row in Delaware for an act of violence that ended with his girlfriend being killed. These two women had become friends and I subsequently learned that they had founded "Because Love Allows Compassion," a Delaware support group for murder victims' families *and* the families of death row inmates.

Anne talks freely about how she came to work for death row inmates and their families, virtually a ministry now, which all began from encountering Barbara Lewis. "We got acquainted at a meeting in Wilmington on the death penalty," which drew people on all sides, including members of the Ku Klux Klan," she told me. "Barbara was there. She stood up and talked about her son on death row and how much pain her whole family was suffering. She said she wished she could give the victim's daughter a hug, but she met with great reluctance on their part to see her."

Anne certainly knew about pain. Her son Daniel was in the army when his sister was murdered. He found out that the police department said they shouldn't expect an arrest because they probably wouldn't find the killer, and Daniel was overwhelmed with anger and depression. He was determined to get revenge, even threatening to get a gun, go to Los Angeles, and kill somebody, anybody. What he really wanted was some kind of justice for his sister. Two years later, Anne stood alongside two graves. Daniel had committed suicide. "I saw what hatred does," she said. "It takes the ultimate toll on one's mind and body."

Hearing Barbara talk at that Wilmington meeting, Anne's painful feelings surfaced, especially when she spoke of the victim's daughter. That was because her murdered Frances also had a daughter, a grandchild Anne had adopted, and she knew the trauma murder caused the child of a victim. She reached out to Barbara, and this mother responded, asking Anne to go to the prison to see her son. "I hadn't contemplated going to prison, but I did. Her son Robert surprised me by asking, 'What are you going to do for other families?' " With that challenge, Anne made appointments to see everyone on death row and has continued this commitment. "Delaware now has eighteen convicted murderers on death row, locked down twenty-three hours a day, surrounded by walls," she said.

The stories Anne can tell, and the people she'll never forget! "When I first met Billy Bailey, he was forty-eight, condemned for a terrible crime. He had been in a halfway house when someone told him he would go to prison for passing a bad check. He went on a drunken rampage and killed an elderly couple. It was pretty terrible." But Anne wonders if he ever had a chance for a good life.

"He was one of twenty-three children. His mother died when he was six months old, his father remarried, and his stepmother had no regard for him. He was abused. He had to steal if he wanted to eat. He stole in order to survive. No one intervened. When he was ten, his father died, his stepmother abandoned him and he stayed with a brother who abused him. When he was twelve, the state said he was socially retarded and had no idea of how one conforms in society.

"I got to know him very well. He was very shy, very traumatized. But in prison he was eventually given a job in the woodworking shop, and this was his forte. He became a foreman and was producing $15,000 a month for the state. This man who had never had a home was settling down, having a 'house,' even if it was prison. This was really something new for Billy, and he was having a pretty good life, finally working, finding he could do something useful. When there were no appeals left, he was put into maximum security and the prison refused to let me visit. It took the intervention of the Governor's Council to get one last visit, on January 19, 1996. When I got there, he was asked to answer a phone call. It was his lawyer, who waited to call till I was there, because he had to tell Billy that the Supreme Court had turned down his final hope. He told me before he left that he never had a friend like me, who wanted nothing from him, only friendship. Billy was hanged on January 25 that month. Two of his brothers witnessed the execution."

Anne then spoke of a woman, charged with murder in a domestic altercation case, who would be going on trial when she was nine months pregnant. "They're asking for a death penalty," Anne said, thinking of the fate of that woman's baby and speaking of how the system ignores the pain of children who survive the execution of a parent.

She feels so strongly about this mainly because she has known Marcus Lowry, a boy who has had to endure such tragedy. His father killed his mother and his two sisters by setting fire to their house; Marcus was a survivor, seven at the time. "He then went to live with his grandmother, Ellie, but kept saying, 'I need my daddy.' When his father was to be executed on April 22, 1999, Marcus was supposed to stay at his aunt's house. My phone rang. Marcus was crying. He wanted to be with his daddy. I took him to the prison, standing as close to the building as possible. I literally held this fourteen-year-old-boy in my arms as his daddy was being killed. It was a nightmare. I don't think I have ever done anything harder in my life.

"We're reaching out to families of death row prisoners to let them know we're there for them. We can't solve anything for them. We know this has to be one of the loneliest things that can ever happen to anyone. The first time I saw Ellie, she cried, telling me, 'You're the first person who ever offered to help.' Nobody cared that she had lost a daughter-in-law and two grandchildren. Victims' families are supposed to receive help. No one ever saw her family as being a survivor of murder victims. She had a terrible time with the system. In the court, great sympathy went out to the father and stepmother of the wife who was killed. Ellie and Marcus were in the courtroom. They were never mentioned. She was regarded only as the mother of a perpetrator, not as victim herself."

Anne started to sound tired as she commented, "In the year 2001, we may have four executions in Delaware, one of them Barbara Lewis's son. I think if he dies, she will become nonfunctional, unable to cope. One of the reasons I started reaching out was because I could see the absolute pain. I agree some prisoners should never get out of prison. But we don't have a right to kill them. Delaware is a violent state. It's not solving anything by the amount of executions taking place here. We had three executions in three months. I was very close to those killed. It took a great deal out of me to have such loss. Now I have to teach myself to detach." Indeed, there comes a point when you have to say, at least temporarily, "Enough!" to pain.

I had talked to Barbara Lewis a couple of years earlier about her son's arrest and conviction. She had a touching story to tell. Her family had lost several members to the violence of murder—an eleven-year-old niece, a twenty-five-year-old nephew, and an uncle. She had survived that pain and now she was at a happy point in her life, having gotten over a divorce, with a good job going well. It was the week before Mother's Day, and on the way home from work she stopped into a local Acme market to pick up some items she needed. As she wrote in the summer 1995 issue of *The Voice*, the publication of Murder Victims Families for Reconciliation: "Suddenly I was drawn to the aisle where greeting cards are found. My eyes fell on one section: 'comfort.' I picked up a card that read, 'I'd like to take the hurt away, but sometimes we must hurt for a while. Know that I am always with you.' I'm not the kind to buy nice cards and send them to people; even when I try my best, I just don't get around to it. Yet this card seemed to stay in my hand. I thought the card would be appropriate for my daughter; she had divorced recently and could use some encouraging words. My world of happiness, though, was about to change forever."

In those very same hours, a tragedy took place. Her only son Robert was involved in a domestic dispute, ending with a shooting that he maintains was accidental. His girlfriend of six years was killed.

"Fate blessed me to receive the news when both my daughters and special friends were with me. It was then that I proceeded to give the card to my daughter. She read it and said, 'Here, Mom, you bought this for yourself.'

"I know now that the message inside was sent from a Higher Source who knows still my destiny. I often repeat the words from that card to get to the next moment of my life," Barbara Lewis affirmed. Since her son has been on death row in Delaware, she has worked actively to help raise consciousness nationwide about why there should be an end to the death penalty in the United States.

As for what a family of a loved one on death row goes through, Barbara Lewis speaks eloquently: "Slowly, you realize that it's just you, your Maker, and your own family that feel and understand your pain. Sometimes words fail you; an expression leads you to embrace each other. You hug each other to squeeze out that gnawing, aching pain that seems to steal in and cause your success to become failure. . . .

"I often want to run away and hide, not for the shame of the crime, but from what I have learned from this experience. I've learned that it's not so much what you did, but who you are and how much you can afford to pay that matters. I've discovered the hopelessness that comes with realizing that, for those who need mercy, the golden rule has no place in this world. I've learned that, with a capital crime, the only recognized victims are the ones lost at the scene of the crime. It is unfortunate that the families of the accused are not recognized as having the greater loss—a loss that includes not just the prospect of our child's death by execution, but the loss of pride and dignity and the loss of friendships. Words cannot describe the suffering we experience."

If anyone can speak eloquently of the devastation that the family of a wrongdoer goes through, it is a man I am privileged to call a friend and brother, with an immediately recognizable name—David Kaczynski. He is the brother of Theodore Kaczynski, the man known as the

Unabomber, convicted of being responsible for a spate of bombings that left three people dead. David had to face one of the hardest decisions a brother could ever make—to turn in his brother for the suspected crime of murder once he could no longer ignore the truth that it was his brother who, for two decades, was mailing homemade bombs to selected victims that left three dead and twenty wounded. The family had had suspicions that Ted, clearly becoming ever more mentally ill, was behind the mailings. But it was only after the Unabomber Manifesto was published in the *Washington Post* that "David finally saw his brother's voice in the writings," said his wife, Linda Patrik, who first suspected the bomber was Ted.

I got to know David and Linda, a philosophy professor at Union College in Schenectady, New York, through Sam Rieger, the president of Survivors of Homicide. We were planning our annual anti-violence conference, and Sam suggested trying to get David Kaczynski as our keynote speaker. Sam had heard that David, who works for troubled teens at a youth shelter in Albany, New York, was deeply concerned about his brother's victims, so much so that he and his wife, had put the bulk of the reward money the family received for identifying the Unabomber in a fund they set up to aid them. He felt that by bringing David to speak to us, we could begin building bridges of understanding between families on both sides who have been victimized by violence.

David agreed to be our speaker that April 1998. Quiet spoken and deeply human, David spoke of the "circle of pain from a violent act that affects us all." He told of the intensity of the pain and loss he, his wife and his mother, Wanda, have felt. He spoke of the love he has for his brother and how he is "puzzled and disquieted" by this "shadow of a brother I knew."

I was deeply touched when he said, "I believe one thing: the brother I grew up with, the person capable of trust and generosity, his forfeited hope, the essential human spark—all live inside him somewhere, however deeply buried they may be. It's precisely because my brother can no longer believe in these that I must."

It took tremendous courage for David to make the choice for life— no more Unabomber victims, even if it meant turning in his brother— precisely because this put him on the horns of a dilemma. David knew Ted could be sentenced to death. "We had to choose between gambling with the lives of people we didn't know and gambling with the life of a family member," he said. "It has been our belief that Ted's crimes were the result of a confused mind, not an evil heart. Indeed, we related to others in condemning his actions, yet we hastened to stop his would-be executioners because we knew they had no insight into the human being they intended to kill." As it turned out, Theodore Kaczynski pleaded guilty to avoid a trial in which his lawyers would have argued that he is mentally ill. He was sentenced to life in prison, without parole, and is serving his sentence at a federal maximum security prison in Florence, Colorado.

Since coming as our speaker that April, David has returned, with Linda, to participate in many of our Survivor of Homicide functions ever since. But I have gotten to know him even better because our paths have crossed in other locations where we have participated in anti–death penalty gatherings. Both of us received an invitation from a group in up-state New York calling itself the Judicial Process Commission to speak in April 2000 at a state-wide anti–death penalty conference, heavily represented by New Yorkers Against the Death Penalty. We had long talks about the importance of remembering the other victims, the families of the wrongdoer, who have to deal with a family's lost honor because of the shamefulness of a member's actions. He told of a remark made by a commentator on the eve of his brother's trial: "Of course David Kaczynski loves his brother and wants to save his life. That's exactly why we shouldn't listen to him." David's response was "It's a strange sense of justice. I think, that holds itself indifferent to love. . . . Can we judge human beings at all if judgment is not tempered by love?"

After his brother's trial, David had a long phone conversation with Anne Marie Salvi, whose son John shot and killed two abortion clinic workers in Boston and then committed suicide in prison. "Her grief, regret, and unending questions were so much like our own that I could identify with her instantly and saw how closely her struggle mirrored that of my own mother. Her heart was torn out twice, first when she learned what her son had done, and then when she learned that he had killed himself."

David, a Buddhist, spoke from the heart and his own experience when he said, "Some crimes are so heinous, we are told, that the perpetrators don't deserve life. But that's where the thinking of the most casual death penalty proponents begins and ends, supported and strengthened by their fear of violent crime, and by a perfectly human sympathy for the victim. There's no arguing with outrage, yet we know that the human tragedies that surround these crimes and outlast them cannot be resolved by outrage."

When I heard David speak against the death penalty, I asked for, and received, his permission to quote what I consider a telling commentary on the death penalty. In David's words:

"The question of the death penalty is a question of justice. Justice invokes so many other virtues: wisdom, insight, compassion—all gathered together in a recognition of the extraordinary complexity of human beings and human life. It's a communal rather than a personal virtue, but it shapes personal consciousness too. Ultimately, it describes the field of understanding which makes it possible for human beings to live together at all.

"Those of us who oppose the death penalty dream of a criminal justice system that reflects what's best rather than what's worst in our national character, of a justice system that taps into the deepest sources of human wisdom. Instead, we are confronted by justice that is blind in precisely the wrong sense of the word. It's supposed to be blind to wealth and privilege. But we know (indeed, everybody knows) it's anything but that. We see our justice system hopelessly engulfed and overwhelmed by the human tragedies it was designed to address. It seems ironic to attach the word 'justice' to the haphazard products of the system. Yet it is this imperfect system, devised and administered by frail human beings, that we have invested with a God-like authority: the power over life and death itself.

"Every year, the killing pace accelerates. Governors' hearts are hardened by political calculation. Along with the scores of innocent people who have been sentenced to die, we routinely execute the mentally ill, the mentally retarded, and people who committed murder as juveniles. Nearly all of these put to death are poor people with underfunded defenses and inexperienced or incompetent lawyers. Few of them are the human monsters we have been led to believe. . . .

"Ultimately, capital punishment asks us to deny our human kinship—and that, I believe, is a grave mistake, a confusion that makes it all too easy to judge others while making it more difficult to know ourselves."

Shakeerah Hameen is one who truly can address David's belief that "capital punishment asks us to deny our human kinship." Her husband, Abdullah Hameen, is on death row in Delaware; his appeals are running out and she's "not doing well." She admits honestly, "I'm afraid of losing him. But I'm realistic. We probably will not win on this. We're Muslims. He's at peace. And he's helping me get through this. He's very strong, much stronger than I am." Abdullah received two death sentences for murder during a drug deal gone bad. "It was an unintentional killing. I know he didn't wake up that morning and say, I'm going to kill somebody today," she commented.

Shakeerah is truly in a unique position. She works for the system, with all the prisons in Delaware, as director of Adult Offender Services with the Delaware Center for Justice. "I met Abdullah through my work. I married him after he was incarcerated. Because of that, I left my job, but they asked me to come back, and I did." Now she works with death row inmates and families, with prisoners up for pardon and parole or prerelease in prison; she monitors state grievance complaints and is a liaison between inmates and their families after release. She also runs victims' sensitivity programs, for example, helping families deal with the death of a member who died from a drug overdose.

From what she has seen and learned in her work, Shakeerah says succinctly, "Our society is a mess. With mandatory sentencing, kids under twenty-one are getting outrageous sentences. One in ten minority males will come in contact with the criminal justice system. No one personalizes a case. People don't understand the difference between this and other crimes." If there's a killing, "everyone gets a death sentence and is put into a box, locked down twenty-three hours a day, no contact. They literally have to earn the right to write letters and visit. We're warehousing people. People are afraid of crime, I know that. But this is not the way, not the answer."

Working with inmates is not for the naïve, as Shakeerah knows. "I believe in incarceration, but also rehabilitation. I see some crazy inmates. And some crimes are hard to deal with. I try to get to know them as a person first, and about the crime later. I've found some beautiful inmates, and some lunatics. I just had a real letdown with an inmate I had worked with. He's a sex offender, and a month after I went to the parole board on his behalf, I find out he's involved in all kinds of stuff. That hurt me," and she disclosed an additional reason why, "I'm a survivor of rape, when I was sixteen."

Because of that devastating teenage experience, Shakeerah says she has been "a control freak. I hold so much stuff inside me. Everybody thinks I'm fine." But she is facing a doomsday, with the clock running out on her husband's appeals. "I'm so fearful of losing him. The guys on death row are like my kids. And I work with the people who are going to kill them. Will I be able to look them in the eye?" she asks. She tries to mask her pain, but it comes through.

We cannot talk honestly about the "other victims" of criminal behavior unless we examine the issue of innocence. Most people in the criminal justice system scoff at the mention of innocence. How often I have heard police or corrections officers say, sarcastically, "Yeah, they're all innocent." I am not naïve, and I know that prisons house con-artists and people who don't know the difference between a lie and the truth. But when a person arrested or on trial claims innocence, it is also possible that the prosecutors, judges, and juries may not really know the difference between what is the truth, what is circumstantial evidence, and what constitutes a forced "confession." The emphasis is on getting a conviction, not finding the truth. Among those who claim innocence, many may be guilty of a crime, true, but not the deadly one they are accused of. When the sentence is death, the question of innocence must, absolutely must, be given every conceivable examination. "The U.S. guaranteed due process, not justice," says Lawrence Hayes.

In late April 2000 I got to meet Lawrence Hayes at the anti–death penalty conference in Binghamton, New York. This man spent twenty years in prison, two of these on death row. What kept him sane in this solitary place, where death hung over his head, was that he did a lot of reading and art work. As an aside, he told us of just one sadistic incident. "An officer gave me a sandwich with a dead mouse. I could hear his laughter." He got out of death row because of the activists who stirred consciences that had the death penalty declared unconstitutional in 1972.

Lawrence's story begins with the activism that sprouted in the Brownsville section of Brooklyn in the late 1960s, with blacks emerging to find their own power. He joined the Black Panthers in 1968 to set up a breakfast program for children, give them a basic education, and teach them martial arts. This program had come out of a study by the Brownsville Board of Education that determined black children in school were hungry and therefore unable to learn effectively; they wore dirty clothes and felt ashamed of this; and they had few role models to boost their self-image. "We went to colleges and got professors to speak to the children; we brought in African Americans in uniform. We wanted to find role models for the children," Lawrence said.

But things went wrong. By 1969, "a lot of kids in the city started to die of drugs." The Black Panther party offices were in shambles as the FBI sought to destroy this organization, along with Vietnam war resisters groups. "We were a ragtag bunch of guys with a cause. We thought we could end the drug problem."

Not only was Lawrence wrong, but, trying to help his nephew, he was caught in the middle of a drug deal that found "people shooting all over." When a man fell from a bullet in his forehead, in the ensuing chaos Lawrence stooped and picked up the gun. This was the beginning of his nightmare. The man who had fallen, killed, was a police officer. Lawrence was arrested two weeks later. He was beaten, made to sign a confession and to this day has "a problem trying to describe what happened. I was railroaded." He says he was never accused of possessing or firing a weapon in the incident, but an all-white jury, whose average age was fifty-five, convicted him of murder in 1971 and sentenced him to death.

Lawrence's sentence was commuted to twenty years to life in 1974, and he was released on parole in 1992. While serving that sentence, he earned a master's degree. Ironically, Lawrence reports that "the prosecutor in my case was later disbarred for taking bribes and the judge was cited by the *New York Times Magazine* as one of the state's ten worst because of his favoritism toward organized criminals." When he was released, Edward Hammock, former New York State Parole Board chairman, noted, "The release of Lawrence Hayes... is obviously long overdue.... Arbitrary and capricious conduct are not appropriate to state agencies with the enormous power that the Board and Division of Parole have over those under their supervision. Such conduct should not be repeated and should be resoundingly condemned."

After his release, Lawrence became active in his downstate New York community, doing counseling and job training with at-risk youth. He also is a founding member of the Campaign to End the Death Penalty, addressing gatherings at such prestigious places as Harvard and Columbia. He says, from his personal experience, "In the death house, I realized we live in a society that has great absence of value and respect for human life. I've made it my mission to use the death penalty as a way of getting society to think about how we really deal with life, to develop a greater appreciation for life."

In a conversation I had with Lawrence, I found his ordeal had not really ended. As he told me, "The death penalty came back to New York State in 1995. I had helped to organize an anti–death penalty organization. A New York newspaper did a story on the death penalty and quoted me." He had been out of prison for six and a half years when the parole board, on the ruse that he had not reported to his officer on the right date, sent him back to prison in August 1998. Lawrence believes they were angry at him for being quoted in the newspaper. "They violated me... gave me five years to life. I lost my apartment, my job, and a year and a half of being able to see my daughter Isis. They let me out on December 8, 1999, but only on the condition that I forfeit my right to sue them." In his case, he says, "the state will never exonerate me for this crime. They will never admit they made a mistake."

Sonia "Sunny" Jacobs of Los Angeles, California, is another victim of the death penalty craze. I met her, too, in Binghamton, and found her story so unbelievable that it should have been fiction, not memoir. On a day in 1976, Sunny was in a car with her common-law husband, Jesse Tafero, and her two children, a young son and a ten-month-old daughter. A friend of her husband was driving. They stopped at a rest area, and a police car pulled up. It turned out the friend was on parole, so the police checked the car. They said they saw a gun, ordered the two men out of the car, and told Sunny not to move. Suddenly there were shots. Sunny bent down, covering the children. When the firing stopped, the "friend" virtually took her hostage, making her and the children get into the police car and taking off, leaving two police officers behind, dead.

Soon apprehended, all three adults were charged with murder. The man who actually did the killing took a plea bargain, lied, and avoided a conviction that would have put him on death row. Sunny and her husband were left as the guilty ones. At age twenty-seven, this innocent mother was put on death row in Florida for murders she did not commit. She spent five years on death row, in solitary confinement, and the next twelve years in prison. Jesse Tafero was executed in 1990, before his innocence could be proven. "My husband was executed on a lie," she maintains.

The other victims in this tragic case were the children. They were left homeless, until grandparents were able to care for them. But then another tragedy struck when, five years later, the children lost their grandparents in a plane crash. "After that, I didn't get to see them any more," Sunny said. Just before her daughter's eighteenth birthday, in 1992, her daughter got into trouble and was sent to a school for troubled youth. "They told my daughter she had 'bad genes,'" Sunny said, pointing out yet another way people are victimized, by being stigmatized.

Sunny's story and innocence came to light when a childhood friend of hers wanted to make a film about incarcerated mothers. When the truth finally came to light, Sunny was exonerated and released in 1992, after seventeen years in a Florida prison for murders she did not commit. Now her children, who had been so angry that at first they did not want to reconcile with her, are living with her. She speaks regularly against the death penalty and works with young people to promote nonviolent conflict resolution. "My daughter came to one of my programs. She also talked, and everyone applauded."

Sunny and I were staying at the same motel in Binghamton, and I had the chance to ask her the main question on my mind: "How did you stay sane in solitary, especially knowing that you were innocent and that you could not care for your children?"

She answered that she did yoga, and credits this soulful practice for her survival and sanity during those solitary years. Now she is a certified yoga instructor and presents workshops across the country on "survival yoga," sharing the techniques she used to turn her solitary cell into a "sanctuary."

"They had taken enough of my life, and I was determined they'd take no more. To be bitter and angry would have given them more of my life," Sunny answered. "I was determined to recover and fill my life with love, not hatred, and to share this love with my children."

Sunny, like myself, is a member of Murder Victims Families for Reconciliation. She lends her voice to this organization: "Life has given me many challenges, which I choose to take as opportunities to learn and to grow. This is my choice. I learned this on death row. I chose life, health, forgiveness, and love. That choice saved me from bitterness and hatred that would have destroyed me from within. I have dedicated myself to an end to violence—in all its forms. This is the way I honor the lives that were sacrificed along the way. This is the way I give back to the universe. Love is the answer. Fear is the enemy. We must choose the world we want and work toward making it happen every day in our own lives."

What Sunny told me that day we spoke at the motel still rings in my heart. She had been talking of the pain she suffered for all that her children had to endure because of what had been done to her. And then she repeated, "I'm so grateful that I chose not to be bitter. The world you want—you have to create that for yourself. I have, and now I have something to give to others." As I left her, I wondered how many of us, trapped in the situation that imprisoned Sunny, would have moved on to the place of active peace she worked for and achieved in making her death row cell a "sanctuary."

The "other victims" of the criminal justice system who are so often overlooked are the children of inmates. The number of women prisoners has been increasing at a faster rate than that of men since 1981. Most women inmates are also mothers. Estimates put the number of their children at over 160,000. Scott Christianson's research shows: "Virtually all inmates, men and women alike, have families. Prison not only affects the individual who is locked up; it can also injure others, both immediately and over the long term. The incarceration of one single husband, wife, sister, brother, son, daughter, cousin, niece, or nephew exacts a heavy toll on a large circle of relatives; given its impact on the girls and boys among them, imprisonment is increasingly an intergenerational problem."

I have come to know April Grosso, who has had to live her life without a father in the house. Her father, Charlie, introduced me to her at Greenhaven prison at one of the annual Holy Name Society family picnic days, and we have stayed in touch. April is beautiful, with expressive blue-grey eyes. When she looks at her father, sometimes I note tears, but they are tears of joy that she is with him, that she can look at him. She was only four when her father, who had never been arrested and had no record at all, was taken away from their California home and brought to New York, charged with a double homicide that had happened about nine months earlier. He left two little children and a pregnant wife.

April's mother and relatives brought her as a child to visit her father, after he was convicted on the word of a jailhouse informant in exchange for a light sentence, the evidence being a half fingerprint found on a business card in a thrown-away wallet owned by one of the victims. I have read all the documents and the summation given by his lawyer, and I know why April claims her father is innocent.

For twenty years, April has been faithfully connected to her father, a relationship that has helped Charlie to stay strong, grounded, and close to God, knowing how important he is to the daughter he so dearly loves. It wasn't an easy choice to be linked with him when she was a child. She remembers being "kind of ashamed when I was younger. I would tell the kids in school that my dad was an artist in California. Then I got over this. I said the hell with it. I was just sad. My brother Charlie was angry. But I wasn't. I just wanted my father here, so I could walk with him. My younger brother, Ronnie, wanted his dad, too."

The family lived with hardships. It was difficult for her mother, Sarah, to be a single mom, with not enough resources to support the family. "I had to work at a young age. I wanted to get us out of this poverty. I felt I could be there to help my mother," said April, who took on a leadership role in the family. She credits her father for helping her with this. "My father always smartened me up." April's love comes through in her words: "What's most important to me is the relationship between a father and daughter. I always wanted to know my dad. My reality was that he was in prison. I have had to deal with this. It made me strong. If

I closed him out, I would be cheating myself. That would be the hardest thing of all. He depends on me. But who else does he have? As for what he needs, it's only love. I don't want people to know how much hurt I feel when I visit my father and have to watch him walk away. I worry about his safety, about his being alone and not able to hug me, about his being in there—as a number. That's when it hits me how two wrongs don't make a right. Who is this government to make a decision about how my father will spend his life?"

It was wrong for him to be convicted and it is wrong for him to be in prison, April maintains, as she continues to talk about the love she has for her father and the way they have been able to maintain a remarkable relationship in spite of these twenty years of separation. April smiled as she told me of the decision she made early on. "I would never let the criminal justice system come between me and my father."

We mustn't gloss over the fact that whenever a person is sentenced to a prison term or put on death row, we have new victims—their family members. All the proposals for "victims' rights" should fairly and honestly acknowledge that the Aunt Margies, the Barbara Lewises, the David Kaczynskis, the Shakira Hameens, the Lawrence Hayeses, the Sonny Jacobses, the April Grossos—and others like them—are victims who need compassion and understanding as much as do we who are survivors of murdered loved ones.

It struck me as I wrote about "the other victims" that there is one more I should remember. Mary, the mother of Jesus, had a son on death row, innocent, but condemned, and put to death by the state. I can't imagine what she went through as she stood at the foot of the cross and watched her beloved son die an agonizing death.

Chapter Nine

LEADERSHIP FROM
THE PULPIT

Above my computer I have a bulletin board with a newspaper article pinned on it dating back to Thursday, November 25, 1976, published in *The Evangelist,* the official publication of the Diocese of Albany, New York. The headline reads, " 'Prison Bishop' Condemns 'Hanging Judge' Mentality." The story is about Texas bishop Joseph A. Durick, who served as a chaplain at the Federal Correctional Institution in Segoville, Texas, near Dallas, and had become known as the "prison bishop."

The Supreme Court had just reinstated the death penalty as not contrary to the Constitution and this bishop was concerned. "I am deeply saddened when I see what appears to be a hanging judge mentality growing in our country. . . . I am . . . saddened when I read that the warden of the Utah State Prison has received numerous requests from individuals who wish to volunteer as members of the firing squad.

"Have we come no further than this in our quest for a more humane and compassionate society?" he asked. "Have we learned so few lessons from all the centuries when the state was used to strike out in vengeance and deal out death to those who have failed and upon whom we have turned in fear? Capital punishment is wrong and should be abolished."

Bishop Durick indicated we should learn from history. "Back in 1764, a wise and compassionate Christian lawyer in Italy, Cesare Bonesana Beccaria, made the first great plea to end capital punishment. Among other things he pointed out that ferocity of punishment breeds ferocity of character, even in the noncriminal public. This is as true today as it was in Beccaria's day."

Years earlier this admirable bishop issued a pastoral letter calling for sweeping changes in the nation's prisons, including the elimination of capital punishment, replacing big, isolated prisons with small regional prisons where inmates could be near their families, and even allowing conjugal visits for married prisoners.

This bishop wasn't the only one speaking out against the death penalty at the time. Many of the nation's churches and religious organizations of all denominations were becoming outspoken advocates of abolition. Since then, the strongest voices emerging against the death penalty are coming from the religious arena, including mainline churches. Among these are Roman Catholic, Baptist, Episcopal, Evangelical Lutheran, Presbyterian, Unitarian, and Methodist, joining many other communities, such as the American Friends Service Committee, the Bruderhof Communities, the Mennonite Church, the Orthodox Church in America, the Rabbinical Assembly, and some twenty other high-profile faith groups.

Polls continue to show that about two-thirds of Americans say they are for the death penalty, though this percentage drops slightly if there is the alternative of life in prison without parole. Many, if not most, of these Americans would admit to being affiliated with one of the religious bodies opposed to the death penalty, either in name only, or in the past, or actively in the present. One has to wonder why so many still hold to capital punishment.

The Philadelphia-based American Friends Service Committee's criminal justice program has long reached out to official religious bodies to develop strategies and promote anti–death penalty activism within each faith tradition. The program launched the Religious Organizing Against the Death Penalty Project, coordinated by Pat Clark, "to galvanize and empower the religious community in the United States to work against capital punishment." The project, seeking "to build a powerful coalition of faith-based activists," in Pat Clark's words, since 1980 has sought out statements by different religious groups and published them in a booklet. The latest, thirty-two pages of extraordinary testimonies affirming life, lists thirty-two faith groups, with information on how to contact each one.

Pat's determination to arouse people of faith to seek an end to the death penalty is rooted in her own experience. "I had an uncle and a first cousin murdered, six months apart, when I was very young. My grandmother's response was that only God could make this situation right. She was a strong, quiet, deeply religious black matriarch. Her faith and ultimate belief in people was memorably displayed when the son of the woman who killed my uncle came to her house to play with my cousins. To the shock and horror of other family members, my grandmother welcomed him in. Her loving example helped lay the foundation of my opposition to capital punishment.

"But I was young and at the time didn't internalize what that meant," Pat said. It was later, after working with the Southern Poverty Law Center, that she became involved with the Alabama Prison Project and came face-to-face with what death by execution looked like. She also saw "the pain of the inmate's families, who were not allowed to be victims." Now believing executions to be morally wrong and remembering her grandmother's turning to God, she began to work to challenge religions to focus on the immorality of these killings and work to end them.

What she found was that, while most denominations were anti–death penalty, people in the pews didn't know that. They weren't hearing sermons or homilies on this issue. "The flocks were not informed," said Pat. "I spoke in Kentucky, to a Disciples of Christ church. The people didn't know the position of their church. Afterward, many came to me to say my talk had been enlightening and that they had never thought of the death penalty as a moral issue," said Pat.

The Religious Organizing Against the Death Penalty Project now has working with them Sister Helen Prejean, author of *Dead Man Walking,* who has become a national leader in the campaign to end the death penalty. "And there's been tremendous activity in the Catholic Church, in the statements of the pope and those of the Catholic bishops. We're working on Moratorium 2000, getting people to sign petitions asking for states to put a moratorium on executions. We're getting most signatures from religious groups," Pat pointed out.

If I could have a wish come true, it would be that everyone in the country read the booklet coordinated by Pat Clark and titled *The Death Penalty: The Religious Community Calls for Abolition.* As a taste of the faith-based declarations, consider this, by the Evangelical Lutheran Church in America: "The human community is saddened by violence, and angered by the injustice involved. We want to hold accountable those who violate life, who violate society. Our sadness and anger, however, make us vulnerable to feelings of revenge. Our frustration with the complex problems contributing to violence may make us long for simple solutions....

"It is because of this church's ministry with and to people affected by violent crime that we oppose the death penalty.... Executions focus on the convicted murderer, providing very little for the victim's family or anyone else whose life has been touched by the crime. Capital punishment focuses on retribution, sometimes reflecting a spirit of vengeance.

Executions do not restore a broken society and can actually work counter to restoration....

"Executions harm society by mirroring and reinforcing existing injustice. The death penalty distracts us from our work toward a just society.... It perpetuates cycles of violence.

"It is because of this church's commitment to justice that we oppose the death penalty. Lutheran Christians have called for an assault on the root causes of violent crime, an assault for which executions are no substitute.... "

The statement by the Union of American Hebrew Congregations begins strongly: "We believe it is the task of the Jew to bring our great spiritual and ethical heritage to bear upon the moral problems of contemporary society." There is no leaning on Old Testament quotes here to justify capital punishment. On the contrary: "One such problem which challenges all who seek to apply God's will in the affairs of men is the practice of capital punishment. We believe that in the light of modern scientific knowledge and concept of humanity, the resort to or continuation of capital punishment either by a state or by the national government is no longer morally justified.

"We believe there is no crime for which the taking of human life by society is justified, and that it is the obligation of society to evolve other methods in dealing with crime. We pledge ourselves to join with like-minded Americans in trying to prevent crime by removal of its causes, and to foster modern methods of rehabilitation of the wrongdoer in the spirit of the Jewish tradition of tshuva (repentance)."

A statement by the United States Catholic Conference, pointing out that the use of the death penalty crosses the broad lines of moral and religious questions and political and legal issues, indicates the strong and longstanding anti–death penalty position taken by the Catholic Church: "In 1974, out of a commitment to the value and dignity of human life, the Catholic Bishops of the United States declared their opposition to capital punishment. We continue to support this position in the belief that a return to the use of the death penalty can only lead to the further erosion of respect for life in our society.

"Violent crime in our society is a serious matter which should not be ignored.... Past history, however, shows that the death penalty in its application has been discriminating with respect to the disadvantaged, the indigent and the socially impoverished....

"The critical question for the Christian is how can we best foster respect for life, preserve the dignity of the human person, and manifest the redemptive message of Christ. We do not believe that more deaths are the response to the question. We therefore have to seek methods of dealing with violent crime which are more consistent with the Gospel's vision of respect for life and Christ's message of God's healing love. In the sight of God, correction of the offender has taken preference over punishment, for the Lord came to save and not condemn."

The teaching is clear, from the pope, our bishops, and leaders of most of the churches and religious bodies in our country that "we must turn away from the culture of death," as Brooklyn's Bishop Thomas Daily says, repeating the plea of the pope, in a video put out by the Sanctity of Life Commission of his diocese.

I had the privilege of being interviewed for this eighteen-minute video in the fall of 1999. I had gotten a call from Frank DeRosa, who has long worked for New York's Brooklyn Diocese, to come to participate in making a video that would look at why Catholics should be opposed to the death penalty. Frank told me that the video would feature me and two other Catholic parents who, like myself, are parents of murder victims and who oppose the death penalty for the killers of our children. Bishop Daily would introduce the program, which would include an interview with Kevin Doyle, a lawyer who is the director of New York State's Capital Defender Office and has defended many capital cases. The video would be made available to any and all, from coast to coast, who requested a copy.

While I didn't get to meet the other parents, Camille Bodden and Bud Welch, in person, when I saw the tape, titled *Mercy and Justice: The Morality of the Death Penalty,* I knew we were linked by our faith. We echoed each other. "It's not in our hands to take a life. God is in control of life and death," said Camille, whose son Andrew, getting out of his car, was shot in the back of his head. Bud Welch, whose daughter Julie was killed in the infamous Oklahoma bombing, said, "I simply don't believe that Jesus would pull the switch." And I emphasized that followers of Christ must remember that the "biggest message in Christ's life was forgiveness." Kevin Doyle expressed his fear that "the death penalty currently represents something of a social hygiene approach," meaning we tell ourselves that this is a way to "clean" our society of crime, a delusion which justifies not doing what we should be doing—dealing with the root causes of crime.

I've been told by people who have seen the tape that it is especially powerful because of the credibility of the three of us who are parents of murdered children. We aren't talking from a theology textbook, but from what we have learned in our hearts. Even Catholics who disagree with us find themselves thinking about what we say. I know that from experience.

Brooklyn isn't the only diocese that has put out an educational tool on the death penalty. The bishops of Indiana, through the Indiana Catholic Conference, have also produced a video, a ten-minute film titled *Talking about the Death Penalty*, available to all Indiana parishes. It was released just before July 9, 2000, Jubilee Day for Prisoners. The tape is needed, according to Bishop William L. Higi of the Diocese of Lafayette, because "church teaching on this life issue is not widely understood, much less widely accepted."

If every diocese, and every Christian church, in the country began a strong effort to educate members on why the death penalty is incompatible with being a follower of Christ, I believe this could have a powerfully positive effect in "presenting capital punishment for what it is: the taking of human life," as Bishop Higi expressed it.

After making the Brooklyn Diocese video, I felt even more strongly that it was up to each one of us, believers in life, to become activists for abolition of the death penalty, not as lone voices, but in community. I started to hear of more people who were willing to go the distance in working for forgiveness and reconciliation to overcome the killing mentality, and none who inspired me more than Bud Welch.

I had expected to meet Bud about six months before Frank de Rosa called me about the Brooklyn video. Both of us had been asked to speak at a two-day May rally against capital punishment organized by the Bruderhof community in Rifton, New York. I had been associated with the members of this unusual Christian community for about a dozen years, when, as editor of a newspaper in Connecticut, I heard about them and wrote feature stories on their way of life, their principles and values, and their work. Comprised of families and single men and women who share all things in common and strive in their daily lives to practice Christ's teachings as he gave them to us in the Sermon on the Mount, I had tremendous admiration for them. When they spoke of their desire to be connected with others who could share their hopes for justice, peace, and love in today's world, I became an immediate friend.

From the beginning of our connection, we talked about the injustice of the death penalty. Among their many reasons for calling for the abolition of executions in the entire world, they have stated: "We oppose the death penalty in all cases, out of reverence for human life and for God, the Creator of life.... We yield to God alone the power over death and life.... Christ was sent ... to bring a new dimension to human life, the possibility of reconciliation with God through repentance.... The death penalty, however, denies Christ's power to transform and restore even the most depraved human being.... While there is no proof that the death penalty deters crime (contrary to the claims of some proponents) it does brutalize our society and creates an atmosphere in which crime flourishes."

The May 1999 rally at the Bruderhof in Rifton was a two-day educational event, covering every aspect of executions, including a chilling photo display of juveniles on death row. It ended with a call for mobilizing people from coast to coast to work for abolition, "the next step," as the motto went.

There was a long list of speakers, and it turned out that Bud Welch and I spoke on different days, so I never got to meet him then, nor in making the video in Brooklyn. I finally got to meet him about five months after that. We were both speakers at the New York statewide anti–death penalty conference in Binghamton. It was instant friendship.

Bud told how he led a quiet, unassuming life running a gasoline service station in Oklahoma until April 19, 1995. That was the infamous day when the nation reeled from the news that the Oklahoma City Federal Building had been destroyed by a bomb. When the final tally of the dead was done, we learned that 168 people had been killed in the blast. One of them was Bud Welch's daughter Julie Marie.

"Temporary insanity is real, it exists, I can assure you. I've lived it," Bud said, referring to the rage that consumed him for nine months after burying Julie. But then he began to look inward and found a new question. If they convict the accused bomber, Timothy McVeigh, and execute him, "how is that going to help me?" It wouldn't bring Julie back, "I realized that it's all about revenge and hate. And revenge and hate is why Julie and 167 others are dead today."

Bud said his change of heart was also inspired by Julie herself, recalling her words to him after listening to a radio report of an execution in Texas. "Dad, that makes me sick. All those Texans are doing is teaching all the children down there to hate. The murderer did wrong, but now the government has stooped to his level."

From that day on, Bud Welch said, he has worked to end the death penalty, traveling the country, speaking to legislatures and groups. But even more admirable is his outreach to another hurting man, to Bill McVeigh, the father of the convicted Oklahoma City bomber. Bud saw him working on his flower bed on television and felt immediate empathy.

The pain in this father's eyes was the same as his. Then he did something incredible. He visited Bill McVeigh at his home. He soon recognized how deeply Bill McVeigh loves his son, "because we, as parents, have a way of loving our children more the more they need us," Bud says.

After that visit, Bud said he went home and sobbed. "But I have never felt closer to God in my life than I did at that moment." Reconciliation was for him the greatest balm. That's what he shares with all who listen to him.

What a contrast between Bud's action and those of others, as noted by the Most Rev. Charles J. Chaput, archbishop of Denver, who wrote on June 6, 1997: "On the heels of the Timothy McVeigh verdict, a local radio station set up a kind of drive-by jury near Denver's federal court house. The idea, literally, was to honk if you wanted to execute (or 'fry') the killer. By the end of Wednesday, June 4, more than 24,000 Coloradans had done so.

"Let's overlook for a moment the circus-like indignity this brought to a moment of almost unbearable remembering for those who lost family and friends in the Oklahoma City bombing. Instead, let's acknowledge a fact: a large majority of Americans support the death penalty. And so do most Catholics. Decent people are understandably tired of the violence in society. They need to defend their children and themselves. They want a deterrent. And even when the deterrent might fail, goes the reasoning, at least it can bring justice and emotional closure for the relatives of murder victims.

"These are powerful arguments, especially today, as we grapple with vivid and terrible memories of the bombing. But they are wrong. . . . What the death penalty does accomplish is closure through blood-letting, violence against violence—which is not really closure at all, because murder will continue as long as humans sin, and capital punishment can never, by its nature, strike at murder's roots. Only love can do that.

"I am aware, as I write these words, that the reality of capital crime is heart-breaking beyond words. I do not presume to understand the deep and bitter personal wounds suffered by those who lose their loved ones through murder. I would gladly give away whatever I have in life to bring back just one of the children lost in the Oklahoma City bombing. As a people we must never allow ourselves the luxury of forgetting the injustice done to victims of murder and terrorism who cannot speak for themselves—or our obligation to bring the guilty to full accounting.

"But as Jesus showed again and again by His words and in His actions, the only true road to justice passes through mercy. Justice cannot be served by more violence. 'Frying the killer' may sound funny to some, righteous to others. But make no mistake: Capital punishment is just another drug we take to ease other, much deeper anxieties about the direction of our culture. Executions may take away some of the symptoms for a time (symptoms who have names and their own stories before God), but the underlying illness—today's contempt for human life—remains and grows worse."

Although we have seen much activism in the churches against abortion, fighting against the contempt for human life—"the culture of death," to use the phrase popularized by the pope—too often has stopped with that one issue, ignoring assisted suicide and the death penalty issues. Stephen Russo, who belongs to the fifteen-member Respect Life Committee of Our Lady of the Lakes parish in New Milford, Connecticut, has been trying to get people to understand that to be "pro-life," one must be opposed to capital punishment. "I've been trying to put this into focus," he told me, "but it's an issue people don't want to deal with. We have a Respect Life bulletin board. I've put clips about the death penalty on it, but have gotten no response at all. I believe the correlation between abortion and the death penalty has been overlooked because abortion is perceived as the taking of innocent life, and capital punishment as the taking of guilty life. But," he went on, quoting a Catholic paper, "the moral underpinning of both positions is identical: human life, as a gift from God, is sacred—the direct taking of life is immoral."

Pointing out that he has continued support from his pastor, Father Tom Ptaszynski, Stephen told about an unusual project a few of them in the parish had come up with. The parish had had a billboard made by professionals to protest abortion. They decided to temporarily change the message, headlining it "U.S. Capital Punishment," showing that we average two executions a week in the U.S. and pointing out that for every seven persons executed in the past twenty-five years, one on death row has been proven innocent. This was the first time the billboard was used other than for abortion, but, from the lack of vocal response, it apparently went practically unnoticed, Stephen said. "The first weekend it was up, a woman stopped and took pictures. She said she was from California and she wanted to bring the pictures back to show her parish." He was happy that the billboard had at least caught some attention.

I congratulated Stephen and encouraged him to keep trying to get parishes to wake up and recognize that now is the time for them to speak up against the death penalty because with the new attention being focused nationally and internationally on our nation's dependence on death to punish people who murder, this is the time that, together, we can make a difference. Yet, I know this can be discouraging work, and I shared a story of a parish with him.

In July 1999, I received a letter from Father James Fanelli, pastor of St. Christopher Church in East Hartford, Connecticut. First he expressed deep sympathy that I had lost a son and daughter-in-law to murder, and then he went on: "With the approach of possible executions in Connecticut, the death penalty is receiving more publicity and discussion. This adds to the need to help people understand and evaluate the issue from a Christian perspective. The need for that help is felt very strongly in our parish because two young men of our church were murdered a year ago at a party in Glastonbury. The whole parish shared in the families' grief and shock.

"As one who experienced that shock and grief, your views carry much weight with others. The fact that you also oppose the death penalty is a powerful witness. Would you be willing to speak to our parishioners at an open meeting some time in August or the Fall? I plan to preach on the topic of capital punishment on July 18. We plan to have a showing of the film *Dead Man Walking* in August. Printed material will be distributed in church at the August film session.

"Do you think this is a good sequence and would you be able to be with us? I look forward to hearing from you."

This was the first time I had received an invitation from a parish to speak specifically on the death penalty, and I was impressed, especially because the talk would be part of a larger teaching "sequence" he had planned to stir awareness on the issue. I also wondered how Father Fanelli had heard of me. When I called, he told me. I had been on a half-hour radio interview, taped for a Hartford station, on the death penalty with three other members of Survivors of Homicide. They were all for the death penalty; I was the lone voice against it. I was told the program would run at six in the morning, and I asked the interviewer, laughing, who listens at that hour? I don't know how many others did, but Father Fanelli was one.

As we talked, I sensed Father Fanelli's concern and honesty on this issue and his sense of responsibility to get the word out to his parishioners that it was important to listen to what the pope and the American bishops, especially in their 1999 "Good Friday Appeal to End the Death Penalty," were urging us Catholics to understand and accept. He sent me a copy of the Sunday talk he gave on July 18. Again I admired him for his truthfulness and openness: "I have to tell you that I myself long accepted the death penalty as a right thing for governments to be able to do," he wrote. "It was a position approved by the church and I thought the reasons for it were good ones. But now we know much more about the death penalty and the circumstances in which it is imposed. And now, our church, yours and mine, is asking all of us to look at this issue in a different light."

Father Fanelli did a lot to try to generate interest in this issue among his parishioners. But when I arrived to talk at his parish in late September, the turnout was a discouraging handful of under fifteen adults. This pastor had also arranged to have the Confirmation class, about forty teenagers, present, and the evening turned out to be a moving one for me, as I reflected on and answered the thoughtful questions raised by these young Christians. Later, Father Fanelli dropped me a line to say that in talking afterward to these teenagers about my message, he could say "they learned a lot and had much to think about." His letter got me thinking about the importance of bringing young people into the death penalty debate. They are, after all, the ones who will really make a difference in the future.

My experience at St. Chrisopher's, along with what Pat Clark and Stephen Russo had told me, was an eye-opener about the hard work that lies ahead if we are to get the people in the pews of the many churches to care enough to get involved with the death penalty issue. At the Binghamton conference, one of the sessions was titled "From the Pulpit, to the Pew, to the Pavement," precisely to look at how much of the statements by religious groups condemning the death penalty have actually filtered down to individuals. The twenty or so of us in the room all concurred that little was being done "to get the message out." The question was asked, "What do we need to do to convert the membership? How do we build a groundswell of awareness?"

Co-leading the group was Rev. Thomas Costello, auxiliary bishop of the Syracuse, New York, diocese. He acknowledged his frustration that with all the teaching against the death penalty coming out under church auspices, not much has been achieved from the pulpit. "People have to interact. We've got to work with smaller groups of people than we're confronted with on a Sunday morning" when it comes to changing hearts and minds on this issue, he said. But then he told us he had "a model" plan for what a parish could do, referring to St. Andrew's in Syracuse, a two-hundred-family parish, with a part-time priest, and calling the members "a unique group of people." Later, Bishop Costello put me in touch with Bill Cuddy, a parishioner, who has long worked in jail ministry and is outspoken against the death penalty. From these two fine men, I learned how, in twenty months, a parish went from forming a committee made up of people for, against, and unsure of their position on the death penalty to actually crafting a plea for a federal and state moratorium on executions, signed by St. Andrew's and sent to New York State's Governor George Pataki, to state legislators, to human rights groups, to Equal Justice USA, which sponsors the national "Moratorium Now" campaign, and to newspapers.

The effort began when Bill Cuddy asked the Parish Council if they would agree to making a one-year commitment to educate parishioners on the death penalty, by means of adult education programs and prayers. "They committed," he said, and "we formed a committee of about a dozen to take responsibility." Acting quickly, the committee initiated a series of events, the first being a talk by Bud Welch, a staunch opponent of the death penalty.

This was followed with a talk by Kathy Dillon, who lives near Syracuse, and a panel discussion with Bishop Costello and U.S. Attorney John Duncan, who, while not personally pushing for the death penalty, "could see it. He was the strongest voice we had in favor of it," said Bill.

Most of the attention that night centered on Kathy, who told them how in 1974, when she was fourteen, her father, Emerson J. Dillon, a New York state trooper, was shot and killed in the line of duty on the New York State Thruway after he pulled over a car whose occupants had been involved in a robbery. The shooters sped away, but were later caught and charged with first degree murder. Ten years later, her boyfriend, David Paul, was also shot and killed and left on a roadside.

Kathy, asking herself, "What am I to learn from these two murders?" came to believe the answer is "forgiveness." She believes that the death penalty, with its outright violence, only undermines the efforts of those seeking a more peaceful world. "She touched a lot of hearts," Bill said. And Bishop Costello concurred: "Storytelling sends a message that can't be sent in any other way."

The next offerings at St. Andrew's were open forums, so that all people could have a chance to be heard. A man in favor of the death penalty gave a talk and some were strongly in agreement with him. "A number of other things surfaced, like a man in the parish telling us that his brother had been killed by someone who was never convicted, pleading self-defense. He had never dealt with his feelings or his own healing process," Bill said. In one session, they brought in Stewart Hancock, a former New York State Supreme Court Justice, who spoke about the death penalty as being inconsistent with the New York state constitution. "He gave us good data and statistics," Bill said.

Keeping up the momentum, the committee then offered a movie night, where they showed *Dead Man Walking*, Sister Helen Prejean's story of her association as a spiritual counselor with a killer on death row, following their relationship up to the time when he was executed. The book and film, which starred Susan Sarandon, has brought so much attention to Sister Helen's anti-execution position that she has become a leading spokesperson in the country for abolition. After the movie, St. Andrew's parish, characterized by Bill Cuddy as having "some very strong peace and justice advocates," engaged in a lively dialogue on the pros and cons of the death penalty.

Prayer, reflecting the mercy of God, was an important part of this parish project to become educated on the death penalty. The parishioners agreed to pray monthly by name for someone facing execution, and for the families of the victims.

When this much work had been done, the committee "tried to draft a resolution that the Parish Council would unanimously agree to," said Bishop Costello. They brainstormed and came up with a consensus to write a strong statement that would be St. Andrew's parish plea for a moratorium on the death penalty. "They made some changes at the Parish Council's suggestion and then presented it to the entire parish. And wonder of wonders, it was adopted unanimously," said Bishop Costello.

What was done at St. Andrew's to raise the consciousness of parishioners on the death penalty issue "is the most successful effort that I am aware of," said Bishop Costello, who believes their six-step process could be a model for other parishes to follow.

When it comes to the anti-execution work done under the auspices of religious groups and people, no one has inspired me more than Sister Camille D'Arienzo, president of the Brooklyn Regional Community of the Sisters of Mercy of the Americas. Shortly after I pledged to work against the death penalty, I heard about the "Declaration of Life," a document stating that if the signer were to be murdered, he or she would not want the killer to be put to death for this crime, because "I believe it is morally wrong for my death to be the reason for the killing of another human being." The document was available through the Cherish Life Circle, a group founded by Sister Camille D'Arienzo in 1994 when it became clear that George Pataki, who campaigned calling for capital punishment, would be elected governor of New York State. In a conversation, she told me that she and about twelve others—sisters of Mercy, St. Joseph, St. Dominic, priests, and lay people—wanted to do something to balance this pro–death position, "agreeing to preach, write, work with anybody, whenever invited, if we can possibly do it."

Diane Shea, a member of the Circle, had heard of the Declaration of Life, being circulated by the national group Catholics Against Capital Punishment. "She came up with the idea that this could be a good teaching tool. It is a dramatic statement, devised by Vic Hummert, a former Maryknoll priest. It is to be signed and notarized and given to prosecutors and the judge after a suspect is convicted of murdering the person who signed it," Sister explained, adding that "thousands have been signed."

Concerned also about family members of murder victims, the Cherish Life Circle offers ecumenical services where they can come together in an atmosphere of faith. "There is no mention of the death penalty. These gatherings are done in an atmosphere of faith to be an evening of compassion, with no talk of violence."

Sister Camille is soft-spoken but direct when she says her position is not an indictment of those who support the death penalty—which include some members of her own family. Nevertheless, she wants to be respected for "my perception of the truth," which is "to do only what Christ asks." She admits that when people she loves are angry with her for her position, that's hard to take. What causes her great pain is "anything that separates me from others."

Most of us need an "eye-opener" before we look at an issue from the heart, and that happened to Sister Camille when she had been going through her community's archives. There she found an item about "Prisoner Greenwall," a convicted murderer in a Brooklyn jail, visited by members of her order in the early 1860s. He insisted he was innocent but went to the gallows in spite of his pleas. Later, the real murderer confessed to the crime. The story touched Sister Camille, who then determined to work "on a larger scale" to seek an end to the death penalty.

In the years since, besides forming the Cherish Life Circle and disseminating the Declaration of Life document, she has written extensively on this issue, led retreats on forgiveness, written to governors pleading clemency for people about to be executed and become spiritual adviser to men on death row. She has also brought Sister Helen Prejean to Brooklyn, introducing her, and her message, to adults and high school students. Sister Helen and Susan Sarandon, who portrayed her in *Dead Man Walking*, have both signed the Declaration of Life.

Sister Camille, who is president of her congregation and involved with the Leadership Conference of Women Religious, admits she is on overload and "torn in a thousand ways." Yet, "As a follower of Jesus, I don't expect wrestling with life and death questions is going to be easy. I never thought I'd be involved like this. I've learned so much more than I ever wanted to know about prison. But sin..." she hesitated, "took on a human face. And now I can never go away."

As the months went by in the new millennium it had become clear that the pro–death penalty climate was changing, with much credit due to the leadership of religious denominations and groups. Catholic bishops were among those calling for an end to executions or at least the adoption of a state-by-state moratorium to study a punishment system that many have called "fatally flawed." A group of about one thousand New York State religious leaders, led by Bishop Howard Hubbard of Albany, prepared petitions calling for a one-year moratorium "to allow for prayerful reflection and debate" and presented these to Governor George Pataki, a Catholic and outspoken supporter of the death penalty. In California, which has 565 inmates on death row, the most in the nation, Cardinal Roger Mahoney, head of the Archdiocese of Los Angeles, urged Governor Gary Davis, also a Catholic and an ardent supporter of capital punishment, to declare a moratorium and appoint a bipartisan committee to do a "comprehensive and objective study." He believes this "will provide substantial factual data to support moral and ethical questions raised by the Catholic bishops of California and the United States regarding the death penalty."

The Joliet Diocese of Illinois, headed by Bishop Joseph L. Imesh, has taken on the death penalty as "the social justice issue" of our time. Cardinal Francis George of Chicago, with leading clergy throughout Illinois, has signed a decree opposing the death penalty. Bishop Joseph A. Fiorenza, as president of the National Conference of Catholic Bishops, took on as a major focus the sharing of the church's teaching on the sacredness of all life, including the life of murderers, quoting Pope John Paul II, who said in his 1995 encyclical, "The Gospel of Life," that "Not even a murderer loses his personal dignity." Bishop Fiorenza, in a message appropriate for all Right-to-Life groups, reached out to the Knights of Columbus, asking them to battle the death penalty with the same vigor and commitment they had in battling abortion. Pax Christi, the Catholic peace organization, put out a statement confirming its "unconditional opposition" to capital punishment, based on "the Gospel of Jesus Christ and in the consistent ethic of life which teaches that all life is sacred from the moment it begins until its natural death." In agreement that all life is sacred, the National Council of Synagogues and the Committee on Ecumenical and Interreligious Affairs of the National Conference of Catholic Bishops issued a joint statement they titled, "To End the Death Penalty."

The circle being formed by religious groups—finding shared beliefs when it comes to the sanctity of human life, the futility of vengeance and anger, and the error of believing that we have a right to take away what is God-given—grows wider and wider as more voices are being raised to encourage dialogue in the extensive interfaith religious traditions and organizations about the death penalty. In all their teachings and writings, they have not forgotten, but yearn to heal, the victim-survivors.

Rabbi Alan Lew, of the Congregation Beth Shalom in San Francisco, certainly gave me, and hopefully others, a truth to reflect on: "Capital punishment is an absolutely crazy idea. It's a spiritual impossibility and a cruel hoax that is sold to the families of victims. They are so vulnerable, the easiest thing to sell them is anger. It's the biggest disservice we can do to them. It guarantees them a life of pain. The only possible healing comes through forgiveness. The hard choice is the only one that works."

Chapter Ten

CONCERN ABOUT
THE DEATH PENALTY GROWS

Two weeks before the dawn of the new millennium, Pope John Paul II spoke to pilgrims from his study window overlooking St. Peter's Square and praised a project based at Rome's ancient amphitheater to be known as "The Colosseum Illuminates Life." He said this place, where Christians were thrown to the lions and gladiators fought to the death, would now become a symbol of life for opponents of capital punishment worldwide. This was the plan: every time a death sentence was commuted or overturned and if the death penalty was abolished anywhere, in any country of the world, the amphitheater would be illuminated for forty-eight hours.

The first ceremony marked the announcement by Albania that it would end capital punishment. This news was received with great joy and forty spotlights placed within the Colosseum "cast a golden glow into the nighttime sky." The pope repeated that the year 2000, which he proclaimed a Holy Year, would be the perfect occasion "to promote throughout the world more mature forms of respect for life and the dignity of every person....I therefore renew my appeal to all leaders to reach an international consensus on the abolition of the death penalty."

Opposition against capital punishment is especially strong among Europeans, who have vocally termed the American attachment to the death penalty "appalling." Henry Leclerc, president of the Human Rights League in Paris, has been quoted to say, "For us, what the Americans are doing is completely incomprehensible, that such an advanced country can be involved in such an act of barbarism. No European country does this. No advanced country does this. America is doing it along with countries like China and Russia and other countries that have terrible human rights records. To us, it looks the same as if the Americans were endorsing torture or slavery."

In Italy, sentiment is running so strongly against this deadly punishment that one Catholic lay group, San Egidio, reported in spring 2000 that it had collected more than two million signatures from people in 128 countries asking for a worldwide moratorium on capital punishment. Mario Marraziti, a San Egidio spokesman, was quoted to say, "Each one of these signatures is a conscience won over by the value of life."

In 1997, the United Nations Human Rights Commission, upholding Article 3 of the UN Universal Declaration of Human Rights, adopted on December 10, 1948, and stating that everyone shall have a right to life, called on all countries to suspend executions. The members passed its first resolution condemning capital punishment that same year. The United States was the only Western nation voting against that resolution. Then, in 1999, the commission called for a worldwide moratorium on capital punishment. Forty countries carried out executions that year, with the United States linked to China, Iran, and Saudi Arabia when it came to sheer numbers. These four countries alone accounted for 85 percent of the executions.

Concern about the death penalty is growing in our country and worldwide for a smorgasbord of reasons, all with the common denominator that this extreme punishment is blatantly anti–human rights. Many of the reasons cited for justifying the death penalty have been documented and shown to be immoral and discriminatory by watchful groups. A notable one is Amnesty International, a nonpartisan human rights organization with members in over 150 countries, which works for the release of prisoners of conscience and for the end to all use of torture and the death penalty.

Amnesty underscores the human rights violation of capital punishment: "Questions about the death penalty are essentially questions about whether a state has the right to utterly destroy the life of someone it holds captive, to engage in the extermination of selected prisoners.... Because the death penalty is a uniquely irrevocable punishment, it demands perfection of the legal system which imposes it ... [but] even the most extensive safeguards against miscarriages of justice cannot produce an infallible legal system."

Causing a growing concern among Americans is the question of innocence. Research shows an average of four entirely innocent people were convicted of murder each year since 1900; twenty-three of these innocent people were executed. These, of course, are only the well-documented cases of wrongful conviction. Amnesty maintains, "False testimony, mistaken identification, misinterpretation of evidence, and community prejudices and pressures may affect both verdicts and sentencing. An attorney's error of judgment, a prosecutor's misconduct, or delayed access to evidence may also result in the execution of an innocent person."

I first read about the execution of those twenty-three innocent prisoners back in 1985, when the American Civil Liberties Union circulated the study which had uncovered that sobering statistic. The study had been undertaken in the hope of rebutting assertions that the problem of wrongful executions was only theoretical. Most disturbing was a comment by Ernest van den Haag, a professor of jurisprudence and public policy at Fordham University, reported in the *New York Times*. A supporter of the death penalty, he focused on the "infrequency of improper executions over 85 years," saying this buttressed the case for capital punishment, adding that twenty-three wrongful convictions were "a very acceptable number."

I have heard several supporters of the death penalty tell me that the death penalty is too important to stop, and if a few innocent people get killed by mistake, well, that's a small price to pay for maintaining something as needed as executions. Charles Wilson, who works at the Center for Astrophysics in Cambridge, Massachusetts, has written about why some claim it is unreasonable to halt executions because of the possibility of mistakes. They say, "All human endeavors involve taking risks. We do not contemplate the abolition of motor vehicles because of accidental traffic fatalities, even large numbers of them. In the same way, they say, we should not abandon an important part of our criminal justice system because of the possibility of unjust executions.... Yet, it boggles the mind what perverse sort of justice requires that the state be willing to sacrifice innocent victims in order to protect innocent victims."

I wonder if these death penalty proponents would still hold that it's worth some risk of error if it were their loved one who was murdered by the state, though innocent. I would hope that we could rely on our citizens' sense of justice and fairness to raise a public outcry against killing convicted criminals when there is even a grain of doubt about their guilt.

A most important study was released in June 2000 that forced us to take another deep look at the judicial process that deals with the life and death of persons convicted of a capital crime. Conducted by

James S. Liebman and a team of lawyers and criminologists at Columbia University, the study examined appeals in all death penalty cases from 1973 to 1995. What they discovered was disturbing. Nearly 70 percent of murder convictions that would bring the condemned person to death row were overturned on appeal. This study points out the flaws in the legal processes that convict and sentence a person accused of a capital crime. It shows the rate of error is extensive. This study gives clout to the American Bar Association, which in 1997 asked for a moratorium on the death penalty until the judicial process, which is "seriously flawed," is overhauled.

Another concern being voiced focuses on the arbitrariness of the death sentence, which is applied neither fairly nor consistently, according to the Amnesty research. "Race, social and economic status, location of crime and pure chance may be the deciding factors which send some defendants to prison, others to death.... Several thousand defendants are convicted of murder each year, and less than one percent of them receive death sentences.... Prosecutors seek the death penalty far more frequently when the victim is white than when the victim is black." Statistics bear this out. In New York, as one example, since late 1995, a death sentence was sought 18 percent of the time when the victim was white, but only 6 percent of the time when the victim was black. Indeed, evidence for the claim that the death penalty is racist is found in the statistics which show that blacks and Latinos constitute more than half the death row prisoners although they constitute only 18 percent of the U.S. population.

Those who opt for justice find a serious flaw in a commonplace practice in which states assign inexperienced counsel with inadequate resources for proper defense to any prisoners who cannot pay legal fees. Stories have been documented in which such defense lawyers have been ill prepared, do not call important witnesses, and even fall asleep during trial. Amnesty reports, "The court-appointed lawyer for Robert Wayne Williams, electrocuted in Louisiana in 1983, spent only eight hours preparing his case. A warden of San Quentin Prison in California has described the death penalty as a 'privilege of the poor.'"

People are starting to question whether the premeditated killing of convicted murderers is cruel and unusual punishment, in spite of the fact that more states are turning to the lethal injection method, calling this "humane." Connecticut is one of the states that has decided to switch from the electric chair to lethal injection when, and if, the first execution takes place there, as is expected, in 2001. State corrections officials visited prisons in Delaware, North Carolina, and Texas to learn about lethal injection and experience a mock execution. Upon their return, Deputy Commissioner of Operations Peter Matos was quoted as saying, "We were real impressed how dignified the whole procedure was."

That's not how many of us would put it when we're talking about the premeditated murder of a living person. We'd be focusing on what Amnesty International had to say about how cruel and degrading state-controlled killing is, beginning with the "psychological suffering caused by the foreknowledge of death.... The physical pain caused by electrocution, gassing, hanging, poisoning, or shooting—the five methods of execution used in the United States—cannot be quantified. Prisoners undergo paralysis of organs and burning of the flesh during electrocution, asphyxiation during gassing, tearing of the spinal cord or asphyxiation during hanging, respiratory paralysis during poisoning, and destruction of vital organs or the central nervous system during shooting."

In Florida, which still uses the electric chair, a botched execution in 1997 made national news when reports came out that flames shot out from the head of the man being killed because the old chair was falling apart. Later, Florida tried to deny this, saying the burning of the man had happened because of an error in the way the sponges were applied to his head. Anyone who has seen the movie *The Green Mile*—which had a horrendous scene of a man literally burning to death from the inside out because a dry sponge was put on his head, blocking the current needed for a quick death—would never again be able to deny that the electric chair constitutes cruel and unusual punishment. Then, in July 1999, Allen Lee Davis, in Florida's new electric chair, bled profusely as the current was turned on. Before he died, "blood had poured out onto his collar, and blood from his chest spread to the size of a dinner plate, oozing through the bucket holes on the leather chest strap holding him to the chair," according to an Associated Press story.

Florida did make a change. Lawmakers passed a bill making lethal injection the state's primary method of execution, with the electric chair a choice, should a death row inmate want that. But Governor Jeb Bush wouldn't sign this bill without getting what he wanted, and that was to speed up the appeals process so that inmates could be executed more quickly. He wanted a plan that would imitate the appeals process in Texas, the death capital of the nation, overseen by his brother, Governor George W. Bush. The Florida Legislature gave him what he wanted. The bill to speed the legal process for executions was passed on January 8, 2000. "This is going to guarantee the execution of the innocent," said George Kendall, a lawyer with the NAACP Legal Defense Fund in New York, reacting to that legislation. He added, "This system has been tried out in Texas and shown to be a colossal failure."

None of this is pleasant to focus on, but it is the reality of what we're doing in the United States supposedly to make us safer from criminals. Yet, no study has brought out any solid evidence that the death penalty deters crime. In fact, Amnesty reports that "the murder rate in states which use the death penalty is twice that of states which do not, according to FBI statistics."

Then there is the disturbing question of whether mentally ill people should be put to death for a capital crime. While the United States Supreme Court ruled in 1986 that the Eighth Amendment prohibits execution of insane prisoners, questions arise: Who is insane? Who will do the diagnosis? Who will interpret the findings? We find some troubling stories, such as that of James Terry Roach, executed in 1986 in South Carolina. He had pleaded guilty to murdering two teenagers in 1977, when he was seventeen. A trial judge ruled that he was mentally retarded and suffered from a personality disorder, but he was nonetheless sentenced to death. "When the state electrocuted him at age twenty-five, he had the intellectual capacity of a twelve-year-old child," according to Amnesty International.

In the fall of 1999, I was emotionally focused on the case of Larry Keith Robison, a death row inmate in Texas, who had been diagnosed as mentally ill. His case had come to my attention because Robert J. Zani, my friend imprisoned in Texas, had written to me about him, enclosing an article by Lois Robison, Larry's mother. "My husband, Ken, and I are co-directors of HOPE, a chapter of TexasCURE, which deals with the issue of capital punishment," she begins. "I am a retired third grade teacher, and Ken is a college teacher. We have eight children (his, mine, and ours) and fifteen grandchildren. We are just an average family, except that our son is on death row...."

This mother goes on to tell how her son was first diagnosed as paranoid schizophrenic at age twenty-one, how he kept being turned away from hospitals either because the insurance money ran out, they "needed the bed" for another patient, or they couldn't keep him because he was "not violent." The first and only violence he was ever accused of was severe, killing five people, in 1982, when he was twenty-four. "We were horrified, of course, and we thought he would finally be committed to a mental institution, probably for life," wrote this mother, admitting sadly that she was wrong. Instead, in spite of his medical history, he was declared sane and sentenced to death.

As the appeals started running down, in a surprise move, the Texas Appeals Court granted a temporary stay of execution for Larry Robison on August 20, 1999. That day a *Boston Globe* editorial commented about the Texas death penalty system: "There are no provisions for the mentally retarded; five men have been executed there since 1990 with IQ's as low as fifty-eight. The mentally ill also have no protections. Robison will get a hearing before a judge to see if he is legally competent to be put to death. If not, he will be placed under medication in a state psychiatric hospital, which is where he belonged in the first place. When the state's scythe sweeps as broadly and quickly as it does in Texas, it is bound to reap injustice."

Lois Robison wrote that the prosecuting attorney at Larry's first trial told a reporter he knew that Larry was insane but that he thought the death penalty was appropriate in such cases. And she asked "How can a modern, civilized society choose to exterminate their ill citizens rather than treat them? Isn't necessary medical care a basic human right?"

She goes on, "In the last fourteen years since Larry was sent to death row, we have met many families who have mentally ill or mentally retarded relatives in prison. Approximately one-third of the people on death row are mentally ill or retarded. The head prison doctor told us that there are more mentally ill in prison than there are in mental hospitals in Texas."

In the same week that I was reading Lois Robison's tragic story, I saw another one reporting that the nation's prisons are brimming with the mentally ill. The study, carried out by the Justice Department, found that some 283,800 inmates in the nation's jails and prisons were suffering from a mental illness, with many of them convicted of a violent crime. Since the wholesale closing of mental hospitals beginning in the late 1960s, prisons have become the only institution required to take in mentally and emotionally disturbed people. "This study provides data to show that the incarceration of the mentally ill is a disastrous, horrible social issue," was the comment of Kay Redfield Jamison, a professor of psychiatry at the Johns Hopkins School of Medicine. This is a disturbing development in our nation, which bears great shame for punishing, and not helping, its mentally ill members.

At this point I wish I could say that the Larry Robison story had a happy ending, but that was not to be. Larry was executed in Texas on January 21, 2000. He was forty-two years old. Appalled by this situation in America where we do not distinguish mental health from mental illness when it comes to crime, some state legislatures have acted to ban capital punishment for the mentally retarded. In 1999, the Texas Catholic Conference issued a statement by the state's bishops specifically asking lawmakers to stop executing people whose IQ tests came out below 70, the level labeled "mentally retarded" by psychiatric and educational professionals.

There is yet one more death penalty practice that more and more people are finding hard to accept, and that's the killing of people who were juveniles when the crime was committed. So repugnant is the idea of killing child offenders that it is considered a principle of international law to ban executions of those committing a crime as a juvenile. Only six countries have executed youthful offenders since 1990—the United States, Iran, Nigeria, Pakistan, Saudi Arabia, and Yemen, which has now abandoned that practice. The American Bar Association firmly states it is opposed to the execution of juvenile offenders and the mentally retarded.

It disturbs many Americans to know that since 1977 the U.S. has executed sixteen men who committed crimes as juveniles since 1977, yet many more believe that youths know what they are doing and are responsible for their actions.

That was clearly the belief when it came to the Oklahoma trial of Sean Sellers, a pimply-faced sixteen-year-old, who shot his mother and stepfather and a shopkeeper and was sentenced to death. His story was told on the A&E television channel under the title "Dead Kid Walking." It was difficult to watch this boy admit that he felt only "relief" when the killing was done; to hear him confess to having been involved in Satanism; to see the professionals report on his severe mental illness at the time; and then to listen to him talk of how he had changed, accepted God, and wanted to do some good in this world. He had been on death row thirteen years and was up for a clemency hearing. The daughter and son of his murdered stepfather were strongly opposed to clemency, repeating that they wanted the execution carried out.

They won their point and later witnessed the execution, in January 1999. Sean's last words were for them. He told them he knew they would hate him in the morning as much as they hated him at this moment. And he said something like he would pray where he goes that they find comfort and peace. When the television interviewer asked them if they now felt justified and relieved, they spewed out angry comments about Sean's "arrogance" for saying he'd pray for them. And the victim's son went on about how it was all too easy. Sean got a sedative, he said, and felt no pain. He should have felt pain. I am a victim, too, and understand the pain of their loss, but what they said was a complete turn-off for me. I felt they, not Sean, were the arrogant ones.

This happened the same month that Pope John Paul II was in America. He believes so deeply in the need to work for a universal dedication to life that he took an unexpected step when he came here in January 1999. He asked the late Missouri governor Mel Carnahan to commute the death sentence of Darrell J. Mease, convicted of killing three people in 1988. Amazingly, the governor responded with a "yes," commuting the sentence to life imprisonment without parole. He explained he did this not because he changed his mind on the death penalty, but as a tribute to the pope, according to news stories. Shortly after this news story broke, another item appeared, without headlines, saying that Mr. Mease could still be tried on the two murder charges that were dropped after he was convicted on one charge in this triple murder case. Time will tell.

A year later, the same governor, convinced by the pope to commute the death sentence of a convicted killer, would say no to a group of nuns asking that the same clemency be given to another man on death row in Missouri—Robert Walls, a Catholic convert, awaiting execution at Potosi Correctional Institute, about seventy miles from St. Louis.

The initiative for the petition to spare his life came from Sister Eileen Hogan, a Sister of Mercy from Connecticut. I knew about her stand against the death penalty because my diocesan newspaper, the *Fairfield County Catholic,* had carried a feature story about her beliefs and her role in forming an anti-execution group. She, along with nuns from three other religious communities, had formed an organization they called Catholic Women Against the Death Penalty. Their position would be to emphasize the value of all human life. As Sister Eileen stated, "It is our responsibility as religious to help create a culture of life in Connecticut, to oppose the culture of death that supports abortion, euthanasia, and the death penalty."

Her concern for people behind bars grew out of her work in the prison office of Catholic Charities in New York. "A Jesuit priest was leaving Rikers and said prison was ready for a woman chaplain. Cardinal Terrence Cooke had the guts to appoint me." She was, in fact, the first

Catholic woman to be appointed chaplain of a large correctional institution anywhere in the country. "I was there from 1977 to 1986, and back then I knew the names of every woman. But times have changed, and there's no way you could do that now," she said, referring to the vast increase in the prison population in that facility, officially called Rikers Island Correctional Center. When she left, Sister Eileen continued in prison ministry for more than another decade, developing a training program for chaplains of correctional institutions and starting a mentoring program for mothers coming out of prison.

After I read the article about her, I got in touch with Sister Eileen, hoping to be able to join with the religious and lay women who belonged to Catholic Women Against the Death Penalty. Eventually I was able to connect with the organization, which now has a more ecumenical name, Connecticut Action to Stop Executions, in the hopes of broadening membership.

Sister Eileen's connection with Robert Walls came about unexpectedly. She had been in St. Louis in late June of 1999 for the Third Institute Chapter gathering of the Sisters of Mercy and heard about the upcoming execution of Robert Walls, in a prison close to where they were meeting. During Mass, she said in utter sincerity, "I realized a man was to be killed—in our names," and this disturbed her deeply. She talked with the nuns, and then some of them went with her to the prison to meet with this condemned man so they could know him as a person, not just a name. After that, they wrote a petition to be sent to the governor, asking him to spare the life of Robert Walls. All the sisters signed it. They didn't have papal clout. Governor Carnahan said no.

Shortly before the execution, set for June 30, 1999, at 12:01 a.m., Dominican Father Thomas Condon celebrated Mass for the sisters, and they prayed for Robert Walls. It was a blessing for them to pray with this priest, for he was the one who had instructed "Bob" in the Catholic faith and baptized him. As it became clear that nothing was going to stop this killing, Sister Eileen urged the sisters to hold a vigil on the steps of the Municipal Court Building in St. Louis on the eve of the execution. The response was unprecedented. "We had some cars, but we also had to hire a bus—because all the nuns, about 150 of us, went."

Sister Camille D'Arienzo was one of those at the vigil. She said that this number of nuns "more than quadrupled the presence of the city's faithful opponents of capital punishment, giving heart and hope to the event's sponsors." The sisters' final public appeal to the governor was read by candlelight to a background of prayers and songs. Local TV stations recorded and reported 'the largest demonstration of its kind in St. Louis.' "

Sister Eileen recounted, "A group of us went to the prison after 12:01 to pray. I had to do this. It was important to me ... to acknowledge that I was part of a sinful group, and needed to be healed. This execution touched me in a very personal way. Here was someone to be killed in my name...." Her voice drifted off.

Many months later, Father Condon wrote about how he had been affected by being "Called to Death Row," in the April 1, 2000, issue of *America* magazine: "My call to be with Robert Walls in his last month was my most profound ministerial experience as a Dominican. I knew Robert for only a short time, but he was a man who experienced conversion, asked for baptism, and, in death, knew he was 'going home.' He was far from perfect. I do not deny his participation in a brutal crime. But he also possessed the dignity of a child of God. And he did not deserve to be a victim of the state's institutionalized violence. No one does.

"Is Missouri a better place, now that it has executed Robert Walls? I think not. As Bob said, it has just created another victim of violence."

As more and more attention is focused on what executions really are—violent murders—people who have long sought an ending to this deadly practice are beginning to feel hope that perhaps the excessive pro-execution climate is changing. Some are listening again to prophetic voices like that of the late Justice William J. Brennan Jr., retired from the Supreme Court in 1990, who said, at age ninety: "We do not yet have justice for all.... One area of law more than any other besmirches the constitutional vision of human dignity. My old friend Justice Harry Blackmun called it the 'machinery of death.' It is the death penalty.

"The statistics paint a chilling portrait of racial discrimination on death row. Yet, the ultimate problem is more fundamental. The barbaric death penalty violates our Constitution. Even the most vile murderer does not release the state from its obligation to respect dignity, for the state does not honor the victim by emulating his murderer. Capital punishment's fatal flaw is that it treats people as objects to be toyed with and discarded. But I refuse to despair. One day the Court will outlaw the death penalty. Permanently...."

While that is a hope of over a third of the American people, some of us are willing to settle—temporarily—for the interim action of a moratorium, seeking what might be attainable in a country where the majority want the death penalty. First credit for getting the idea of a moratorium to a national audience has to go to the American Bar Association, which on February 3, 1997, asked for an immediate moratorium to halt all executions in the United States until "the judicial system is overhauled," fixing the process, which is "seriously flawed and... unfairly discriminates against minorities." The ABA resolution stated: "In case after case, decisions about who will live and who will die turn not on the nature of the offense the defendant is charged with committing, but rather on the nature of the legal representation the defendant receives."

Nobody could have predicted the action taken by Governor George Ryan of Illinois in January 2000. When he had to confront the fact that thirteen death row inmates in his state had been found to be innocent, he put a halt to executions—and literally changed the death penalty landscape in our country. The governor, a Republican who supports the death penalty, in a courageous act, declared a moratorium until there is reform legislation that can fix the volumes of errors that accompany convictions in capital cases. He said he would never want it on his conscience that he had been a party to "the ultimate nightmare—the state's taking of an innocent life."

Remarkably, it wasn't police, prosecutors, or judges who uncovered these miscarriages of justice. Journalism students at Northwestern University found the evidence that proved innocence and caused the reversal of these mistaken convictions. The *New York Times,* praising Governor Ryan for his "political courage" and "brave example," said: "He has single-handedly instigated a new national debate on capital punishment by acting on conscience when faced with statistical evidence that innocent people stand a very real chance of being executed in Illinois.... That high standard calls into question the record of other death penalty states.... He has instructed the nation on the only morally coherent position for supporters of capital punishment to take, and that is that no execution can go forward when there is abundant evidence that innocent people have been put on death row."

On the same day that Governor Ryan announced the moratorium in his state, Senator Russ Feingold, a Democrat of Wisconsin, on the Senate floor, urged President Bill Clinton to impose a moratorium on federal executions. While no federal executions have taken place for about the last forty years, twenty-one men are now on federal death row. Questions have been raised about fairness in the way the federal death penalty is applied, since of these twenty-one men on death row, seventeen are members of racial minorities, thirteen of them African American. Then there is a question of geographical disparity: fourteen of these inmates are from three states, Texas, Virginia, and Missouri. The *New York Times* stated that "federal prosecutors in a dozen Southern states have accounted for more than half of the federal cases in which the death penalty has been sought. Senator Feingold said: "The problem of inadequate representation, lack of access to DNA testing, police misconduct, racial bias, and even simple errors are not unique to Illinois. These are problems that have plagued the administration of capital punishment around the country."

The federal death penalty was reinstated in 1988, allowing the death penalty for a person who commits murder as part of a drug operation. Then, in 1994, Congress passed the Federal Death Penalty Act, expanding the crimes warranting execution. These are the assassination of a president, big-time drug trafficking even if no murders take place, drive-by killings, sexual abuse resulting in death, and purposeful destruction of a plane, train, or motor vehicle resulting in death.

What happens in the halls of the Senate is a story to-be-continued, but the important development here is that senators, hearing that meaningful word "moratorium," may have their consciences stirred. Meanwhile, on August 3, 2000, President Bill Clinton delayed the execution of Juan Raul Garza, scheduled to die on August 5, who would have been the first federal inmate to be executed in four decades. The president approved new clemency procedures planned for release by the Justice Department. This was a not-so-subtle indication that even the president, soundly pro–death penalty, cannot turn away from a grossly unfair system.

Members of the House of Representatives have also had to consider a moratorium on executions, thanks to HR3612, a bill introduced by Democratic Illinois Congressman Jesse Jackson Jr. His bill, "The Accuracy in Judicial Administration Act of 2000" (AJA), "would impose a minimum seven-year national moratorium on all U.S. executions until all inmates currently sitting on death row have an opportunity to explore potentially exculpatory DNA and similar evidence," reports Equal Justice USA, an abolitionist group associated with the Quixote Center in Maryland.

Some of the death row inmates have been found innocent because they were finally given access to DNA testing, a process that clearly helps to prevent wrongful convictions. Yet, many death row inmates have never had access to DNA testing in cases where sufficient evidence, gathered at the crime scene, could have led to proof of guilt or innocence, either pretrial or postconviction. Only New York and Illinois—no other states at this writing—have laws providing for postconviction DNA testing.

Equal Justice reports that "since 1992, the Innocence Project at the Cardozo School of Law has received thousands of letters from prisoners who claim that DNA testing could prove them innocent. In over 70 percent of these cases, where DNA testing could prove them innocent, the evidence has been destroyed or lost. Further, in two-thirds of the cases where the evidence was found and DNA testing was conducted, the results exonerated the prisoner."

Seeing how important it is for prisoners to have access to DNA testing, Senator Patrick Leahy, a Democrat of Vermont, in February 2000 introduced the "Innocence Protection Act (IPA)," legislation aimed at reducing the risk of executing innocent persons by ensuring that state and federal prisoners have access to DNA testing. For the bill to have meaning, steps must be taken to insure that biological evidence is preserved. The bill would prohibit a state from denying prisoners' requests for DNA testing that could prove their innocence. The IPA seeks other remedies in the rush to kill, including a requirement that "any state receiving federal criminal justice grants establish and maintain an 'effective system' for providing competent legal services to indigent defendants from pretrial proceedings through the appeals process. This part of the bill is especially critical given that many death row prisoners currently have no lawyers to pursue their appeals," Equal Justice USA reports.

As of mid-year 2000, the call for a moratorium on the death penalty, echoing the lead of the American Bar Association and Governor Ryan, was being heard across the land. Equal Justice USA began an active campaign to get a national tidal wave of support for "Moratorium Now! Not One More Execution!" An article in the June issue of the *ABA Journal* quoted Jane Henderson, co-director of the Quixote Center: "Moratorium legislation is now under consideration in six states . . . and is expected to be filed in at least four others. Baltimore's city council recently became the 11th local jurisdiction nationwide to call for a moratorium on the death penalty. And more than 750 groups and 4,100 individuals have joined the movement, including 19 present and former members of Congress, two ex-governors, two former big-city mayors, several retired judges, and the relatives of more than 1,000 murder victims."

A major voice was added to theirs when Sister Helen Prejean and the group she is associated with, the Religious Organizing Against the Death Penalty Project, began seeking supporters for their "Moratorium 2000" project. Their goal was to have one million signatures on a petition calling for a moratorium on the death penalty that they would deliver to the United Nations, in honor of Human Rights Day, on December 10, 2000. Sister Helen's appeal was, "I encourage you to endorse a worldwide moratorium on the death penalty, as a first and necessary step toward the full protection of human rights for all."

In some states where political resistance to a moratorium would be strong, individuals and groups appealed directly to their governors. In New York State, an anti–capital punishment group headed by Bishop Howard J. Hubbard of Albany—New Yorkers Against the Death Penalty—called on Governor George Pataki and prosecutors across the state to establish an immediate moratorium. They pointed out that historically evidence has shown New York to have had more wrongful capital convictions than any other state.

Bishop Hubbard and the members put their appeal in writing: "Existing safeguards are not sufficient to prevent further miscarriages of justice. . . . Above all, it is wrong. We need to join the community of nations who have put the death penalty behind them."

In my own state of Connecticut, with six men on death row and the first executions in nearly forty years set to happen in 2001, the first appeal for a moratorium came from Representative Richard Tulisano in January 1999, when he proposed Bill No. 5051 to the Judiciary Committee. His purpose was clearly stated: "To ensure that the death penalty is carried out in a fair and non-discriminatory manner by placing a moratorium on executions until the state has adopted specific substantive and procedural safeguards recommended by the American Bar Association."

While this proposal didn't get very far in the halls of the capital building, it did encourage some of us in Connecticut to get behind the call for a moratorium in our state. In April 2000, Rev. Walter Everett called on me and five other opponents of the death penalty to go with him to Governor John Rowland's office in Hartford to petition the governor to impose a moratorium. Besides myself and Rev. Everett, two others, Mikki Brady and Art Laffin, had lost loved ones to murder; Joe Grabarz, head of the American Civil Liberties Union in Connecticut, and Kim Harrison from the United Church of Christ were longtime opponents of the death penalty.

Just to be joined with these fine, like-minded people was uplifting. Mikki's story was painful to hear, as are all the tales we, who have suffered news of murder close to home, have endured. In 1992 her daughter Kathy was shot to death by a man she knew. Her body was thrown into a wooded area and discovered after about a week by a mother and daughter taking a walk. The man who murdered her was apprehended and later convicted and sentenced to serve ninety-plus years in prison.

"I was, and still am, in terrible agony, longing for my child," says this mother, who has four sons. "I looked at his [the killer's] life and wondered what had turned him into someone who could do this. He wasn't born a murderer, and I wonder if how he was raised had something to do with this. I know no one has the right to take a life, but this has happened and I had to do what was best. To heal myself, I knew I had to forgive. I believed God would give me the strength. I have a lot of faith. It gets me through," says Mikki, a Catholic.

Like myself and Rev. Everett, Mikki belongs to Murder Victims Families for Reconciliation. She talks with great empathy about prisoners because, by a twist of fate, her position before her daughter's murder had been to work in the prisons as an employment counselor. "I saw so many who had been able to put their lives together. I knew people could change because I had worked with many young men who had, and I had come to love them." A very spiritual woman, she believes her daughter's murderer has found faith in prison, at least this is her hope and prayer. I felt an immediate "sisterhood" with Mikki Brady.

Art Laffin's name was familiar to me, and it soon struck me why. I had read about his brother, Paul Laffin, a man highly respected by all, who worked at Mercy, Housing and Shelter in Hartford, serving the poor with compassion and love. On September 20, 1999, he was stabbed to death and given last rites by Father Frank Scavola, a friend from Paul's parish of St. Patrick–St. Anthony. Art, a member of Pax Christi who lives in the Dorothy Day Catholic Worker Community in Washington, D.C., was in Connecticut that day to be with his mother at the bedside of his father, hospitalized and in poor physical condition after a car crash. In his words:

"Stunned and dazed, my mother and I returned to our family home, where we met my two brothers and their wives and Father Scavola. . . . Later we would find out that Dennis Soutar, a forty-year-old man of Jamaican descent, who suffered from mental illness and had been helped by Paul, was charged with killing him. We cried and prayed.

"After asking God for the faith to endure this terrible tragedy and giving thanks for Paul's life, somehow, through the grace of God, I found myself also praying for the man who stabbed my brother. I remembered Jesus' beatitude: 'Blessed are the merciful, for they will receive mercy.'

"Throughout the night, a rush of emotions permeated my being. I still couldn't believe that Paul, my forty-two-year-old kid brother, who I was with just the day before, had been murdered. Why would anyone do such a thing? . . . How is it possible that a man so sick is out on the streets instead of getting the care he needs? I thought about how this tragedy, and so many other similar tragedies, could be prevented if our society and government placed as its top priority, meeting the needs of the afflicted and eliminating poverty....

"As a youth and a young adult, I believed in 'an eye for an eye....' But when I was introduced to nonviolence in my early twenties by Catholic pacifists and war resisters, I realized how blinded I had been by the culture of violence and war.... After reading about and praying over the teachings of Jesus, learning about the rich history of nonviolence from biblical times to the present, and meeting many peacemakers, I knew that to follow Jesus meant resolving conflict through nonviolent means and seeking reconciliation with those with whom we have differences.

"To be a follower of Jesus means that we must live as Jesus did. Jesus calls each of us to do the works of mercy, to stand with and for the victims, to proclaim God's reign of justice and peace and to be willing to lay down one's life rather than to kill.... The legacy Paul leaves us is a life of love and service. I find great consolation in knowing that Paul died living out the Gospel."

I hadn't found such faith as Art's in a long time, and I am fortunate to have called him friend ever since that morning when we six gathered at the capitol building in Hartford to try to meet with Governor Rowland to petition for a moratorium. Later, I rediscovered another reason why Art's name was familiar to me. He was one of eighteen people arrested for protesting executions at the U.S. Supreme Court on January 27, 1997. The protest was staged to mark the twentieth anniversary of the firing squad death in Utah of Gary Gilmore, the first prisoner executed after the Supreme Court reinstated the death penalty in our land, and to announce that the campaign to stop executions would not end, but escalate. At the time, 362 people had been executed since Gary Gilmore's death, and the protestors had written their names on a large banner spread across the sidewalk in front of the court. A similar demonstration today would require a banner twice that size to fit the 650-plus names we now have of the executed.

Being with these truly remarkable people that April morning made me feel that if those of us who believe in ending state-sanctioned death begin to join forces, our united voice might become strong enough to convince our elected political leaders to follow the lead of Governor Ryan and the American Bar Association and vote for a moratorium. But when we met later with the governor's chief-of-staff, Sidney Holbrook, reality set in.

We would have a tough road ahead before getting Connecticut officials acting on this. He gave us a memorandum:

The Governor cannot unilaterally impose a moratorium on the death penalty. For a moratorium to occur, the following governmental entities would have to act in conjunction with each other in the manner described below:

- The General Assembly must pass legislation temporarily suspending the death penalty statute.

- The Governor must exercise his constitutional authority to grant temporary reprieves of execution.

- The Connecticut Supreme Court must postpone scheduling any executions.

- State's Attorneys must stop requesting the death penalty. (In cases where the death penalty applies, an alternative sentence of natural life imprisonment without parole may be imposed.)

- The Board of Pardons *may* pardon those already sitting on death row.

We decided not to get discouraged by this memorandum. We made it a call to action. Catholic Women Against the Death Penalty met and determined to expand membership by having a more inclusive name. The final agreement would be to call the organization Connecticut Action to Stop Executions, CASE, with a primary first objective: to get a moratorium in our state. A nearly inactive Connecticut Network to Abolish the Death Penalty, CNADP, was reactivated at Rev. Everett's church hall, with Stephen Kobasa at the helm, meeting with CASE to join forces. All agreed we had to get a coalition against the death penalty mobilized statewide by contacting all the known groups we believed would work with us. While all of us want to end executions, we agreed to start first with what might be attainable, a moratorium. By late summer of 2000, we were on our way.

If the momentum that has been building against the death penalty can keep gaining strength, we could perhaps reverse the dreadful course that was set into motion in the 1970s whereby politicians began to believe—unfortunately rightfully—that they had to be for death if they wanted to get elected. People are coming up with creative ideas for getting their anti–death penalty feelings known—like the one told to me by Sister

Dorothy Briggs, a Dominican nun and reader of my syndicated column who has become a telephone friend. Sister Dorothy has become involved with "For Whom the Bells Toll," a new effort to bring attention to the need to stop executions.

As she explained, throughout history, bells have been tolled for good news and bad news—for coming dangers and a war's end; for happy occasions, like weddings, and sad ones, like death. In the Philippines, Jaime Cardinal Sin asked the Catholic churches to toll bells to mourn the execution of a citizen of that country. Bishop Walter Sullivan of Richmond, Virginia, learning of that practice in the Philippines, sent this message to all the churches in his diocese: "I ask all diocesan churches and chapels with bell towers to toll their bells at 9 p.m. on November 9, 1999, and on the evening of every execution until we bring an end to this inhumane practice."

Sister Dorothy heard about this from Charlie Sullivan, director of Citizens United for the Rehabilitation of Errants (CURE), a group she had worked with. She said: "I called Bishop Sullivan to determine if anything was being done to promote the effort on a national level. No such attempt was being made, and I was encouraged to do so if I wished. Charlie continued to encourage me, though by this time I didn't need much encouragement. I called Kay Perry, director of the Michigan chapter of CURE, to explain the project. She shared our enthusiasm. . . .

"We have now launched For Whom the Bells Toll, to encourage all religious communities throughout the country to toll their bells for two minutes at 6 p.m. on the date of any execution. . . .

"We recognize that many churches no longer have bells. We are encouraging them to place a black drape over the outside door of the building and/or to tie black ribbons around the trees and utility poles surrounding the church.

"The tolling bells will be a reminder to all who hear them that all of us are diminished by continuing acts of state-sponsored murder. The churches, monasteries, abbeys, temples, and synagogues that join in this effort will go a long way toward stopping the death penalty in this country.

"The campaign will continue until there is a moratorium on the death penalty or until the death penalty is abolished in this country."

Voices are being raised—and now bells will be ringing—bringing ever more attention to the madness for death that has taken over our land for way too long. Hope is arriving that we may see an end to preventable violent death by official hands.

Chapter Eleven

SO MUCH KNOWN—
SO MUCH TO BE DONE

ᘔᘓᘔᘓᘔᘓᘔᘓᘔᘓᘔᘓᘔᘓ

Once you meet others who believe as you do—that life is too precious to approve its violent ending at the hands of the state—you have made new and lifelong friends. I learned this from my connection with Mimi Klocko of Delaware, dating back to 1995. She had read in her daily paper the anti–death penalty article I had written for the *Hartford Courant,* which was syndicated nationally, and she managed to track down my phone number, wanting to know if I'd come to Delaware to give a talk. I did, and, like "soul sisters," we have stayed in touch ever since.

In late April 1999, Mimi sent me a piece she had written called "Reflections at the Vigil of an Execution." I was deeply moved by her words:

"April 23, 1999. It is shortly after midnight and the group of 75 or 80 of us opposed to the death penalty are standing in a fenced-in pen just outside the Delaware Correctional Center, the maximum security prison in Smyrna, waiting. . . .

"Our eyes look to the distance for the headlights of the car bringing the prison official from the place of execution to make the terse announcement that the sentence has been carried out and David Lawrie, the convicted murderer, is dead. But it is too early and no car comes. . . .

"If one observed this lonely group of pilgrims from a distance, it must have presented a surreal scene. A group of huddling people enclosed by a fence bathed in blinding floodlights, surrounded by armed guards and state police on foot, in cars, and with dogs. Occasionally, the dogs would bark and howl as if they had been taught to hate us. The police took flashlights and visually searched our cars, and we were told that if we left this compound, we could not come back. We would have to leave the grounds. I thought to myself that if I didn't know better, one might

200

think we were criminals. But I did know better and I stood straighter as if to resist the intimidation being thrust upon us.

"The giant bronze bell that accompanies us on all vigils rings out its lonesome toll for the victims and for the condemned.... Everyone waits—even the media is respectful and quiet. It is as if time stands still. It is holy time.

"The wait seems endless in the dark and the cold and the wind. It is strange to know you're standing there while someone is being put to death behind those walls.

"The silence of the vigil is broken ever so quietly by two voices in the corner singing, 'Jesus, remember me when you come into your kingdom....' Over and over and over again, the words are repeated. Each time, the meaning of those words pierces the heart.

"Slowly, the headlights appear over a small knoll and everyone knows that it is over.... The official emerges and appears angry that he has to do this unpleasant task. He makes the cold and emotionless announcement that a man has just been put to death and just as quickly as he appeared, he returns to his car and is driven away.

"The vigilers gather their things and prepare to leave. Some leave in silence and some reach out to each other and hug and weep. Who do we weep for?

"We weep for ourselves because we are a part of this. We weep for the victims and their families. We weep for David Lawrie and pray he made his peace with God before he died. We weep for his family. We weep for the prison officials and for the executioners. We weep for the people of the state of Delaware and for the legislators who misguidedly believe they are doing the right thing. We weep for our country awash in violence. We weep for our children and our grandchildren and we say, 'God have mercy on us all!' "

Mimi's words affected me deeply because I had become concerned about what was happening in my own state of Connecticut. I knew that six men were on death row, but somehow I was living in the fantasy that Connecticut would never really kill someone. No one had been put to death in my state since 1960, when Joseph Taborsky, responsible for pistol whipping and shooting six people, was electrocuted at the state prison in Wethersfield. Connecticut has executed seventy-three people in its history, but had, as Michael Mello, a professor at Vermont Law School, said, "one of the most careful and reliable capital statutes in the country—they made the decision that we want to err on the side of mercy rather than risk executing innocent people."

Yet, Governor John Rowland, a Catholic, signed a bill in 1995 making it much easier for juries to impose the death penalty and for the state to carry it out. The new law simplified the appeals process by eliminating proportionality review, a process by which the state's Supreme Court compared the death sentence to the sentences in similar cases to determine if it was proportional; it allowed juries to weigh aggravating factors in their deliberations and to offset mitigating factors; and it broadened the list of crimes that could merit death. At the April 2000 anti-violence conference initiated by Survivors of Homicide, Connecticut's chief state's attorney, John M. Bailey, indicated the state could see its first execution in the year 2001. Now I was devastated at the realization that in the very near future I might be huddled outside the prison where my fellow state residents would be killing a man, raising my voice, praying, tolling a bell. God, I prayed, please never let that happen!

It became important to me to talk to the defense attorneys who, I knew, have done and would continue to do all in their power to convince juries that a sentence of death is wrong for anyone. I had met Gerard Smyth, chief public defender for the state, at the anti-violence conference, and he had graciously told me I could call and make an appointment to meet with him. Not only did he give me considerable time in response to my questions; he also arranged for me to meet with his Capital Defense Unit, an eleven-member team, consisting of lawyers, one social worker, investigators, and two secretaries they call "indispensable." He started the team to provide the best in legal services for prisoners charged with a capital offense.

For Gerard Smyth, being a public defender is exactly the right position. A student of Catholic schools, from elementary through college, graduating from the Jesuits' Fairfield University in 1967, he gained a strong sense of social and moral responsibility. He went into law, "hopefully to do some good for people who needed help, who were not dealt as good a hand...." Listening to him, you understand why he defends those convicted of a capital offense. This work involves "a lot of pressure and responsibility ... and is very time consuming" because defense lawyers utilize every possible court of review. "And thank God we do," Mr. Smyth says. "You're trying to save your client's life!"

His opposition to the death penalty is "partly based on religion, and partly on my own view," he said, acknowledging that with so many pro–death penalty advocates in the state and country, "sometimes we [defense attorneys] bear the brunt of a lot of anger."

Case in point was the reversal by the state Supreme Court, in May 2000, of a death sentence for Terry Johnson, ordering him, instead, to be imprisoned for life without possibility of release. Johnson and his brother Duane were convicted of shooting State Trooper Russell Bagshaw on June 5, 1991, after the officer, on a routine patrol, interrupted them during a robbery. Terry Johnson, then twenty-one, received a death sentence, while his brother was sentenced to life in prison.

"Our appellate office handled the appeal," said Mr. Smyth. The high court ruled 4–3 that the shooting itself was not cruel or heinous enough to meet the standard for the death penalty. "It was a pretty obvious decision, consistent with case law, and it feels great," said the chief public defender, to know a life will be saved. Many people did not applaud this decision, ridiculing the idea that a murder was not "cruel or heinous enough" to merit the death penalty. Mr. Smyth responded, "It was the right decision for the court to make. But," he added somewhat sadly, "it doesn't play well with the public."

If he has any nightmares about a case, it would be only "that we didn't supply adequate representation," he said firmly, emphasizing that he and his team work to find everything they can about the background and character of their client and the nature of their offense to do everything possible to get the jury to accept a sentence less than death. They try to discover if the clients are mentally impaired, were abused as children, have done good things in their lives, served in the military, supported a family, were good parents, adapted well to incarceration, and anything else that can be seen as "mitigating factors" in judging the crime. According to Connecticut statute, "Mitigating factors are such as do not constitute a defense or excuse for the capital felony of which the defendant has been convicted, but which, in fairness and mercy, may be considered as tending either to extenuate or reduce the degree of his culpability or blame for the offense or to otherwise constitute a basis for a sentence less than death."

"In some ways it's getting harder to prove mitigating factors, and, under the new law, the jury now has to weigh these against the 'aggravating factors,'" said Mr. Smyth. Aggravating factors, as listed in the Connecticut statute are:

- the defendant committed the offense during the commission of, or during the immediate flight from the commission or attempted commission of, a felony and he had previously been convicted of the same felony;

- the defendant committed the offense after having been convicted of two or more state offenses or two or more federal offenses, or of one or more state offenses and one or more federal offenses for each of which a penalty of more than one year imprisonment may be imposed, which offenses were committed on different occasions and which involved the infliction of serious bodily injury upon another person;

- the defendant committed the offense and in such commission knowingly created a grave risk of death to another person in addition to the victim of the offense;

- the defendant committed the offense in an especially heinous, cruel, or depraved manner;

- the defendant procured the commission of the offense by payment, or promise of payment, of anything of pecuniary value;

- the defendant committed the offense as consideration for the receipt, or in expectation of the receipt, of anything of pecuniary value;

- the defendant committed the offense with an assault weapon.

The types of murder that make someone eligible for the death sentence include rape/murder, death of a child under twelve, murder of a police officer who is carrying out the duties of his or her job, murder for hire, murder during the course of a kidnapping, intentional killing during a sexual assault, the killer was serving a life sentence, the killer was previously convicted of murder, murder of two or more persons at the same time or in the same circumstances, and a death caused directly from using cocaine, heroin, or methadone that was illegally sold to that person by the defendant for profit.

Six men are on Connecticut's death row as of this writing—Daniel Webb, for abducting a woman from a downtown Hartford parking garage and killing her; Robert Breton, for killing his ex-wife and sixteen-year-old son; Sedrick Cobb, for kidnap, rape, and murder of a woman who accepted his offer to change her tire; Richard Reynolds, who shot Officer Walter Williams while he was on routine patrol in Waterbury's North End in 1992; Todd Rizzo, a teenager who bludgeoned thirteen-year-old Stanley Edwards to death; and Michael Ross, a serial killer convicted of kidnapping and murdering four young women and raping two of them.

I came to know about one of these men, Richard Reynolds, very well, because I met the mother of the man he murdered through Survivors of Homicide, and I have hugged and cried with her. Helen Williams is still tormented when she remembers getting the call from her granddaughter that would change her life, the one telling her that her beloved son, Walter, a police officer, a father of two, with a pregnant wife close to delivery of a new child, was in the hospital, terribly wounded from a bullet. She feels strongly that the family deserves justice, and the only way they'll ever get it is if Richard Reynolds is put to death. When I asked Helen if she would tell me why she feels so strongly about this, she sent me these three paragraphs, "which best express my feeling on the subject":

"The death penalty should be imposed on convicted murderers. A person who wantonly takes another person's life should expect to be punished by death.

"There can be no excuse for murder except self-defense.

"People who oppose capital punishment are rewarding a murderer with moral and ethical considerations that the killer does not deserve. People who kill other human beings should not be allowed to live in our society nor should society have to feed, shelter, or care for them.

"This applies, of course, if we strive for a civilized, safer society where the rights of the victim are more important than the rights of the criminal."

Helen and I remain good friends, even though we hold different positions on the death penalty, because, as mothers of murdered sons, we have a tremendously strong bond. When she talks about how she used to worry that, because her son wore a uniform, he might be a target one day for someone out to "get a cop," I could relate. My adopted son, Sterling, was on the Illinois State Police force for twenty-eight years, and I was always concerned for his safety. Even now, because his daughter, Julie, and son, Gregory, are police officers, I pray every day to the Lord to keep my two grandchildren in uniform safe. I can relate to Helen's anger and devastation, but I still believe that the way to healing is not to endorse more killing. I hope the day never comes when Helen and I may be standing at opposite poles—where some cheer, and some weep—when the poison is put into a man's veins.

In talking to other survivors of murder victims, I have found that some feel a great resentment toward the capital defense lawyers, upset that they try to find mitigating factors for why someone commits the crime of murder and feeling that they don't empathize with the victims.

I spoke with defense attorneys to find out how they can take it when so much anger is thrown their way. "It strengthens our resolve. You get to know people on a personal level...and you find a lot of redeeming values in each person. I see something good in everyone," said Barry Butler.

In a conversation with him and Ronald Gold, I found real concern for the arrested people they must defend and was comforted to know that in my state, an accused killer would always get the best professional defense possible, delivered by lawyers who see them as people deserving of consideration. Most of the offenders they see "have been molded by negative things. People get very cynical about what they call 'the abuse excuse,' but people aren't natural-born killers. So often we see the worst upbringing. We see clients from horrendous backgrounds. There's got to be a cause and effect.

"Sometimes there's no family. We're it. They're so discarded. Nothing justifies killing anyone, but we're trying to make the process fair."

Barry Butler provided a final comment, "We're public defenders, but we're not in favor of crime. Give up the death penalty, and I'll go back to car accidents!"

Another name I know on death row is Michael Ross, but then everybody knows his name. He is the notorious serial killer-rapist of, according to his count, eight young women in Connecticut and New York. In 1987 he received a death sentence for kidnapping and strangling fourteen-year-old Leslie Shelly and her friend April Brunais, also fourteen, and for raping and killing Wendy Baribeault, seventeen, and Robin Stavinsky, nineteen. He was already serving two life sentences for killing two other women, Debra Smith Taylor, twenty-three, and Tammy Williams, seventeen. He also admits to killing two women in New York State, though he was never prosecuted for those alleged crimes.

Ross's conviction was upheld by the State Supreme Court in 1994, but his sentence was overturned because the trial judge had excluded part of a psychiatric report that might have kept him from getting the death sentence. His defense right along has been that a psychiatric disorder, "sexual sadism," turned him into the monster that raped and killed, and that medication he received in prison has eliminated the uncontrollable urges that drove him to commit the crimes. In Michael Ross's own words, after he received a diagnosis and medical treatment from the Sexual Disorders Clinic at Johns Hopkins Hospital in Maryland, he was cleared of the "vile and noxious thoughts of rape and murder that plagued my mind for so long. The drug—Depo-Lupron—eliminates the previously uncontrollable urges that drove me to commit the crimes that put me here on death row. That monster still lives in my head, but the medication has chained him and banished him to the back of my mind. And while he is still able to mock me, he can no longer control me. I control him. I am human again. . . .

"And it allowed my humanity to awaken—giving me back something that I thought I had lost forever. . . . After my eyes were finally opened and I saw the truth of what I had become and what I had done, . . . I began to feel the terrible agony and distress that I had brought to so many: my victims, the families and friends of my victims, my own family. . . . I felt a profound sense of guilt, an intense, overwhelming and pervasive guilt that surrounds my very soul with dark, tormented clouds filled with a mixture of self-hatred, remorse, regrets and sorrow. All of which leaves me with a deep desire to make amends and achieve reconciliation— something which under the circumstances seems all but impossible."

When his case was sent to the Superior Court for a new trial to determine the penalty, Ross insisted he wanted the death penalty so that the families of his victims would not have to go through the pain of another trial. That request was denied and the new trial went on, ending with a verdict in April 2000. The Superior Court jury deliberated nine days and then, rejecting his "sexual disorder" defense, recommended six death sentences for Ross, now forty.

I hadn't known much about Michael Ross until I got a call in 1997 from Msgr. John Gilmartin, then director of Catholic Charities for the Diocese of Rockville Centre on Long Island. Knowing my stand against the death penalty, he wanted to meet with me to talk about a Connecticut death row inmate, Michael Ross. He told me he had been visiting Michael every month for more than a year. I had thought of Ross as someone most people wouldn't care to know. I was curious.

We met for lunch, and Father Gilmartin told me his personal visits to Michael started after this notorious inmate had sent some anti–death penalty articles to him, asking if they could be published in the magazine he and his Catholic Charities staff put out. His writing was "compelling," Father told me, and he wondered, "Who is this guy? Then I found out he was on death row, and I wanted to see if he was for real. I decided I had to meet him, and so I went to the Northern Correctional Institution in Somers where he was. I was apprehensive. I had no idea what I'd find. His first words were, 'I know why you're here. You're bringing forgiveness. Tell me what that means."

That was a tough question. Michael Ross, a Cornell University gradu-ate, had been doing a lot of writing, and he had said of himself, "I'm the worst of the worst, a man who has raped and murdered eight women, as-saulted several others, and stalked and frightened many more. And when I am finally executed, the vast majority of the people of this state will celebrate my death." I could verify that part regarding "celebrations" from the many and repeated comments I had heard about Michael Ross, particularly from other victims.

Later I read more of Michael Ross's writings. I think he discovered that forgiveness begins when someone reaches out to you with love, not judgment. Listen to his words: "I am grateful and thankful to the Divine Providence that sent me Father John. With his help, and if it is God's will, I will achieve that reconciliation that I so desire and hopefully complete my transformation into one who is worthy of redemption and forgiveness. My journey is still far from over, but at least now I can see that there is a light at the end of the tunnel—and what a glorious light it is! May God give me the strength, perseverance, and moral fortitude to complete my journey and become one with that light."

Father Gilmartin told me the visits to Michael gave him the realiza-tion that this man is not just a heinous rapist/murderer, but an articulate, very real human being, now being helped by drugs that control the men-tal illness that triggered his horrible actions. Working and praying with Michael was an overwhelming experience, he said, touching both the reality of evil in this world and of grace that brings forgiveness and rec-onciliation. Michael told him he hoped one day to forgive himself for his crimes, yearning mostly for reconciliation, with the family and friends of his victims, with himself, and with his God. Father Gilmartin found that, in seeking redemption, Michael was coming alive. "He's a new man; the old man has left."

About a year after my first meeting with Father Gilmartin, I was asked to be one of two speakers for a program at a Connecticut Catholic church, titled "An End to Violence." The other speaker was a for-mer prison chaplain, Larry Deraleau, who had also been working with Michael Ross for five years at that time. He said that back in 1992 he believed the convicted murderer was a "grandstander," looking for attention. But after a five-year relationship with Ross, he had become convinced of his sincerity when he expressed sorrow for what he had done. "He's haunted by the victims," Mr. Deraleau told us. "He's having a hard time forgiving himself. . . . He can't see how God can forgive him."

By this time I had access to more of Michael Ross's writings, thanks to

Father Gilmartin, who passed them on to me. Even though this prisoner was asking to be executed and had, in fact, signed an unprecedented agreement, worked out with a special prosecutor, promising not to oppose the state's efforts to send him to the death chamber, this was not because he believed in the death penalty. Clearly, his conviction was just the opposite, as he wrote, " . . . executions degrade us all." In his words,

"There are acceptable alternatives to capital punishment that are more in line with the values of our supposedly enlightened and humanistic society. The state is supposed to be the pillar of our ideals and its institutions should emulate the best values of our society. Are not the greatest of these values our compassion, our concern for human rights and *our capacity for mercy?* By continuing to conduct executions, aren't we undermining the very foundations of our greatness?

"As Zimbabwe poet Chenjerai Hove wrote: 'The death penalty is abominable, as abominable as the crime itself. Our state must be based on love, not hatred and victimization. Our penal code must be based on rehabilitation rather than annihilation. . . . '

"Individuals who are a danger to society must be removed from society. Society has the right to protect itself—there is no disputing that. . . . The choice is not between the death penalty and unconditional release, but between the death penalty and meaningful long-term sentences. Life without the possibility of parole, or natural life sentences, meet the necessary requirements of society without being excessively brutal or barbaric."

I was actually pleased to read that after Michael Ross's agreement with prosecutors to let him die was thrown out, he then chose to have a strong defense. He was assigned two attorneys from the state's Capital Defense team, Karen Goodrow and Barry Butler, who, acknowledging how difficult and complex their work would be in such a high-profile case with such a notorious defendant, gave a vigorous defense in the courtroom. They found their client to be "very bright, very respectful," his one-time sexual sadism long overcome and controlled by specific drugs. "The Michael Ross we knew was not the Michael Ross of those past years," said Karen Goodrow.

I have met several times with Karen, and we have talked about her work and why she has chosen to defend people facing the death penalty. "It's a job that's awesome in an incredibly frightening way. Here you have someone facing a potential death sentence, and, it sounds hokey, but I see it as an honor to try to save their life. It's very humbling. It affects you in ways you don't realize. You dream about it. You get up to go to the bathroom at one in the morning and you think about it. The responsibility is immense."

Her work was especially difficult in the Michael Ross case, because, as a woman, to hear of his crimes against women could stir up disturbing emotions. Negative reactions were directed at her, including an unsigned piece of hate mail addressed specifically to her. "It was meant to upset me, but you don't draw a line on the death penalty. Defending anyone, even a Michael Ross, is a test of your convictions."

One of the realities a defense lawyer must face is that families of victims will be in the court. "I'm cognizant of the fact that victims will be in the courtroom. Our role is to do what we must do with as much dignity as we can. We make zealous arguments to convince a jury that this person doesn't deserve to be killed, even if these don't make sense to the victims. They're entitled to feel as they do," said Karen, adding her wish that victims could "humanize" her, see her "as a person," and, "on some level, understand and accept me for what I do."

In Karen's words, "The people we defend are often depicted as monsters. It makes it easier for the public if they see them as monsters. But I see them as human. I see their vulnerability and their need for someone to help them."

Karen then brought up the subject of mercy, a quality I seek in all my relations with people and doings in daily life. Often I have consulted the dictionary to remind myself of its meaning: "compassionate or kindly forbearance toward an offender, an enemy or other person in one's power; discretionary power as to clemency or severity, pardon or punishment, or the like: to be at the mercy of a conqueror...." So often, contemplating this definition, I have felt that if there is any place in our day and age where mercy should be remembered and considered, it is in the criminal justice system. Karen spoke of this: "All through law school," she began, "the emphasis is separation of church and state. Religion has no direct role in making legal judgments. Yet, in the courtroom, much of what is presented and argued has its genesis in religion. The statute, which guides the jury to weigh mitigating factors, allows them to make their judgment 'in fairness and mercy.'

"The concept of mercy, as I understand it, has a religious basis," Karen said. "Yet, from the legal standpoint, mercy becomes ambiguous because it invites a jury to decide for or against mercy on its own. They may find mitigating factors, but not want mercy. They may feel, 'Why should someone get mercy if they didn't show mercy?' "

Yet, Karen believes, "You afford mercy to people who need it most, and Michael Ross is the best example of such a person. If mercy is not there for the worst of the worst, it is a hollow concept."

In my dealings with the defense lawyers of my state of Connecticut, I felt great pride for their professional expertise, concern for their clients, and commitment to deliver the best defense possible for them. More than that, I felt a strong empathy with their humanness and determination to work diligently not to just "win a case," but to achieve something much more important: the saving of a life.

Focusing on murderers makes it easy to believe that everyone in prison is bad, or, in words I've heard used, "scum," "human garbage." Yet research shows that as many as 65 percent of prisoners are incarcerated because of mandatory drug laws, because of violation of a previous parole, or because they are mentally ill and psychologically impaired. These people could be helped if alternatives to prison were available, giving them, not cages to live in, but instead drug rehabilitation programs, home surveillance for those on parole, and psychiatric help for those with mental and psychiatric disorders. Most important, too, is that prisoners should not be isolated and should maintain contact with their families.

But it seems we have made the choice to lock them up and punish them instead of helping them. And the numbers keep growing, because as someone put it, we are imprisoning more and more "small fry," making it necessary to build ever more prisons. It should concern us that one out of every 145 Americans is in prison! Statistics have also shown that about 15 percent of the incarcerated are innocent.

From what I have seen and learned, rehabilitation of prisoners is of little or no concern to most public officials. The job of corrections is primarily to see to it that prisoners behave, never escape, have minimal contact with outsiders, especially "do-gooders," stay caged in isolation if they misbehave, make few phone calls—"collect," of course and expensive—and receive only censored mail and packages. What is important in this business of warehousing human beings are jobs for the people who no longer want to be called prison guards, but "corrections officers." In many states, the fastest-growing public employee associations are unions representing corrections officers, assuring them good salaries, ample time off, and impressive benefits.

Take one state, California. I have learned a lot about California from Father Vince Connor, who has been a prison chaplain for twenty-three years, most of these at the Youth Correctional Facility in Chino, California. Father Vince tells me that the California Correctional Peace Officers Association is the strongest union in the state, and it dictates the laws governing the prisons. From another source I learned that in 1998, the California union was given a raise of 12 percent, which brought the salary for a seasoned prison guard up to $51,000.

Father Vince works with eighteen-to-twenty-five-year-olds, and after so many years looking at the system from the inside out, he is more than disillusioned. "We don't rehabilitate these young people; we desocialize them," he says, mentioning as one case in point the fact that "we are the only correctional facility in the United States where all the population sits in their room to eat because we have no dining room. They have to sit on their commode to eat!" he said. The disgust he feels for this situation is evident.

This priest doesn't mince words. "The justice system is crazy, simply insane," he says. "We define rehabilitation as 'to reinvest with dignity,' That's what the word means. People who have been convicted have stained their dignity by their unthinkable acts. Their human dignity's been ruptured. It's our job to reinvest them with dignity, to make them socially conscious. The most effective tools for doing this are education, significant family contact, breaking away from the negative structures and models that helped get them into trouble, and having an individual and lasting religious conviction, through spiritual development and gaining a sense of ethics. Yet these are the things prisons are continually dismantling. They are taking someone who has done some antisocial act and doing nothing other than putting them into an environment designed and geared to desocialize them further. The whole thing is crazy.

"This is my take," he went on. "For anybody who's committed serious crime, give them a life sentence. Then tell them, get a high school diploma, a college degree, individual therapy, and group counseling. Along with developing these skills, develop a good relationship with your family, an ability to earn a living, and grow spiritually. Get all these done, and then come back and we'll talk about parole."

Unfortunately, even if young offenders "have got the incentive, we don't provide the resources. We'd rather spend $60,000 for yet one more security guard, who've become the 'chosen elite,' " said Father Vince.

His work has positioned him strongly against the death penalty, and he counts among his respected acquaintances several high-profile celebrities who are outspoken abolitionists, including actors Mike Farrell and Martin Sheen; David Kelley, scriptwriter for television shows, including *The Practice;* and David Morris, co-star of *The Green Mile,* the unforgettable Tom Hanks film about death row in a prison in the 1930s. "David was a religious volunteer at my Catholic chapel at the youth correctional facility for six years," said the chaplain.

Father Vince speaks of one personal experience that will forever be memorable: "I visited the original death row in Folsom Prison in north California. You go into this big, huge area and see there are cell blocks within cell blocks, made with grey cinderblock—twelve cells in all, six on top, six on bottom. Cell #1 is in front of the noose, which is hanging there, with the trap door. As #1 is executed, you watch, and then you drop down a number. If you're #12, you get to see eleven executed. I learned these people became family as they waited their turn to die."

"This would be an incredible play, wouldn't it?" Father Vince asked. He tells this story because "we need to enlighten people," about the history of institutional violence that has gone on in our American prisons.

Father Vince always takes the opportunity to talk about the young men he has worked with for so many years, pointing out that, with proper rehabilitation, they can leave the prison and become productive citizens. "There's such a phenomenal change between age eighteen and age twenty-five."

One of the stories he tells is about Jason, in trouble at seventeen, convicted of murder about seven years ago. "In those days, there was still a philosophy of hope in California. He got sent to my institution. One day, after about two years, he came into my office and said he wanted to be a doctor." Jason began studying and proved to be diligent.

It so happened that about three years ago, two priest friends from Montana visited Father Vince. They got to meet Jason and were impressed with how brilliant he was. The priests knew that Carroll College in Helena, Montana, the college Father Vince had attended, had a notable pre-med program, and these three priests were determined to get Jason accepted there. They were successful, and Jason is there now, struggling financially, but determined to make it even if he has to live in his car, Father Vince says. "Jason is a poster child for rehabilitation. After his conviction at seventeen, he made a decision not to be a liability to society, but to contribute back to society. He wants to be a trauma care doctor in an inner city emergency room."

There could be many more success stories like this. But Father Vince is not optimistic, not in a state where punishment reigns. Case in point: California's "three strikes and you're out" rule, which mandates prison upon conviction for any third felony, regardless of how minor. "They just gave a guy twenty-five years to life. His third crime was stealing three cups of coffee," said Father Vince. "I think it's crazy."

Prisons can, indeed, be places of despair, but I have corresponded with and met many inmates who seem to be surviving the dehumanizing environment they are in, finding their own ways out of the darkness. Some might find it impossible to believe that persons convicted of serious crimes would actually find a "transformation" in prison that would bring them the internal freedom prerequisite for growing spiritually. I have several times read a paper with the intriguing title of "Despair, Redemption, and Meaning: Transformation in Prison," signed by a man named Mark K. Thomas and sent to me by a prisoner I have come to know well and respect. From his many years in prison, Mr. Thomas could share the truth of his own experience, a remarkable "transformation": "For the most part, prison is an unfortunate and diseased culture. It is a dehumanizing system created consciously by our society to mete out punishment and degradation, and is a result of our collective fear and hostility related to crime and those that commit it.... Its social and psychological environment is typically permeated with separatism, hatred, rage, despair, self-pity, fear, addiction, lust, delusion, and victimization.... [Yet] for me it was a place of redemption and service, because I could see through the darkness and psychic smog to the Light of the Soul that was still there in the troubled humanity about me, though it was obscured....

"People often ask me how I came through thirteen years of prison in the good psychological, moral, and spiritual shape I appear to be in. It was because of the power of the Soul and my identification with the Soul.... It was from my attempt to express spirituality into the darkness of the prison environment.... As a spiritual being, I am beyond abuse, humiliations, punishment, trauma, and degradation. This is how not only I survived, but prospered.... If one does not have a spiritual center to rely on then one will likely be a victim of the dehumanizing culture."

The author of this paper credits his involvement with two programs, the Alternatives to Violence and Hands of Peace workshops, with helping him move out of his isolation. "There we strove to learn together, to work together, to play together, to cry together, to laugh together, to walk together, to meditate and pray together, and to love and have faith together, but most importantly, we learned to have hope together."

I wonder how many prisons in the country care enough to try to bring programs to their people that would replace despair, which is common in prisons, with hope?

Sometimes I am humbled by the letters I receive from inmates who have become my friends. One man, gentle, devoted to his faith, is among them. I asked him to write to me about his prison experience and he did. I have known this man—who I shall not name for fear of repercussions—over four years, and he is solid and honest. His response is a truthful one.

"I have so much that I could say about the criminal justice system. It is difficult to find a starting point and focus. The system and its concomitant problems are very complex and multifaceted. One thing is for sure, there is no simple panacea to be advocated as a solution. Deep philosophical questions are raised—about ourselves, about who we are, what our beliefs are, and what kind of civilization have we made.

"To me, prison represents the dark side of humanity. It seems to bring out the worst in everyone. In a way, though, prison has enabled me to rediscover myself. The lyrics, 'I once was lost but now I am found,' have a much deeper meaning for me now. It wasn't until I was thrown into a cage, alone with nothing, that for the first time in my life I was honest, brutally honest, with myself. I questioned myself about many things: What kind of contribution have I made to the world? Am I a man of integrity? Morality? Honor? I didn't like the answers I gave myself. I felt so worthless. I was so tormented that I wanted to die. I seriously contemplated suicide. The only thing that prevented me from going through with it was my family. How much further grief would I cause them by doing that? After all the disappointment and embarrassment that I caused them, they gave me unconditional love and support. It was their love that saved my life. The glimmer of hope of one day being reunited with them kept me from taking my own life.

"Soon after, I experienced a spiritual awakening. I gained a sense of purpose. Intuitively, I knew what I had to do to make myself whole in mind, body, and spirit. I began going to school (GED and college). I stopped abusing my body with cigarettes, marijuana, and alcohol, and I renewed my faith. For a while I started feeling good about myself. I was healthy, doing well in college, and my spirit was growing each day. But prison is not a cooperative place. I was injured, the college program was discontinued, and the confinement, deprivation, and psychological abuse are a constant assault on the spirit.

"I began suffering from severe bouts of depression. I once asked my former psychology teacher (and special academic program director) about it when she came back to the prison to speak to us. She said it was a normal response to an abnormal environment. I found a little solace in that thought. However, the depression has been more frequent and intense. There's a wide range of emotions involved. I try to fight it but sometimes it feels as though it's futile. The biggest obstacle is the constant psychological abuse from the administration and officers. Their dehumanizing treatment, degradation, humiliation, and cruelty induce hopelessness and despair. It's not something that can adequately be explained in detail. It's a cumulative thing. Unfortunately, it must be experienced to be completely understood. It's like an insidious culture that casts a shadow over people.

"I remember reading about an experiment at the university in Berkeley, California. They took a group of college students, some of whom had the role of corrections officers and others that of prisoners. They reported that the 'corrections officers' became abusive and cruel to the 'prisoners.' The researchers, all of them psychologists, thought that it was the power, that it was some kind of catharsis. I don't know why it happens, but I know that it does. I've witnessed new officers, some of them just kids and seemingly good people, who, after a while, suddenly become malevolent....

"I hope I haven't been 'bumming you out' with all of this stuff. I'm afraid that I've been babbling on. This stuff has been bottled up inside of me for so long....

"Of course, the criminal justice system is much larger in scope than just prisons. There are many social, economic, political, and judicial issues that require redress for there to be any meaningful reform. I'm very pessimistic about reform, however, given the level of public discourse. Public officials and the news media in particular have been egregiously irresponsible at informing (or should I say dis-informing) the public regarding criminal justice issues. So many people seem to form their opinions from an assimilation of twenty-second sound-bytes. This news-speak has a tremendous influence on the political climate and ultimately public policy. Everyone seems to be so agenda-driven and predisposed without knowing the facts or thinking things through. It is all so very discouraging."

I simply cannot understand why inmates like this man, who so clearly has a fine mind and much goodness, cannot be treated with respect and given some opportunities to get an education and meaningful employment.

Many survivors of murder victims counter my willingness to believe that a person who committed a terrible crime can be transformed into a good, productive member of our human race. They point out that many of them never take full responsibility for the heinous act they committed, believing often that they, and not the one they hurt or killed, are the "victims" because their early environment was unjust, the people around them were abusive, and all they found was a "dog-eat-dog" cruel world as they went through adolescence and early adulthood.

John MacKenzie tells me he was one of these angry young men, removed from his home when he was six, "separated from the only connection to life I had," then catapulted from foster home to Catholic Charities back to foster home, never experiencing love or a connection to anything. "Today," he said, "when a child is physically admonished, it's called child abuse; when I was beaten by people entrusted with my welfare, it was called corporal punishment."

I met John after a Catholic service at Greenhaven prison when he approached me and wanted me to participate in a group he had been running there to bring victims and prisoners together so that his fellow inmates could learn first hand what a crime like theirs does to victims. "I started talking to men in prison about taking responsibility for their crime," he said. He had "an epiphany," after years as an angry young man believing everybody was out to get him. He was convicted in 1975 for a crime that resulted in the death of a police officer, a tragedy that was "nonintentional," not premeditated, he says. "I believed I was 'railroaded,' and that I was the victim. I was only worried about getting a reversal." Then, in 1983, at a conference at Attica prison, he met George Grobe, then chairman of the Crime Victims Board, and listened to him speak in a very emotional way about the rights of victims.

Still feeling like a victim himself, sentenced to twenty-five years to life, John challenged that man. Then something happened. "There was a warmth running through my body. I immediately went over to him and apologized for challenging him in the group. He commended me on how prepared I was and added that if I put as much energy into trying to understand victims, I'd be a worthy proponent. So began my journey into victims and how they are treated, how they feel, how they are in fact, mothers, fathers, brothers, sisters, sons, and daughters—how they are family." He became overwhelmed with remorse, thinking about the family of Officer Matthew Giglio, who died ten weeks after he shot him.

John started to talk to his fellow inmates about victims and learned how many of them were in the same, wrong place he had long been in—feeling themselves the victim. "It took years of group meetings, class discussions, and personal interaction with men to finally convince enough of them that they would have to start thinking about victims." He says he spent the next decade and a half taking courses, designing classes, getting men interested in starting a Victims Awareness group.

John eventually was able to start this program at Greenhaven, designed to get men convicted of a crime to take full responsibility for their actions, express sincere remorse, and not blame the rest of society for their failures. In meeting victims face to face, the men could feel the pain and suffering they caused others. John had a long-range vision for this program, the hope that when a man was released from prison, being with victims would have changed him enough so that he would not return to the community with the same mentality that led him to prison in the first place. In a statement about his years of working to bring victims and prisoners together, John addresses all of us: "Why care at all about this? Because most of the people in prison will eventually return to their communities, more specifically, the very same neighborhoods they left. How they return is not only your concern, but also your responsibility, your responsibility to ensure they reintegrate with a different attitude, one that encourages them to sublimate their energy into more productive life styles. The only way to accomplish this is to offer them a chance to effect positive change, and to do that, you must provide a vehicle—a vehicle guided by a sincere desire to make amends for one's immorality."

So much needs to be done to humanize the criminal justice system. One of the best ways this can be done is to give inmates their own "sacred space" for religious services and private prayer, but I've come across one story that shows how limited this opportunity is in many prisons. It reminded me of many years ago when I saw a movie called *A Bell for Adamo,* set in a village in Italy. The people had lost their church bell because of World War II's destruction, and all they wanted was to have a bell again. It was an important symbol; it made them a community. I felt something similar going on when I talked to Deacon Richard Rosado, a Catholic prison chaplain, telling me about how badly the men he works with want their own place to worship the Lord. A movie about them could be called *A Chapel for Mid-Orange.*

Deacon Rosado has been at Mid-Orange, a correctional facility in New York State, for the past ten years. He told me that out of a prison population of some 750 men, about 300 are Catholic. For religious services, only one room is available, and this has to accommodate men belonging to all other religious faiths.

"We all have to share the multipurpose room. My altar is a table on wheels. After Mass, God forbid the priest and I leave anything behind. The cross, the statue of the Blessed Mother, and the tabernacle go in a closet," said Deacon Rosado, who described the multipurpose room as a "sandwich": "Above the room is the gym, so we hear all the noise, especially the sound of dropping weights. Below us is the recreation room, with the TV blaring. Then there's the PA system. So much noise. We're fighting all this."

Deacon Rosado sees an even deeper problem for weekdays. "As Catholics, we should be able to have here what we have on the outside—sacred space, a place to join others in prayer, or seek repentance, or just find solace alone from everyday pressure."

Several years ago representatives from the Archdiocese of New York asked for and received permission to build a chapel on prison grounds from the state commissioner of corrections, but under the condition that the chaplain raise the money. Deacon Rosado says that because the men would provide the labor, the chapel could be built for about $110,000. Yet, even a tax-deductible donation seems to be a low priority for people who could contribute. To date, the chaplain has been able to raise less than $40,000.

What you hear when you talk to this chaplain is how much he cares for the prisoners. "It is a pleasure working with the men. I want to be here till I die," says this family man, who left a big company twenty-two years ago to be ordained a deacon. He has opened doors for many men, fallen away from the faith, to come back to the church.

His dream for a chapel is a realistic one, because he has a model, the beautiful St. Paul's Catholic Chapel at Greenhaven prison, built in the 1960s by the inmates. It was the determination of the chaplain, Father Edward J. Donovan, now a monsignor and retired after nearly forty years of working with the men imprisoned here, that made this dream of having their own chapel a reality. Designed with a semicircle floor plan, it has wood ceiling beams that converge over the altar to center on a simple, large cross. Considering that the daily wages for an inmate then was ten cents a day, the money for materials had to be raised elsewhere, and they put out an appeal for "Green Stamps," which were a popular money-back item then. Father Donovan once told me that the chapel was literally built by the hands of inmates and Green Stamps! He and the inmates even wrote a poem, about their joy and their need, on the back of a card showing a photo of the impressive chapel.

> St. Paul's Chapel is surrounded
> By walls impressively high.
> There, as the days go by,
> Mass becomes special for men here
> Bringing hope and God's Love to cheer.
>
> Savings stamps are important now,
> PLAID, GREEN and TRIPLE s blue.
> All that are given by you,
> From the goodness of your heart
> Will make your love a special part....

I have often been to Greenhaven, and I see the joy it brings the men to have their own Catholic chapel. It warms the heart to see some as altar servers and hear all of them sing out, led by their own inmate-formed music group. How important it is for Catholic prisoners to meet Christ behind bars in the person of a chaplain, and better yet, if they have their own "sacred space." I pray that Deacon Rosado's dream for a chapel comes true. I pray that prisons become more than warehouses stacked with discarded human beings.

POSTSCRIPT

In the summer of 2000, I was asked to be the guest speaker for the tenth annual ecumenical Remembrance Day service to be held in Worcester, Massachusetts, sponsored by Project Hope to Abolish the Death Penalty. The call came from Tanya Connor, who explained that HOPE, a nonsectarian organization, was started in 1989 by death row inmates in Alabama, along with abolitionists outside prison walls. One of the co-founders was her friend Wallace Thomas, who was executed on July 13, 1990. Every year since that day, on or near the July 13 anniversary, Tanya has invited people to observe a Remembrance Day in Massachusetts, joining with people in and outside the prisons in Alabama and Louisiana to mourn all victims of violent crimes.

"We value life, oppose killing by the state and individuals, and invite all to help end the cycle of violence, seeking restitution to victims' families, rehabilitation of offenders, and reconciliation between both groups," Tanya wrote in her letter to me.

Those words expressed exactly what I have long stood for and prayed for. It was an honor for me to accept the invitation.

I had a surprise coming when I finished talking and answering questions from the many people who filled Our Lady of Fatima Church, where, welcomed graciously by the pastor, Father Louis Gould, the Project Hope to Abolish the Death Penalty program was being held. A dozen or so youngsters—who were youth group members from St. Mary Parish in Uxbridge, I later found out—went up to the altar, papers in their hands. One by one, they began to read names—the names of the 651 people who, by mid-July 2000, had been executed in the United States since 1976. It surprised me that I knew so many of the names, so many of their stories. I felt I was attending a massive wake.

This was sobering, powerful, disturbing. We in that church were mourning, not anonymous "prisoners" or "inmates" or "criminals," but people who had a name, who once had faces, personalities, bodies, and souls. The wretchedness of how we kill in the name of "justice" became more and more thundering as the young ones kept voicing the names of people we took it upon ourselves to judge as unworthy of life. I started to pray—"God, forgive us!"

Ahead of us is a huge challenge. First we have to stop the lie that has been built into our society: that killing is an acceptable way to handle those we judge to be aggressors. What an insane logic we ascribe to— that the state should kill to show others that killing is wrong! There's no way we can cover up the truth that putting a fellow human being to death in the cold-blooded, planned, bureaucratic way that executions are carried out is nothing less than barbaric and horrifying.

Still, some make a joke of this. Consider what Gail Collins wrote for a July column in the *New York Times*: "Just outside our nation's capital, kids of all ages have been flocking to an arcade in Rockville, Maryland, to ride on The Shocker, an electric chair simulation that challenges patrons to hang on until smoke comes out of their skulls." And then there was another *Times* story by Kari Haskell entitled "Never Say Die, Just Execute." This was about how we can now buy a toy called "Death Row Marv," put out by McFarlane Toys, and by pulling a tiny switch, carry out a miniature execution. "Watch Marv convulse as the switch is thrown," say the words on the box, then hear him say, "That the best you can do?" His eyes "glow red as he fries." According to the marketing director of the toy company, they sold out in preorder sales before Marv was even in the stores, and sales are booming, with the typical buyer being a fifteen-to-forty-five-year-old male.

Some supporters of the death penalty take great offense with my position that we must end this death penalty madness, maintaining this abolitionist stance "corrodes American trust in the democratic system," as David Frum, an author, wrote in an Op-Ed column in the *New York Times*. Claiming death penalty opponents "are hoping to persuade governors who support executions to flip flop after the election," he says that what's really being asked is that governors "flout democratically enacted laws," inviting them "to abuse their power, alienating and embittering their electorates."

On national television Ohio's Governor Frank Keating made the point that "capital punishment, in most cases, works very well." When asked how he, a Catholic, feels about the pope's strong anti–death penalty stand, the governor responded that the pope "was wrong" on this one.

Clearly, people holding to our right to kill murderers feel very justified in taking that position. Very often they point to people like me, a victim who has mourned the deaths of my son and his wife from the day I got word of the murders and will continue to mourn till the day I die and become reunited with them. They say the only way I can have "justice" is to see the murderer killed. But I ask, what good can come of heaping more violence upon the violence already done? I beg, please, don't ask to kill in my name.

I would urge people of conscience throughout America to get on the bandwagon calling for a moratorium on all executions until the system is fixed, guaranteeing that never again would an innocent person be put on death row, that American "justice" is no longer riddled with racial and ethnic bias, and that mentally incapable people and juveniles get treatment and punishment commensurate with their level of capability and understanding at the time they committed a crime. This would at least be a first step toward restoring human rights in our land.

I believe we must protest a criminal justice system that, in effect, regards innocence as "irrelevant." Innocence is relevant and should be considered whenever new evidence is presented that could determine if the right person is incarcerated for a given crime. Congress should abolish its 1996 Anti-Terrorism and Effective Death Penalty Act that puts a time limit of one year on a prisoner's direct appeal (a habeas corpus petition) to the federal court for a review of a case. This simply results in prisoners "running out of time" for a hearing on their case. Most of us would like to believe that gross injustice does not happen in our country. But it does when it comes to an "actual innocence" appeal for a new trial. As stated in the *New York Times,* "Once a jury has reached a verdict or a judge has ruled, lawyers say, the odds are overwhelmingly against reopening a case, no matter how compelling the new information is." This is incomprehensible, and as citizens, we should be protesting this.

An immediate change needed throughout our nation is the radical reform of our prison system. Because of our mandatory drug laws, people arrested for handling sometimes very small amounts of illegal drugs are sent to prison for terms that defy logic. Nearly a half million people are behind bars for crimes involving drugs—ten times more than twenty years ago—nearly a third of them for simply possessing an illicit drug. When you read of the thousands behind bars, who have no history of violence, confined for decades, with no possibility of parole because of the way these laws are written, we have to conclude that this is inhumane—or maybe insane.

While these mandatory long sentences account for much of the increase in the total prison population—rising from about a quarter million twenty-five years ago to two million in 2001—they're not the entire reason. Convicted people are getting longer sentences, and prison is becoming the accepted punishment for what once might have been considered a minor crime. Then, in the effort to prove they're getting "tough on crime," people in powerful corrections positions have "taken deliberate, progressive steps to hold criminals more accountable for the consequences of their acts," as stated by Connecticut's Department of Corrections. How? They "minimize the opportunities for early releases" in several ways, such as denying parole and eliminating "good time" credits. In Connecticut, for example, the department says, "Time served has been restored to meaningful levels." In 1989, inmates served 31 percent of their sentence as compared to 1999 when they served 78 percent. The states also have a decided incentive for keeping inmates locked up for a long time. "A Federal law passed in 1994 provides matching funds to states to keep violent criminals in prison longer by denying parole. This act and other so-called truth-in-sentencing laws are reasons why the ranks of prisoners will not soon drop, even as crime levels off," reports the *New York Times*.

Because of the climbing numbers of prisoners, incarcerated for such long terms, we've had an enormous prison-building boom going on, often in communities that were economically depressed. No more. Now there are jobs, lots of them, permanent ones, high-paying and with excellent benefits. We have become a prison-building society, which means we're going to have to keep these places filled, and it won't matter if many of the people there are nonviolent and in need of medical help, drug rehabilitation, or mental health services. They won't get help, because our prisons today are for punishment, not rehabilitation. It's not surprising that prison becomes a revolving door for all too many of those who do get out. The recidivism rate stays all too high.

"We've created a monstrous operation, and it's growing," said Father Mike Bryant, a prison chaplain for twenty years in Washington, D.C., in the *National Catholic Reporter*. "Our prisons are social trash compactors: We believe that if you stick everybody together—the medically unhealthy and the mentally ill, the socially deviant and those with AIDS—that we'll come out with something magically different. Well, we do," he said, pointing to the recidivism rate—70 percent among juveniles, 63 percent among adults.

As the prison-industrial complex continues to grow, and all the signs are that it will, not enough attention has been given to the price we're paying to put nearly one out of every 150 people in our country into prison. In dollars, it costs well over $20,000 a year in most states— $66 to $156 a day in Connecticut—to house a prisoner; that escalates to about $50,000 for the thousands who are in Special Housing Units (SHUs). California will soon be reporting that it costs the state nearly $4 billion a year to run its gigantic prison system. With so much money going for prisons, what's left for social services, children's needs, the homeless, low-income mothers, job training, low-income housing, you name it. When it comes to what we've done about crime in this country, there's only one way to describe this mess—it's a crime!

Some people have been confused by my strong anti–death penalty beliefs. A few have accused me of caring more for murderers than for victims. I make my position clear: I believe people who commit crimes must be punished, and the punishment should fit the crime, and I also believe that life in prison, without parole, fits the crime of murder very well. I don't believe we should rob thieves, rape rapists, burn an arsonist, or kill a killer. They must be punished, but this is done by taking them out of circulation, protecting society by removing them from the population.

I am certainly aware that some people are entrenched in their violence and that the job of a corrections officer can be very dangerous when having to deal with the worst of the worst. This very day as I am writing this, I read a news story of an inmate attack on the warden and four corrections officers at Connecticut's Northern Correctional Institution, which houses the most violent prisoners as well as those on death row. Warden Lawrence Myers was slashed in the face by John Barletta, who had made a knife out of a razor blade. Barletta, twenty-nine, is serving a life sentence without the possibility of parole for killing a cell mate at another prison where he had been serving two concurrent sixty-year sentences for driving a car involved in a drive-by shooting, leaving a woman dead. The corrections officers suffered lacerations when they tried to restrain Barletta. Stories like this show that some inmates— who may be amoral or insane—need to be kept away from the general population. No one would want to see him kill another person—inmate, warden, or guard.

Another serious problem I hear of, from the prisoners themselves, concerns the escalating prison gangs, power-wars behind the walls. One good inmate I know told me that years ago when young ones like he was then came into the prison, the older men would take them under their wing and show them the ropes on how to survive, stay out of trouble, and do well. Today, he said, the younger ones don't listen; they either don't want to, or they're afraid of repercussions. They're taken into a gang, most often defined by ethnic kinship—White vs. Black vs. Hispanic vs. Asian—and that's where their loyalty stays. "And gangs tend to be predators in a prison population," he said.

The prison gang problems are the reason given for why Control Units or Special Housing Units (SHUs) are being built in increasing numbers. But what kind of a human being is going to emerge from these places, where they have been denied human contact for a long period, degraded, threatened, and deprived of just about everything but food and a toilet? An Investigative Report on the A&E cable network gave a graphic and disturbing look at these control units, interviewing psychiatrists, like Dr. Stuart Grassian of Chestnut Hill, Massachusetts, who studied people confined in them. The devastating effects of such "sensory deprivation" are vast, including restlessness, banging on walls, yelling, incoherent, confused states, hallucinations, regression, disassociation, weakness, and exhaustion. Early in the twentieth century, the nation closed down the one solitary prison that had been built, in Pennsylvania, for being "inhumane." Early in the twenty-first century we build such places of human destruction, with high-tech cruelty added to them. Are SHUs really the way to attack the gang problem in our prisons? Couldn't we work out constructive ways to treat human beings, helping them to emerge healed instead of destroyed? I believe SHUs, which are vehicles for physical, mental, psychological, and spiritual breakdowns, are immoral and inhumane and that Americans should demand that they be abolished.

I don't deny we have major problems with crime in America. But I also believe we have put our resources primarily into punishing offenders, all too many of them young. Far too little is being done to discover ways we could make them see a better path. Gangs are *chosen* families, where young people—who may be disadvantaged, lonely, mentally unstable, unguided by an adult, failing in school—get approval for acting out their fantasies of self-power through violence, as they are television-taught. We haven't given them other options.

I also believe that victims have rights, and that these in many ways have been overlooked by the criminal justice system. Anyone who has ever been the victim of a crime knows how devastating this violation of your person and your life can be. Depending on the severity of the crime, a victim can be permanently damaged, physically and emotionally, by the trauma. And one of the added pains is that victims are often made to feel that no one really cares enough about their wounds to help them. It is easier for all just to forget the crime and to tell the victims to get up and get on with their life.

To address the fact that the justice system too often ignores the victims of crime, there has been a proposal in Washington for a Constitutional Amendment to right a number of wrongs done to victims of crime and their families, including: to insure that victims are told when court proceedings will take place and that they have the right to attend them; to give victims the right to make a statement in court about bail, sentencing, and a plea bargain; to keep victims informed about parole hearings and give them the right to speak at these; to have victims notified if the convicted criminal should escape from prison or will come up for early release because of "good time."

Such a Constitutional Amendment wouldn't change the present adversarial system of prosecution and defense. Its purpose would be to end confusion about just what are victims' rights, and make sure that victims get treated with fairness and respect. Certainly, as a victim, I believe we should have access to information about the arrest, be allowed to communicate with the prosecution, be allowed to make a statement to the court at sentencing, and have the right to get needed help, be it counseling or financial. But I also believe that nothing should happen in a courtroom that would diminish the constitutional tenet that an accused is innocent until proven guilty. I also have some real concerns about victims' rights versus the rights of the accused in death penalty cases. For example, I would oppose any law that would give us, murder victims' survivors, the right to address the jury in a death penalty case, telling them of the impact of the crime on us. Such an emotional account could wrongly influence a jury.

I have known the pain of murder and have grieved with many other parents of murdered children. We are all victims, and through Survivors of Homicide, we advocate changes in the court system. It is devastating when you can't get information from the system that would help you cope with the tragic death.

If we need something like a Constitutional Amendment to guarantee victims' rights, the reason for this is simply because the criminal justice system and the courts have failed us. Voices are being raised by people whose lives have been shattered by the senseless acts of another; they're demanding to be heard. As always, there must be caution, to make sure

that in guaranteeing rights to victims, rights are not taken away from
the accused, who could be innocent.

I believed that the death penalty was wrong, but it took a tremendous
tragedy to bring me to a point where I would actively go out and speak
passionately of this belief. First I had to grieve, in my own way and in
my own time. Grieving is essential because it keeps us from suppressing
the truth of our pain and the fact that we are permanently altered by
such an immense loss. With grieving we acknowledge our pain and our
anger and learn that these are prerequisites for the next step we must
take. That step begins with questions: Who am I going to become now
that I have been seared by evil? What am I supposed to do with my
life now?

Buoyed by the grace of God, I found my answer. It is not to want
more death. It is ever to work for and celebrate *life*.

SOURCES AND NOTES

ᏸᏯᏸᏯᏸᏯᏸᏯᏸᏯᏸᏯᏸᏯ

Sources used by the author have been many and varied, gathered primarily from books, magazine articles, newspaper features, personal interviews, talks covered from a journalist's perspective, and published stories and opinion pieces by-lined by the author. The major resources are here presented, chapter by chapter.

Chapter One: The Murders

"Deaths of Pair Probed," *Daily Inter Lake,* August 20, 1993.

"Couple Murdered in Ferndale Home," *Bigfork Eagle,* August 25, 1993. Note: All the news stories from the *Bigfork Eagle* listed below were written by William Simonsen.

Raymond Moody, *Life after Life: The Investigation of a Phenomenon—Survival of Bodily Death* (Harrisburg, Pa.: Stackpole Books, 1976).

"Shadow Clark Arrested in Bosco Slayings," *Bigfork Eagle,* December 15, 1993.

"Investigators Want to Know: Was Nancy Bosco Molested?" *Bigfork Eagle,* December 29, 1993.

"Dear Judge, Please Ask Why," editorial, *Bigfork Eagle,* July 28, 1994.

"Teen Pleads Guilty to Killings," *Daily Inter Lake,* June 28, 1994.

"Man Admits to Double Murder," *Associated Press,* June 28, 1994.

"Clark Says Murders Prompted by Dreams," *Bigfork Eagle,* September 7, 1994.

Chapter Two: Beginning the Healing Process

"Albany Murder," *Albany Times Union,* November 8, 1926.

"Sentence Doran to Chair," *Albany Times Union,* May 9, 1927.

"Doran Has Lost All Hope," *Albany Times Union,* January 3, 1928.

"Smith Gives His Reasons in Denying Clemency," *Albany Times Union,* January 6, 1928.

"How Doran Died," *Albany Times Union,* January 6, 1928.

Antoinette Bosco, *The Pummeled Heart: Finding Peace through Pain* (Mystic, Conn.: Twenty-Third Publications, 1994).

Survivors of Homicide, 530 Silas Dean Highway, Suite 108, Wethersfield, Conn.

Antoinette Bosco, "Best-Selling Author Revisits His Alma Mater—Dominick Dunne Shares Experiences," *Litchfield County Times,* February 25, 1994.

Antoinette Bosco, "Candidates Callously Ride the Death Penalty Bandwagon... (speaking with Bill Pelke)," *Litchfield County Times,* November 4, 1994.

Antoinette Bosco, "No Benefit from Increase in Executions" (Raulerson, Skillern executions), *Litchfield County Times*, February 15, 1985.

Sister Helen Prejean, *Dead Man Walking: An Eyewitness Account of the Death Penalty in the United States* (New York: Random House, 1993).

Debbie Morris, *Forgiving the Dead Man Walking* (Grand Rapids, Mich.: Zondervan, 1998).

"Where Healing Begins—'I Forgave My Rapist,'" [by Debbie Morris, as told to Antoinette Bosco], *Clarity* (February–March 1999).

Chapter Three: Raising My Voice

"Justice Is Served," *Daily Inter Lake,* May 10, 1995.

"Death Penalty Delays Cruel, Unusual Punishment for Victims' Families," editorial, *Bigfork Eagle,* May 3, 1995.

Antoinette Bosco, "A Mother Comes to Terms with her Son's Killer," *Hartford Courant,* June 20, 1995.

"Inner Peace Restored for Victims' Families When Murderer Is Executed," *National Catholic Reporter,* July 2, 1999.

"Divisive Case of a Killer of Two Ends as Texas Executes Tucker," *New York Times,* February 4, 1998.

Antoinette Bosco, "Not All Victims of Murderers Demand Vengeance" (after Richard Thornton's positive reaction to the Tucker execution), *Danbury News-Times,* February 22, 1998.

"Texas Executes Killer of Two As Families of Victims Watch," *New York Times,* February 10, 1996.

Chapter Four: Plunging into the Debate

"Forgiving the Unforgiveable" (the Marietta Jaeger story), *Detroit Free Press Magazine,* August 21, 1994.

"Death Penalty Protects the Social Contract" (Charles Olivea), *Litchfield County Times,* February 15, 1985.

"A Friendship Rooted in Tragedy, Based on Forgiveness" (Rev. Walter Everett story), *New York Times,* October 30, 1994.

Save Our Sons and Daughters (SOSAD), 2441 Grand Blvd., Detroit, MI 48208, 313-361-5200, *SOSADB@aol.com.*

Teresa Mathis, "A New Look at the Victims' Movement," *The Voice, Murder Victims Families for Reconciliation* (Summer 1995).

Charley Reese, "Benefits of the Death Penalty," *Conservative Chronicle,* February 15, 1989.

"In Death Row Dispute, a Witness Stands Firm" (on Gary Graham execution), *New York Times,* June 16, 2000.

"With Bush Assent, Convict Executed" (Gary Graham), *New York Times,* June 23, 2000.

Charles Wilton, "Innocence Is Irrelevant," Peacework, Global Thought and Local Action for Nonviolent Social Change, American Friends Service Committee.

Chapter Five: A New Door Opens—and Prisoners Become Kin

"Prison a Punishment, Influx of Inmates Burdening System" (American Correctional Association Convention, Denver), August 24, 1976.

"Moral Sense Lacking, 2 Judges Criticize Failures of Society" (American Correctional Association), *Denver Post,* August 25, 1976.

"Colson, Others...Urge Simplifying Criminal Justice System" (American Correctional Association), *Denver Post,* August 26, 1976.

Antoinette Bosco, "Judges, Prison Officials Confess They Don't Know How to Rehabilitate," *St. Louis Review,* October 1, 1976.

Herbert H. Haines, *Against Capital Punishment: The Anti–Death Penalty Movement in America, 1972–1994* (New York: Oxford University Press, 1996), 53, with permission.

"Attica Revisited: Conditions Are As They Were Before '71 Riot," *Sunday News,* September 5, 1976.

"Ex-Attica Inmates Recount Shattered Lives and Dreams," *New York Times,* February 15, 2000.

" 'Prison Bishop' Condemns 'Hanging Judge' Mentality," *The Evangelist* (Albany), November 25, 1976.

Antoinette Bosco, "For Women in Prison and Their Warden—Not an Easy Life," *Woman Magazine,* November 1996.

"The Utmost Restraint and How to Exercise It—The Incarcerated-Minded Meet to Buy Mobile Cells, Ballistic Batons and More," *New York Times,* August 23, 1996.

Antoinette Bosco, "They're Not Human Garbage" (Catholic News Service), *Catholic Free Press* (Worcester, Mass.), August 29, 1997.

"Basic Prison and Jail Fact Sheet," February 2000, Correctional Association of New York, 135 E. 15th St., New York, NY 10003, 212-254-5700.

"Prisons, the New Growth Industry," *National Catholic Reporter,* July 2, 1999.

Chapter Six: Calls Come In—and I Am the Learner

"Committee Hears Death Penalty Testimony; Bishop Reilly: Dignity of Life Is Most Powerful Principle," *Catholic Free Press* (Worcester, Mass.), March 26, 1999.

"Execution for Juveniles: New Focus on an Old Issue" (includes Charles Rumbaugh), *New York Times,* September 10, 1985.

"Texan Put to Death for a Murder Committed at 17" (Charles Rumbaugh), *New York Times,* September 11, 1985.

"Texas Legislator Proposes Death Penalty for Murderers as Young as 11," *New York Times,* April 18, 1998.

"Boy Who Killed Gets 7 Years; Judge Says Law Is Too Harsh" (Nathaniel Abraham), *New York Times,* January 14, 2000.

Antoinette Bosco, "Guns in Hands of Children, a Lethal Combination," *Litchfield County Times,* January 27, 1989.

"Death Penalty Punishes Us All" (Renny Cushing), *Concord Monitor,* April 5, 1998, with permission.

"Is the Death Penalty Good for Us?" (Bruce Ledewitz), *The Voice* (Winter 1995).

Chapter Seven: Behind the Bars, Seriously Flawed Prison System

"Number in Prison Grows Despite Crime Reduction," *New York Times,* August 10, 2000.

Scott Christianson, *With Liberty for Some: 500 Years of Imprisonment in America* (Boston: Northeastern University Press, 1998), 299–313, with permission.

Cardinal John J. O'Connor, "The Rockefeller Drug Laws" *Catholic New York,* February 3, 2000.

"New York's Harmful Drug Laws," editorial, *New York Times,* May 12, 2000.

"Drug Laws That Destroy Lives," editorial, *New York Times,* May 24, 2000.

"Drug Laws That Misfired," editorial, *New York Times,* June 5, 2000.

"Bills Aim to Reroute Minority Prisoners" (Connecticut drug offenders), *Danbury News-Times,* April 6, 1999.

George Anderson, S.J., "Supermax Prisons," *America,* December 4, 1999, with permission.

Paul Grondahl, "Lockdown—Sensible Control or Senseless Cruelty?" *Albany Times Union,* March 26, 2000.

"As More Prisons Go Private, States Seek Tighter Controls," *New York Times,* April 15, 1999.

"Privately Run Juvenile Prison in Louisiana Is Attacked for Abuse of 6 Inmates," *New York Times,* March 16, 2000.

"When Johnny Calls Home, from Prison," editorial, *New York Times,* December 5, 1999.

Antoinette Bosco, "Prison Rate: $3.33 for the First Minute," Catholic News Service, *Catholic Free Press* (Worcester, Mass.), January 14, 2000.

Campaign to Promote Equitable Telephone Charges, c/o MI-CURE, P.O. Box 2736, Kalamazoo, MI 49003-2736.

Chapter Eight: The Other Victims

Barbara Lewis, "A Son on Death Row," *The Voice,* MVFR (Summer 1995).

"A Tale of Intuition and Trust, an Interview with David Kaczynski and Linda Patrik," *Journal of Family Life* 4 (November 3, 1998), with permission.

Sonia "Sunny" Jacobs, "Not in Our Name, Murder Victims' Families Speak Out against the Death Penalty," 3d ed., 1999.

Chapter Nine: Leadership from the Pulpit

"Prison Bishop Condemns 'Hanging Judge' Mentality," *The Evangelist,* November 25, 1976.

"The Death Penalty: The Religious Community Calls for Abolition, Statements of Opposition to Capital Punishment," Religious Organizing Against the Death Penalty, c/o American Friends Service Committee, *pclark@afsc.org,* with permission.

"Catholic Opposition to Death Penalty Forefront in Many States," *Long Island Catholic,* June 2000.

"Statement of Catholic Bishops of Connecticut regarding Capital Punishment," *Hartford Catholic Transcript,* March 31, 1995.

"Building Consensus on the Death Penalty," Bishops of Missouri, *Origins,* CNS Documentary Service, Washington, D.C., February 5, 1999.

Mercy and Justice—The Morality of the Death Penalty, videotape by the Diocese of Brooklyn, Public Relations Office, Diocese of Brooklyn, P.O. Box C, Brooklyn, NY 12202.

"Statement on the Death Penalty," The Bruderhof Communities, P.O. Box 903, Rifton, NY 12471.

Most Rev. Charles J. Chaput, "The True Road to Justice," Archdiocese of Denver, June 6, 1997, with permission.

"A Closer Look: After Much Study, St. Andrew's Parish Crafts Death Penalty Moratorium," *Syracuse Catholic Sun,* September 16–22, 1999.

"Declaration of Life," Cherish Life Circle, Convent of Mercy, 273 Willoughby Avenue, Brooklyn, NY 11205.

"Diocese Makes Death Penalty Priority Issue for Jubilee Year," *Long Island Catholic,* January 25, 2000.

Catholics Against Capital Punishment, P.O. Box 3125, Arlington, VA 22203.

Chapter Ten: Concern about the Death Penalty Grows

"Colosseum Symbol of Life for Capital Punishment Foes," *National Catholic Reporter,* December 1999.

"Europeans Deplore Executions in the U.S.," *New York Times,* February 25, 2000.

"More Vehemently Than Ever, Europe Is Scorning the U.S.," *New York Times,* April 8, 2000.

"2 Million-Plus Sign Anti–Death Penalty Petition," *Catholic Free Press* (Worcester, Mass.), March 10, 2000.

"Is the Death Penalty a Human Rights Issue?" Amnesty International USA, 322 Eighth Avenue, New York, NY 10001.

"25 Wrongfully Executed in the U.S., Study Finds," *New York Times,* November 14, 1985.

"Death Sentences Being Overturned in 2 of 3 Appeals," *New York Times,* June 12, 2000.

"Bloody Death Prompts Call for Executions Halt," *Danbury News-Times,* July 9, 1999.

"Florida OK's Bill to Speed Executions," *Danbury News-Times,* January 8, 2000.

"Prisons Brim with Mentally Ill," *New York Times,* July 11, 1999.

"Why Our Son, Larry Robison, Is on Death Row," *Works in Progress,* September 1999.

"Governor Grants Pope's Plea for Life of a Missouri Inmate," *New York Times,* January 28, 1999.

Sister Eileen Hogan, R.S.M., "Women Religious in State Oppose Death Penalty," *Fairfield County Catholic,* October 1998.

Sister Camille D'Arienzo, "The Quality of Mercy Confronts a Killer," *National Catholic Reporter,* August 27, 1999.

Father Thomas Condon, "Called to Death Row," *America,* April 1, 2000, with permission.

"Governor Ryan's Brave Example," editorial, *New York Times,* July 3, 2000.

"Illinois Governor Halts Executions," *Moratorium News!* Equal Justice USA, Quixote Center, Spring 2000.

Senator Russ Feingold, "Clinton Urged to Declare Moratorium," *Moratorium News!* Equal Justice USA, Quixote Center, Spring 2000.

"The Federal Death Row," editorial, *New York Times,* July 8, 2000.

"Charges of Bias Challenge U.S. Death Penalty," *New York Times,* June 24, 2000.

"U.S. Plans Delay in First Execution in Four Decades," *New York Times,* July 7, 2000.

Senator Patrick Leahy, " 'Innocence Protection Act' Introduced in Senate," *Moratorium News!* Equal Justice USA, Quixote Center.

"Death Knell for Death Row?" *ABA Journal,* June 2000.

Art Laffin, "My Brother's Murder and the Gospel Call of Mercy and Nonviolence," *Catholic Peace Voice,* Fall 1999, with permission.

Sister Dorothy Briggs, O.P., "For Whom the Bells Toll," PO Box 2736, Kalamazoo, MI 49003-2736.

Chapter Eleven: So Much Known—So Much to Be Done

Michael Mello, "Connecticut's Death Penalty Bills Would Ease Way to Executions" (quote, Rowland bill), *New York Times,* April 10, 1995.

Michael Ross, "My Journey toward the Light," *Passage,* Catholic Charities, Diocese of Rockville Centre, Spring 1996, with permission.

"New York Priest Visits Connecticut Serial Killer," *Hartford Catholic Transcript,* October 27, 1995.

Chaplain Larry Deraleau, "Chaplain Believes Ross Truly Sorry for Killing," *The Day* (New London, Conn.), September 19, 1998.

Karen Goodrow, "Woman Seeks to Save Ross" (public defender), *Hartford Courant,* March 26, 2000.

"Less Crime, More Criminals" (California statistics), *New York Times,* March 7, 1999.

Mark K. Thomas, "Despair, Redemption and Meaning: Transformation in Prison," a paper written for a course at the California Institute of Integral Studies, September 23, 1996.

Antoinette Bosco, "Needed: A Chapel for Mid-Orange Prison," *Catholic News Service,* April 10, 2000.

Postscript

"Murder Victim's Mother 'Choosing Mercy,' " *Worcester Telegram and Gazette,* July 11, 2000.

"Mother of Murder Victim Argues against the Death Penalty," *Catholic Free Press* (Worcester, Mass.), July 14, 2000.

Project Hope to Abolish the Death Penalty, 11076 CR 267, Lanett, AL 36863, and Tanya Connor, 41 White Avenue, Worcester, MA 01605.

Gail Collins, "An Ode to July," Op-Ed, *New York Times,* July 11, 2000.

Kari Haskell, "Never Say Die, Just Execute," *New York Times,* July 2000.

David Frum, "The Justice Americans Demand," Op-Ed, *New York Times,* February 2, 2000.

"Justice System Riddled with Bias, Studies Say," *Danbury News-Times,* May 7, 2000.

"The Death Penalty on Trial" (includes 1996 Anti-Terrorism and Effective Death Penalty Act), *Newsweek,* June 12, 2000.

State of Connecticut, Department of Corrections, Public Information Office, Wolcott Hill Road, Wethersfield, CT 06109, (860) 692-7783.

"Inmate Attacks Warden," *Danbury News-Times,* August 4, 2000.

"Jubilee in Jail, a Call for Clemency—Pope Backs Prison Reform; U.S. Bishops Plan Document," *National Catholic Reporter,* July 28, 2000.

" 'God Forgives'—New York Bishops Join Pope in Offering Prison Masses for Jubilee Year," *Catholic New York,* July 13, 2000.

"Gore Seeks Constitutional Guards for Crime Victims," *New York Times,* July 19, 2000.

RECOMMENDED BOOKS

Arnold, Johann Christoph. *Why Forgive?* Farmington, Pa.: Plough Publishing House, 2000.

Bedau, Hugo Adam, ed. *The Death Penalty in America: Current Controversies.* New York: Oxford University Press, 1997.

Cabana, Don. *Death at Midnight: The Confession of an Executioner.* Boston: Northeastern University Press, 1996.

Christianson, Scott. *With Liberty for Some: 500 Years of Imprisonment in America.* Boston: Northeastern University Press, 1998.

———. *Condemned: Inside the Sing Sing Death House.* New York: New York University Press, 2000.

Cole, David. *No Equal Justice: Race and Class in the American Criminal Justice System.* New York: New Press, 1999.

Conover, Ted. *Newjack: Guarding Sing Sing.* New York: Random House, 2000.

Dwyer, Jim, Peter Neufeld, and Barry Scheck. *Actual Innocence: Five Days to Execution, and Other Dispatches from the Wrongly Convicted.* New York: Doubleday, 2000.

Haines, Herbert H. *Against Capital Punishment: The Anti–Death Penalty Movement in America, 1972–1994.* New York: Oxford University Press, 1996.

Jackson, Rev. Jesse. *Legal Lynching: Racism, Injustice, and the Death Penalty.* New York: Marlowe, 1996.

McFeely, William S. *Proximity to Death.* New York: W. W. Norton, 2000.

Megivern, James J. *The Death Penalty: An Historical and Theological Survey.* New York: Paulist Press, 1997.

RESOURCE GROUPS AGAINST CAPITAL PUNISHMENT

᭡᭢᭡᭢᭡᭢᭡᭢᭡᭢᭡᭢᭡᭢

The American Friends Service Committee, and
Religious Organizing Against the Death Penalty
1501 Cherry Street
Philadelphia, PA 19102
215-241-7130

National Coalition to Abolish the Death Penalty
1436 U Street NW #104
Washington, DC 20009
202-387-3890 (Dial this number for the National
Execution Hotline and current information about
scheduled executions and the number of prisoners
executed to date)

Citizens United for Alternatives to the Death Sentence
US Highway #1
Box 297
Tequesta, FL 33469
800-973-6548

The Judicial Process Commission
121 N. Fitzhugh Street
Rochester, NY 14614
716-325-7727

Peacework
New England Regional Office
American Friends Service Committee
2161 Massachusetts Avenue
Cambridge, MA 02140
617-661-6130

Amnesty International USA
600 Pennsylvania Avenue, 5th floor
Washington, DC 20003
202-675-8582

Amnesty International USA
322 Eighth Avenue
New York, NY 10001

Murder Victims Families for Reconciliation
2161 Massachusetts Avenue
Cambridge, MA 02140
617-868-0007

Religious Organizing Against the Death Penalty
1501 Cherry Street
Philadelphia, PA 19102
202-588-5489

Quixote Center, and
Equal Justice USA
P.O. Box 5206
Hyattsville, MD 20782
301-699-0042

New Yorkers Against the Death Penalty
40 North Main Avenue
Albany, NY 12203
888-224-6579; 914-946-4456; 518-453-6797

The November Coalition
795 South Cedar
Colville, WA 99114
509-684-1550

Families Against Mandatory Minimums
1612 K Street NW, Suite 1400
Washington, DC 20006
202-822-6700

Death Penalty Information Center
1320 Eighteenth Street NW, 5th Floor
Washington, DC 20036
202-293-6970